SPSS for Introductory Statistics

Use and Interpretation

Second Edition

SPSS for Introductory Statistics

Use and Interpretation

Second Edition

George A. Morgan
Colorado State University

Nancy L. Leech
University of Colorado at Denver

Gene W. Gloeckner
Karen C. Barrett
Colorado State University

In Collaboration With
Joan Naden Clay, Laura Jensen, and Don Quick

2004

LAWRENCE ERLBAUM ASSOCIATES, PUBLISHERS
Mahwah, New Jersey   London

Lawrence Erlbaum Associates, Inc., Publishers
10 Industrial Avenue
Mahwah, New Jersey 07430

Library of Congress Cataloging-in-Publication Data

SPSS for introductory statistics : use and interpretation / George A. Morgan ... [et al.] ; in collaboration with Joan Naden Clay, Laura Jensen, and Don Quick. — 2nd ed.
p. cm.

Includes bibliographical references and index.

ISBN 0-8058-4789-8 (pbk.)
1. SPSS for Windows. 2. SPSS (Computer file). 3. Social sciences—Statistical methods—Computer programs.   I. Morgan, George A. (George Arthur), 1936–
HA32.S572 2004
300'.285'555—dc22

                                                                    2004040383
                                                                         CIP

Books published by Lawrence Erlbaum Associates are printed on acid-free paper, and their bindings are chosen for strength and durability.

Printed in the United States of America
10 9 8 7 6 5 4 3 2

Contents

100475282
300.
2854
SP3

Contents

Appendices

PREFACE

This book is designed to help students learn how to analyze and interpret research data with basic statistics. It is intended to be a supplemental text in an introductory (undergraduate or graduate) statistics or research methods course in the behavioral sciences or education and it can be used in conjunction with any mainstream text. We have found that the book makes SPSS for Windows easy to use so that it is not necessary to have a formal, instructional computer lab; you should be able to learn how to use SPSS on your own with this book. Access to the SPSS program and some familiarity with Windows is all that is required. Although SPSS for Windows is quite easy to use, there is such a wide variety of options and statistics that knowing which ones to use and how to interpret the printouts can be difficult, so this book is intended to help with these challenges.

SPSS 12 and Earlier Versions
We use SPSS 12 for Windows in this book, but, except for enhanced tables and graphics, there are only minor differences from versions 10 and 11. In fact, as far as the procedures demonstrated, in this book there is only one *major* difference (in how data are entered) between versions 7 and 12. We also expect future Windows versions to be similar. You should not have much difficulty (except in Chapter 2) if you have access to SPSS versions 7 through 9. Our students have used this book, or earlier editions of it, with all of these versions of SPSS; both the procedures and outputs are quite similar. We will point out some of the changes at various points in the text.

Goals of This Book
This book demonstrates how to produce a variety of statistics that are usually included in basic statistics courses, plus some (e.g., reliability measures) that are useful for doing research. Our goal is to describe the use and interpretation of these statistics as much as possible in nontechnical, jargon-free language.

Helping you learn how to choose the appropriate statistics, interpret the outputs, and develop skills in writing about the meaning of the results are the main goals of this book. Thus, we have included material on:
1) How the appropriate **choice of a statistic** is based on the design of the research.
2) How to use SPSS to **answer research questions**.
3) How to **interpret SPSS outputs**.
4) How to **write about the outputs** in the Results section of a paper.

This information will help you develop skills that cover the whole range of the steps in the research process: design, data collection, data entry, data analysis, interpretation of outputs, and writing results. The modified high school and beyond data set (HSB) used in this book is similar to one you might have for a thesis, dissertation, or research project. Therefore, we think it can serve as a model for your analysis. The compact disk (CD) packaged with the book contains the HSB data file and another data set (called the College Student data) that is used for the extra problems at the end of each chapter. However, **you will need to have access to or purchase the SPSS program.**

Partially to make the text more readable, we have chosen not to cite many references in the text; however, we have provided a short bibliography of some of the books and articles that we have found useful. We assume that most students will use this book in conjunction with a class that has a textbook; it will help you to read more about each statistic before doing the assignments. Our "For Further Reading" list should also help.

Our companion book, Leech, Barrett, and Morgan (2004), *SPSS for Intermediate Statistics: Use and Interpretation,* also published by Lawrence Erlbaum Associates, is on the "For Further Reading" list at the end of this book. We think that you will find it useful if you need to do complex statistics including ones such as Cronbach's alpha, multiple regression, and factorial ANOVA that are introduced briefly in this book.

Special Features

Several user friendly features of this book include:
1. The **key SPSS windows** that you see when performing the statistical analyses. This has been helpful to "visual learners."
2. The **complete outputs** for the analyses that we have done so you can see what you will get (we have done some editing in SPSS to make the outputs fit better on the pages).
3. **Callout boxes** on the outputs that point out parts of the output to focus on and indicate what they mean.
4. For each output, a boxed **interpretation section** that will help you understand the output.
5. Chapter 6 provides specially developed flow charts and tables to help you **select an appropriate inferential statistic** and **interpret statistical significance and effect sizes**. This chapter also provides an extended example of how to identify and write a research problem, several research questions, and a results paragraph.
6. For the inferential statistics in Chapters 7-11, an example of **how to write about the output** and make a table for a thesis, dissertation, or research paper.
7. **Interpretation questions** that stimulate you to think about the information in the chapter and outputs.
8. Several **extra SPSS problems** at the end of each chapter for you to run with SPSS and discuss.
9. A **Quick Reference Guide** to SPSS (Appendix A) which provides information about many SPSS commands not discussed in the chapters.
10. Appendixes B, C, and D, which provide examples of how to **write research problems and questions/hypotheses** (B) and how to **get started with SPSS** (C), and how to **make tables and figures** (D).
11. **Answers** to the odd numbered interpretation questions (Appendix E).
12. **Two data sets on a CD.** These realistic data sets are packaged with the book to provide you with data to be used to solve the chapter problems and the extra problems at the end of each chapter.

Overview of the Chapters
Our approach in this book is to present how to use and interpret SPSS in the context of proceeding as if the HSB data were the actual data from your research project. However, before starting the SPSS assignments, we have three introductory chapters. The first chapter describes research problems, variables, and research questions, and it identifies a number of specific research questions related to the HSB data. The goal is to use SPSS as a tool to help you answer these research questions. (Appendix B provides some guidelines for phrasing or formatting research questions). Chapter 2 provides an introduction to data coding, entry, and checking with sample questionnaire data designed for those purposes. We developed Chapter 2 because many of you may have little experience with getting "messy", realistic data ready to analyze. Chapter 3 discusses measurement and its relation to the appropriate use of descriptive statistics. This chapter also includes a brief review of descriptive statistics.

Chapters 4 and 5 provide you with experience doing exploratory data analysis (EDA), basic descriptive statistics, and data manipulations (e.g., compute and recode) using the high school and beyond (HSB) data set. These chapters are organized in very much the way you might proceed if this were your project. We calculate a variety of descriptive statistics, check certain statistical assumptions, and make a few data transformations. Much of what is done in these two chapters involves preliminary analyses to get ready to answer the research questions that you might state in a report.

Chapter 6 provides a brief overview of research designs (between groups and within subjects). This chapter describes flowcharts and tables useful for selecting an appropriate statistic. Also included is an overview of how to interpret and write about the results of an inferential statistic. This section includes not only testing for statistical significance but also a discussion of effect size measures and guidelines for interpreting them.

Chapters 7-11 are designed to answer the several research questions posed in Chapter 1 as well as a number of additional questions. Solving the problems in these chapters should give you a good idea of the basic statistics that can be computed with SPSS. Hopefully, seeing how the research questions and design lead naturally to the choice of statistics will become apparent after using this book. In addition, it is our hope that interpreting what you get back from the computer will become more clear after doing these assignments, studying the outputs, answering the interpretation questions, and doing the extra SPSS problems.

Our Approach to Research Questions, Measurement and Selection of Statistics
In Chapters 1, 3, and 6, our approach is somewhat nontraditional because we have found that students have a great deal of difficulty with some aspects of research and statistics but not others. Most can learn formulas and "crunch" the numbers quite easily and accurately with a calculator or with a computer. However, many have trouble knowing what statistics to use and how to interpret the results. They do not seem to have a "big picture" or see how research design and measurement influence data analysis. Part of the problem is inconsistent terminology. We are reminded of Bruce Thompson's frequently repeated, intentionally facetious remark at his many national workshops: "We use these different terms to confuse the graduate students." For these reasons we have tried to present a semantically consistent and coherent picture of how research design leads to three basic kinds of research questions (difference, associational, and descriptive) which, in turn, lead to three kinds or groups of statistics with the same names. We realize that these and other attempts to develop and utilize a consistent framework are both nontraditional and somewhat of an oversimplification. However, we think the framework and consistency pay off in terms of student understanding and ability to actually use statistics to answer their research questions. Instructors who are not persuaded that this framework is useful can skip Chapters 1, 3, and 6 and still have a book that helps their students use and interpret SPSS.

Major Changes and Additions to This Edition
The following changes and additions are based on our experiences using the book with students, feedback from reviewers and other users, and the revisions in policy and best practice specified by the APA Task Force on Statistical Inference (1999) and the 5th Edition of the *APA Publication Manual* (2001). We have included more discussion of:
1. *Effect size.* We discuss effect size in each interpretation section to be consistent with the requirements of the revised APA manual. Unfortunately because SPSS doesn't provide effect sizes for all the demonstrated statistics, we often had to show how to estimate or compute them by hand.

2. ***Writing about outputs.*** We include examples of how to write about and make APA type tables from the information in SPSS outputs. We have found the step from interpretation to writing quite difficult for students so we now put more emphasis on research writing.
3. ***Assumptions.*** When each statistic is introduced, we have a brief section about its assumptions and when it is appropriate to select that statistic for the problem or question at hand.
4. ***Descriptive statistics and testing assumptions.*** We have expanded emphasis on exploratory data analysis (EDA) and how to test assumptions. Also there is more on data file management than was in the first edition.
5. ***Reliability assessment.*** We present some ways of assessing reliability in the crosstabulation, correlation, and *t* test chapters of this book. More emphasis on reliability and testing assumptions is consistent with our strategy of presenting SPSS procedures that students would use in an actual research project.
6. ***One-way ANOVA and t tests.*** We have made separate chapters for these statistics. In the ANOVA chapter, we also include an introduction to factorial ANOVA.
7. ***Nonparametric statistics.*** We include the nonparametric tests that are similar to the *t* tests (Mann-Whitney and Wilcoxon) and single factor ANOVA (Kruskal-Wallis) in appropriate chapters as well as several nonparametric measures of association. This is consistent with the increased emphasis on checking assumptions because it provides alternative procedures for the student when key assumptions are markedly violated.
8. ***Data entry and checking.*** Chapter 2, on data entry, variable labeling, and data checking is based on a small data set (6 variables and 12 participants) developed for this book. What is new and unusual is that the data are displayed as if they were on copies of actual questionnaires answered by participants. We built in problematic responses that require the researcher or data entry person to look for errors or inconsistencies and make decisions. We hope this quite realistic task will help students be more sensitive to issues of data checking *before* doing analyses.
9. ***Interpretation questions.*** We have added more interpretation questions to each chapter because we have found them useful for student understanding. We include the answers to the odd numbered questions in Appendix E for self-study.
10. ***Extra SPSS problems.*** We have developed additional extra problems to give you more practice in running and interpreting SPSS.
11. ***SPSS syntax.*** We show the syntax along with the outputs because a number of professors and skilled students like seeing and prefer using syntax to produce outputs. How to use SPSS syntax is presented in the Quick Reference Guide.
12. ***Quick Reference Guide for SPSS procedures.*** We have condensed several of the appendixes of the first edition into the alphabetically organized Appendix A, which is somewhat like a glossary. It includes how to do basic procedures like print and save, which are tasks you will use several times and/or may already know. It also includes brief directions of how to do things like import a file from Excel or export to PowerPoint, do split files, and make 3-D figures.
13. ***An Instructor CD.*** This manual is available to course instructors who request it from LEA. It contains aids for teaching the course, including PowerPoint slides, the answers to the even numbered Interpretation Questions, and information related to the Extra SPSS Problems.

Bullets, Arrows, Bold and Italics
To help you do the problems with SPSS, we have developed some conventions. We use bullets to indicate actions in SPSS Windows that you will take. For example:

- Highlight *gender* and *math achievement*.
- Click on the arrow to move the variables into the right hand box.

- Click on **Options** to get Fig 2.16.
- Check **Mean, Std Deviation, Minimum,** and **Maximum.**
- Click on **Continue.**

Note that the words in italics are variable names and words in bold are words that you will see in the SPSS Windows and utilize to produce the desired output. In the text they are spelled and capitalized as you see them in the Windows. Bold is also used to identify key terms when they are introduced, defined, or important to understanding.

To access a Window from what SPSS calls the **Data View** (see the Quick Reference Guide or Chapter 2), the words you will see in the pull down menus are given in bold with arrows between them. For example:

- Select **Analyze => Descriptive Statistics => Frequencies.**
(This means pull down the Analyze menu, then slide your cursor down to Descriptive Statistics and over to Frequencies, and click.)

Occasionally, we have used underlines to emphasize critical points or commands.

Acknowledgements
This SPSS book is consistent with and could be used as a supplement for Gliner and Morgan, (2000) *Research Methods in Applied Settings: An Integrated Approach to Design and Analysis,* also published by Erlbaum. In fact, some sections of Chapters 1, 3, and 6 have been only slightly modified from that text. For this we thank Jeff Gliner, the first author of that book. Although Orlando Griego is not an author on this revision of our SPSS book, it still shows the imprint of his student friendly writing style.

We would like to acknowledge the assistance of the many students who have used earlier versions of this book and provided helpful suggestions for improvement. We could not have completed the task or made it look so good without our technology consultant, Don Quick, our word processor, Linda White, and several capable work study students including Rae Russell, Katie Jones, Erica Snyder, Jennifer Musser, and Catherine Lamana. Jikyeong Kang, Bill Sears, LaVon Blaesi, Mei-Huei Tsay, and Sheridan Green assisted with classes and the development of materials for the DOS and earlier Windows versions of the assignments. Lisa Vogel, Don Quick, James Lyall, Joan Anderson, and Yasmine Andrews helped with writing or editing parts of the manuscript or earlier editions. Jeff Gliner, Jerry Vaske, Jim zumBrunnen, Laura Goodwin, James O. Benedict, Barry Cohen, John Ruscio, Tim Urdan, and Steve Knotek provided reviews and suggestions for improving the text. Joan Clay, Laura Jensen, and Don Quick wrote helpful appendixes for this edition, and Joan Clay wrote the Instructor's Manual. Bob Fetch and Ray Yang provided helpful feedback on the readability and user friendliness of the text. We also acknowledge the financial assistance of two instructional improvement grants from the College of Applied Human Sciences at Colorado State University. Finally, the patience of our spouses (Hildy, Susan, and Terry) and families enabled us to complete the task, without too much family strain.

G. M., N. L., G. G., and K. B.
Fort Collins, Colorado
December, 2003

CHAPTER 1

Variables, Research Problems and Questions

Research Problems

The research process begins with an issue or problem of interest to the researcher. This **research problem** is a statement that <u>asks about the relationships between two or more variables</u>[1]. Almost all research studies have *more* than two variables. Appendix B provides templates to help you phrase your research problem, and provides examples from the expanded high school and beyond (HSB) data set that will be described in this chapter and used throughout the book.

The process of moving from a sense of curiosity, or a feeling that there is an unresolved problem to a clearly defined, researchable problem, can be a complex and long one. That part of the research process is beyond the scope of this book, but it is discussed in most books about research methods and books about completing a dissertation or thesis.

Variables

Key elements in a research problem are the variables. A **variable** is defined as a characteristic of the participants or situation for a given study that has different values in that study. A <u>variable must be able to vary or have different values</u>. For example, *gender* is a variable because it has two values, female or male. *Age* is a variable that has a large number of values. *Type of treatment/intervention* (or *type of curriculum*) is a variable if there is more than one treatment or a treatment and a control group. *Number of days to learn something or to recover from an ailment* are common measures of the effect of a treatment and, thus, are also variables. Similarly, *amount of mathematics knowledge* is a variable because it can vary from none to a lot.

If a concept has only one value in a particular study it is not a variable; it is a constant. Thus, ethnic group is not a variable if all participants are European American. Gender is not a variable if all participants in a study are female.

In quantitative research, variables are defined operationally and are commonly divided into **independent variables** (active or attribute), **dependent variables**, and **extraneous variables**. Each of these topics will be dealt with in briefly the following sections.

Operational definitions of variables. An operational definition describes or <u>defines a variable in terms of the operations or techniques used to make it happen or measure it</u>. When quantitative researchers describe the variables in their study, they specify what they mean by demonstrating how they measured the variable. Demographic variables like age, gender, or ethnic group are usually measured simply by asking the participant to choose the appropriate category from a list.

---

[1] To help you, we have identified the SPSS variable names, labels, and values using italics (e.g., *gender* and *male*) and have put in bold the terms used in the SPSS windows and outputs (e.g., **SPSS Data Editor**), and we use bold for other key terms when they are introduced, defined, or are important to understanding. Underlines are used to focus your attention on critical points or phrases that could be missed. Italics are also used, as commonly the case, for emphasizing a word or two and for the titles of books.

Types of treatment (or curriculum) are usually operationally defined much more extensively by describing what was done during the treatment or new curriculum. Likewise, abstract concepts like mathematics knowledge, self-concept, or mathematics anxiety need to be defined operationally by spelling out in some detail how they were measured in a particular study. To do this, the investigator may provide sample questions, append the actual instrument, or provide a reference where more information can be found.

Independent Variables

There are two types of independent variables **active** and **attribute.** It is important to distinguish between these types when we discuss the results of a study. As presented in more detail below, an active independent variable is a necessary but not sufficient condition to make cause and effect conclusions.

Active or manipulated independent variables. An active independent variable is a variable, such as a workshop, new curriculum, or other intervention, at least one level of which is given to a group of participants, within a specified period of time during the study.

For example, a researcher might investigate a new kind of therapy compared to the traditional treatment. A second example might be to study the effect of a new teaching method, such as cooperative learning, on student performance. In these two examples, the variable of interest was something that was *given to* the participants. Thus, active independent variables are *given* to the participants in the study but are not necessarily given or manipulated by the experimenter. They may be given by a clinic, school, or someone other than the investigator, but from the participants' point of view, the situation was manipulated. Using this definition, the treatment is always given *after* the study was planned so that there could have been (or preferably was) a pretest. Other writers have similar but, perhaps, slightly different definitions of active independent variables. **Randomized experimental** and **quasi-experimental** studies have an active independent variable.

Attribute or measured independent variables. A variable that cannot be manipulated, yet is a major focus of the study; can be called an attribute independent variable. In other words, the values of the independent variable are preexisting attributes of the persons or their ongoing environment that are not systematically changed during the study. For example, education, gender, age, ethnic group, IQ, and self-esteem are attribute variables that could be used as attribute independent variables. Studies with only attribute independent variables are called **non experimental** studies.

In keeping with SPSS, but unlike authors of some research methods books, we do not restrict the term independent variable to those variables that are manipulated or active. We define an independent variable more broadly to include any predictors, antecedents, or *presumed* causes or influences under investigation in the study. Attributes of the participants as well as active independent variables fit within this definition. For the social sciences and education, attribute independent variables are especially important. Type of disability or level of disability may be the major focus of a study. Disability certainly qualifies as a variable since it can take on different values even though they are not *given* during the study. For example, cerebral palsy is different from Down syndrome, which is different from spina bifida, yet all are disabilities. Also, there are different levels of the same disability. People already have defining characteristics or attributes that place them into one of two or more categories. The different disabilities are already present when we begin our study. Thus, we might also be interested in studying a class of variables that are not given or manipulated during the study, even by other persons, schools, or clinics.

Other labels for the independent variable. SPSS uses a variety of terms such as **factor** (Chapter 10), and **grouping variable** (Chapter 9). In other cases, (Chapters 7 and 8) SPSS and statisticians do not make a distinction between the independent and dependent variable; they just label them **variables.** For example, there is no independent variable for a correlation or chi-square. However, even for chi-square and correlation, we think it is sometimes educationally useful to think of one variable as the predictor (independent variable) and the other as the outcome (dependent variable), as is the case in regression.

Type of independent variable and inferences about cause and effect. When we analyze data from a research study, the statistical analysis does not differentiate whether the independent variable is an active independent variable or an attribute independent variable. However, even though SPSS and most statistics books use the label independent variable for both active and attribute variables, there is a crucial difference in interpretation.

A major goal of scientific research is to be able to identify a causal relationship between two variables. For those in applied disciplines, the need to demonstrate that a given intervention or treatment causes change in behavior or performance is extremely important. Only the approaches that have an active independent variable (randomized experimental and, to a lesser extent, quasi-experimental) can provide data that allow one to infer that the independent variable caused the change or difference in the dependent variable.

In contrast, a significant difference between or among persons with different values of an attribute independent variable should *not* lead one to conclude that the attribute independent variable caused the dependent variable to change. Thus, this distinction between active and attribute independent variables is important because terms such as **main effect** and **effect size** used by SPSS and most statistics books might lead one to believe that if you find a significant difference the independent variable *caused* the difference. These terms can be misleading when the independent variable is an attribute.

Although non experimental studies (those with attribute independent variables) are limited in what can be said about causation, they can lead to solid conclusions about the differences between groups and about associations between variables. Furthermore, if the focus of your research is on attribute independent variables, a non experimental study is the *only* available approach. For example, if you are interested in learning how boys and girls learn mathematical concepts, you are interested in the attribute independent variable of gender.

Values of the independent variable. SPSS uses the term **values** to describe the several options or values of a variable. These values are *not* necessarily ordered, and several other terms, **categories, levels, groups,** or **samples** are sometimes used interchangeably with the term values, especially in statistics books. Suppose that an investigator is performing a study to investigate the effect of a treatment. One group of participants is assigned to the treatment group. A second group does not receive the treatment. The study could be conceptualized as having one independent variable (*treatment type)*, with two values or levels (*treatment* and *no treatment*). The independent variable in this example would be classified as an active independent variable. Now, suppose instead, that the investigator was interested primarily in comparing two different treatments but decided to include a third no-treatment group as a control group in the study. The study still would be conceptualized as having one active independent variable (*treatment type*), but with three values or levels (the two treatment conditions and the control condition). This variable could be diagrammed as follows:

Variable Label	Values	Value Labels
	1	= Treatment 1
Treatment type	2	= Treatment 2
	3	= No treatment (control)

As an additional example, consider *gender*, which is an attribute independent variable with two values, as *male* and *female*. It could be diagrammed as follows:

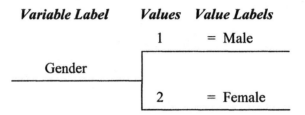

Variable Label	Values	Value Labels
	1	= Male
Gender		
	2	= Female

Note that in SPSS each variable is given a **variable label;** moreover, the values, which are often categories, have **value labels** (e.g., male and female). Each value or level is assigned a number used by SPSS to compute statistics. It is especially important to know the value labels when the variable is **nominal;** i.e., when the values of the variable are just names and, thus, are not ordered.

Dependent Variables

The **dependent variable** is assumed to measure or assess the effect of the independent variable. It is thought of as the presumed outcome or criterion. Dependent variables are often test scores, ratings on questionnaires, readings from instruments (electrocardiogram, galvanic skin response, etc.), or measures of physical performance. When we discuss measurement in Chapters 2 and 3, we are usually referring to the dependent variable. Dependent variables, like independent variables must have at least two values; most dependent variables have many values, varying from low to high so they are not as easy to diagram as the independent variables shown above.

SPSS also uses a number of other terms for the dependent variable. **Dependent list** is used in cases where you can do the same statistic several times, for a list of dependent variables (e.g., in Chapter 10 with one-way ANOVA). The term **test variable** is used in Chapter 9 for the *t* test.

Extraneous Variables

These are variables (also called nuisance variables or, in some designs, covariates) that are not of interest in a particular study but could influence the dependent variable. Environmental factors (e.g., temperature or distractions), time of day, and characteristics of the experimenter, teacher, or therapist are some possible extraneous variables that need to be controlled. SPSS does not use the term extraneous variable. However, sometimes such variables are "controlled" using statistics that are available in SPSS.

Research Hypotheses and Questions

<u>**Research hypotheses**</u> <u>are predictive statements about the relationship between variables.</u>
<u>**Research questions**</u> <u>are similar to hypotheses, except that they do not entail specific predictions</u>
and are phrased in question format. For example, one might have the following research
question: "Is there a difference in students' scores on a standardized test if they took two tests in
one day versus taking only one test on each of two days?" A hypothesis regarding the same issue
might be: "Students who take only one test per day will score *better* on standardized tests than
will students who take two tests in one day."

We divide research questions into three broad types: **difference, associational,** and **descriptive**
a*s* shown in the middle of Fig 1.1. The figure also shows the general and specific purposes and
the general types of statistics for each of these three types of research question.

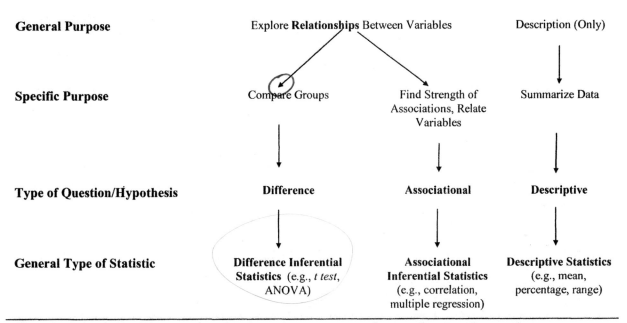

**Fig. 1.1. Schematic diagram showing how the purpose and type of research question
correspond to the general type of statistic used in a study.**

Difference research questions. For these questions, we compare scores (on the dependent
variable) of two or more different groups, each of which is composed of individuals with one of
the values or levels on the independent variable. This type of question attempts to demonstrate
that groups are not the same on the dependent variable.

Associational research questions. Here we associate or relate two or more variables. This
approach usually involves an attempt to see how two or more variables co-vary (e.g., higher
values on one variable correspond to higher, or lower, values on another variable for the same
persons) or how one or more variables enables one to predict another variable.

Descriptive research questions. These are not answered with inferential statistics. They merely describe or summarize data, without trying to generalize to a larger population of individuals.

Figure 1.1 shows that both <u>difference and associational questions</u> or hypotheses <u>are similar in that they explore the relationships between variables</u>.[2] Note that difference and associational questions differ in specific purpose and the kinds of statistics they use to answer the question.

Difference versus associational inferential statistics. We think it is educationally useful to divide inferential statistics into two types corresponding to difference and associational hypotheses or questions[3]. **Difference inferential statistics** (e.g., *t* test or analysis of variance) are <u>used for approaches that test for differences between groups</u>. **Associational inferential statistics** <u>test for associations or relationships between variables</u> and use, for example, correlation or multiple regression analysis. We will utilize this contrast between difference and associational inferential statistics in Chapter 6 and later in this book.

Table 1.1 provides the general format and one example of a basic difference question, a basic associational question, and a basic descriptive question. Remember that research questions are similar to hypotheses, but they are stated in question format. We think it is advisable to use the question format when one does not have a clear directional prediction and for the descriptive approach. More details and examples are given in Appendix B. As implied by Fig. 1.1, it is acceptable to phrase any research question that involves two variables as whether or not there is a relationship between the variables (e.g., is there a relationship between *gender* and *math achievement* or is there a relationship between *anxiety* and *GPA*?). However, we think that phrasing the question as a difference or association is desirable because it helps one choose an appropriate statistic and interpret the result.

Complex Research Questions

Some research questions involve more than two variables at a time. We call such questions and the appropriate statistics **complex**. Some of these statistics are called **multivariate** in other texts, but there is not a consistent definition of multivariate in the literature. We provide examples of how to write certain complex research questions in Appendix B, and in Chapters 8 and 10 we introduce complex statistics, multiple regression and factorial ANOVA.

---

[2]This similarity is in agreement with the statement by statisticians that all common parametric inferential statistics are relational. We use the term associational for the second type of research question rather than relational or correlational to distinguish it from the *general purpose* of both difference and associational questions/hypothesis, which is to study relationships. Also we wanted to distinguish between correlation, as a specific statistical technique, and the broader type of associational question and that group of statistics.

[3] We realize that all parametric inferential statistics are relational so this dichotomy of using one type of data analysis procedure to test for differences (when there are a few values or levels of the independent variables) and another type of data analysis procedure to test for associations (when there are continuous independent variables) is somewhat artificial. Both continuous and categorical independent variables can be used in a general linear model approach to data analysis. However, we think that the distinction is useful because most researchers utilize the above dichotomy in selecting statistics for data analysis.

Table 1.1. *Examples of Three Kinds of Basic Research Questions/Hypotheses*

1. *Basic Difference (group comparison) Questions*

   - Usually used for Randomized Experimental, Quasi-Experimental, and Comparative Approaches.
   - For this type of question, values or categories of the independent variable (e.g., anxiety) are used to categorize the participants into groups (e.g., high and low), which are then compared to see if they differ in respect to the average scores on the dependent variable (e.g., GPA).
   - Example: Do persons with low and high anxiety differ on their average grades? In other words, will the average GPA of the high anxiety persons be significantly different from the average GPA for low anxiety persons?

2. *Basic Associational (relational) Questions*

   - Used for the Associational Approach, in which the independent variable is usually continuous (i.e., has many ordered levels).
   - For this type of question, the scores on the independent variable (e.g., anxiety) are associated with or related to the dependent variable scores (e.g., GPA).
   - Example: Will students' degree of anxiety be associated with their overall GPA? In other words, will knowing students' level of anxiety tell us anything about their tendency to make higher versus lower grades? If there is a *negative* association (correlation) between anxiety scores and grade point average, those persons who have high levels of anxiety will tend to have low GPAs, those with low anxiety will tend to have high GPAs, and those in the middle on anxiety will tend to be in the middle on GPA.

3. *Basic Descriptive Questions*

   - Used for the Descriptive Approach.
   - For this type of question, scores on a single variable are described in terms of their central tendency, variability, or percentages in each category/level.
   - Example: What percentage of students make a B or above? What is the average level of anxiety found in 9th grade students? The average GPA was 2.73, or 30% had high anxiety.

A Sample Research Problem:
The Modified High School and Beyond (HSB) Study

The SPSS file name of the data set used with this book is *hsbdata.sav*; it stands for high school and beyond data. It is based on a national sample of data from more than 28,000 high school students. The current data set is a sample of 75 students drawn randomly from the larger population. The data that we have for this sample includes school outcomes such as *grades* and the *number of mathematics courses* of different types that the students took in high school. Also, there are several kinds of standardized test data and demographic data such as *gender* and *mother's* and *father's education*. To provide an example of rating scale questionnaire data, we have included 14 items about *mathematics attitudes*. These data were developed for this book and, thus, are not really the math attitudes of the 75 students in this sample; however, they are based on real data gathered by one of the authors to study motivation. Also, we made up data for *religion, ethnic group,* and *SAT-math,* which are somewhat realistic overall. These inclusions enable us to do some additional statistical analyses.

The Research Problem

Imagine that you are interested in the general problem of what factors seem to influence mathematics achievement at the end of high school. You might have some hunches or hypotheses about such factors based on your experience and your reading of the research and popular literature. Some factors that might influence *mathematics achievement* are commonly called demographics: e.g., *gender, ethnic group,* and *mother's* and *father's education.* A probable influence would be the mathematics courses that the student has taken. We might speculate that *grades in mathematics* and in other subjects could have an impact on *math achievement.*[4] However, other variables, such as *students' IQs* or *parents' encouragement* and assistance, could be the actual causes of both high grades and math achievement. Such variables could influence what courses one took, the grades one received, and might be correlates of the demographic variables. We might wonder how spatial performance scores, such as pattern or *mosaic test scores* and *visualization scores,* might enable a more complete understanding of the problem, and whether these skills seem to be influenced by the same factors as *math achievement.*

The HSB Variables

Before we state the research problem and questions in more formal ways, we need to step back and discuss the types of variables and the approaches that might be used to study the above problem. We need to identify the independent/antecedent (presumed causes) variables, the dependent/outcome variable(s), and any extraneous variables.

The primary dependent variable. Given the above research problem, which focuses on achievement tests at the end of the senior year, the primary dependent variable is *math achievement.*

Independent and extraneous variables. The *number of math courses taken* up to that point is best considered to be an antecedent or independent variable in this study. What about *father's* and *mother's education* and *gender*? How would you classify *gender* and *parents' education* in terms of the type of variable? What about *grades*? Like the *number of math courses,* these variables would usually be independent variables because they occurred before the math achievement test. However some of these variables, specifically parental education, might be viewed as extraneous variables that need to be "controlled." *Visualization* and *mosaic pattern scores* probably could be either independent or dependent variables depending upon the specific research question, because they were measured at approximately the same time as math achievement, at the end of the senior year. Note that student's class is a constant and is not a variable in this study because all the participants are high school seniors (i.e., it does not vary; it is the population of interest).

Types of independent variables. As we discussed previously, independent variables can be **active** (given to the participant during the study or manipulated by the investigator) or **attributes** of the participants or their environments. Are there any **active** independent variables in this study? No! There is no intervention, new curriculum, or similar treatment. All the independent variables, then, are attribute variables because they are attributes or characteristics of these high school students. Given that all the independent variables are attributes, the research approach

---

[4] We have decided to use the short version of mathematics (i.e., math) throughout the book to save space and because it is used in common language.

<u>cannot be experimental</u>. This means that we will *not* be able to draw definite conclusions about cause and effect (i.e., we will find out what is related to math achievement, but <u>we will not know for sure what causes or influences</u> math achievement).

Now we will examine the *hsbdata.sav* that you will use to study this complex research problem. We have provided a CD that contains the data for each of the 75 participants on 38 variables. The variables in the *hsbdata.sav* file have already been labeled (see Fig 1.2) and entered (see Fig 1.3) to enable you to get started on analyses quickly. The <u>CD in the back of this book</u> contains SPSS data files for you to use, but it <u>does not include the actual SPSS program</u>, which you will have to have access to in order to do the assignments.

The SPSS Variable View

Figure 1.2 is a piece of what SPSS calls the **variable view** in the **SPSS Data Editor** for the *hsbdata.sav* file. Figure 1.2 shows information about each of the first 17 variables. When you open this file and click on **Variable View** at the bottom left corner of the screen, this is what you will see. We will describe what is in the variable view screen in more detail in Chapter 2; for now focus on the Name, Label, Values, and Missing columns. **Name** is a short name for each variable (e.g., *faed* or *alg1*) [5]. **Label** is a longer label for the variable (e.g., *father's education* or *algebra 1 in h.s.*). The **Values** column contains the **value labels,** but you can see only the label for one value at a time (e.g., 0=male). That is, you cannot see that 1=female unless you click on the value column. The **Missing** column indicates whether there are any special, user identified missing values. **None** just means that there <u>are no special missing values</u>, just the usual *SPSS system missing* value, which is a blank.

	Name	Type	Width	Decimals	Label	Values	Missing	Columns	Align	Measure
1	gender	Numeric	1	0	gender	{0, male}.	None	6	Right	Nominal
2	faed	Numeric	2	0	father's educati	{2, < h.s. grad}	None	6	Right	Ordinal
3	maed	Numeric	2	0	mother's educ	{2, < h.s.}.	None	6	Right	Ordinal
4	alg1	Numeric	1	0	algebra 1 in h.	{0, not taken}.	None	6	Right	Nominal
5	alg2	Numeric	1	0	algebra 2 in h.	{0, not taken}.	None	6	Right	Nominal
6	geo	Numeric	1	0	geometry in h.	{0, not taken}.	None	6	Right	Nominal
7	trig	Numeric	1	0	trigonometry in	{0, not taken}.	None	5	Right	Nominal
8	calc	Numeric	1	0	calculus in h.s	{0, not taken}.	None	5	Right	Nominal
9	mathgr	Numeric	1	0	math grades	{0, less A-B}.	None	6	Right	Nominal
10	grades	Numeric	1	0	grades in h.s.	{1, less than D	None	6	Right	Ordinal
11	mathach	Numeric	4	2	math achievem	{-8.3, low}.	None	6	Right	Scale
12	mosaic	Numeric	3	1	mosaic, patter	{-4, Low}.	None	6	Right	Scale
13	visual	Numeric	4	2	visualization te	{-4.0, low}.	None	6	Right	Scale
14	visual2	Numeric	4	2	visualization re	{.00, Lowest}.	None	6	Right	Scale
15	satm	Numeric	3	0	scholastic apti	{200, minmum	None	5	Right	Scale
16	ethnic	Numeric	2	0	ethnicity	{1, Euro-Amer}	98, 99	6	Right	Nominal
17	religion	Numeric	2	0	religion	{1, protestant}.	98, 99	6	Right	Nominal

Fig. 1.2 Part of the hsbdata.sav variable view in the SPSS data editor.

Variables in the Modified HSB Data Set

The 38 variables shown in Table 1.2 (with the values/levels or range of their values in parentheses) are found in the *hsbdata.sav* file. Also included, for completeness, are seven variables (numbers 39-45) that are not in the *hsbdata.sav* data set because you will compute them

---

[5] In SPSS 7-11 the variable name had to be 8 characters or less. In SPSS 12, it can be longer, but we recommend that you keep it short. If a longer name is used with SPSS 7-11, the name will be truncated. SPSS names must start with a letter and must not contain blank spaces or certain special characters (e.g., !, ?, ', or *).

in Chapter 5. Note that variables 33-38 have been computed already from the math attitude variables (19-32) so that you would have fewer new variables to compute in Chapter 5.

The variables of *ethnic* and *religion* were added to the data set to provide true nominal (unordered) variables with a few (4 and 3) levels or values. In addition, for *ethnic* and *religion*, we have made two missing value codes to illustrate this possibility. All other variables use blanks, the SPSS system missing value, for missing data. For *ethnicity*, 98 indicates multi-ethnic and other. For *religion*, all the high school students who were not *protestant* or *catholic* or said they had *no religion* were coded 98 and considered to be missing because none of the other religions had enough members to make a reasonable size group. Those who left the ethnicity or religion questions blank were coded as 99, also missing.

Table 1.2 HSB Variable Descriptions

	Name	Label (and Values)
		Demographic School and Test Variables
1.	gender	gender (0 = male, 1 = female).
2.	faed	father's education (2 = less than h.s. to 10 = PhD/MD).
3.	maed	mother's education (2 = less than h.s. grad to 10 = PhD/MD).
4.	alg1	algebra 1 in h.s. (1 = taken, 0 = not taken)
5.	alg2	algebra 2 in h.s. (1 = taken, 0 = not taken)
6.	geo	geometry in h.s. (1 = taken, 0 = not taken)
7.	trig	*trigonometry in h.s.* (1 = taken, 0 = not taken)
8.	calc	*calculus in h.s.* (1 = taken, 0 = not taken)
9.	mathgr	*math grades* (0 = low, 1 = high)
10.	grades	*grades in h.s.* (1 = less than a D average to 8 = mostly an A average)
11.	mathach	*math achievement score* (-8.33 to 25) [6]. This is a test something like the ACT math.
12.	mosaic	*mosaic, pattern test score* (-4 to 56). This is a test of pattern recognition ability involving the detection of relationships in patterns of tiles.
13.	visual	*visualization score* (-4 to 16). This is a 16-item test that assesses visualization in three dimensions (i.e., how a three-dimensional object would look if its spatial position were changed).
14.	visual2	*visualization retest* – the visualization test score students obtained when they retook the test a month or so later.
15.	satm	*scholastic aptitude test – math* (200 = lowest, 800 = highest possible)
16.	ethnic	*ethnicity* (1 = Euro-American, 2 = African-American, 3 = Latino-American, 4 = Asian-American, 98 = other or multi ethnic, chose 2 or more, 99 = missing, left blank)
17.	religion	*religion* (1 = protestant, 2 = catholic, 3 = no religion, 98=chose one of several other religions, 99=left blank
18.	ethnic2	*ethnicity reported by student* (same as values for ethnic)
		Math Attitude Questions 1 – 14 (Rated from 1 = very atypical to 4 = very typical)
19.	item01	*motivation* - "I practice math skills until I can do them well."
20.	item02	*pleasure* - "I feel happy after solving a hard problem."
21.	item03	*competence* - "I solve math problems quickly."

---

[6]Negative test scores result from a penalty for guessing.

22.	item04	*(low) motiv* - "I give up easily instead of persisting if a math problem is difficult."
23.	item05	*(low)comp* - "I am a little slow catching on to new topics in math."
24.	item06	*(low)pleas* - "I do not get much pleasure out of math problems."
25.	item07	*motivation* - "I prefer to figure out how to solve problems without asking for help."
26.	item08	*(low)motiv* - "I do not keep at it very long when a math problem is challenging."
27.	item09	*competence* - "I am very competent at math."
28.	item10	*(low)pleas* - "I smile only a little (or not at all) when I solve a math problem."
29.	item11	*(low)comp* - "I have some difficulties doing math as well as other kids my age."
30.	item12	*motivation* - "I try to complete my math problems even if it takes a long time to finish."
31.	item13	*motivation* - "I explore all possible solutions of a complex problem before going on to another one."
32.	item14	*pleasure* – "I really enjoy doing math problems".

New Variables Computed From the Above Variables

33.	item04r	*item04 reversed (4 now = high motivation)*
34.	item05r	*item05 reversed (4 now = high competence)*
35.	item08r	*item08 reversed (4 now = high motivation)*
36.	item11r	item11 reversed (4 now = high competence)
37.	competence	*competence scale. An average computed as follows: (item03 + item05r + item09 + item11r)/4*
38.	motivation	*motivation scale (item01 + item04r + item07 + item08r + item12 + item13)/6*

Variables to be Computed in Chapter 5

39.	mathcrs	*math courses taken (0 = none, 5 = all five)*
40.	faedRevis	*father's educ revised (1 = HS grad or less, 2 = some college, 3 = BS or more)*
41.	maedRevis	*mother's educ revised (1 = HS grad or less, 2 = some college, 3 = BS or more)*
42.	item06r	*item06 reversed (4 now = high pleasure)*
43.	item10r	*item10 reversed (4 now = high pleasure)*
44.	pleasure	*pleasure scale (item02 + item06r + item 10r + item14)/4*
45.	parEduc	*parents education (average of the <u>unrevised</u> mother's and father's educations)*

The Raw HSB Data and Data Editor

Figure 1.3 is a piece of the *hsbdata.sav* file showing the first 11 student participants for variables 1 through 17 (gender through religion). Notice the short variable names (e.g., *gend, faed,* etc.) at the top of the hsbdata file. Be aware that the participants are listed down the left side of the page, and the variables are always listed across the top. <u>You will always enter data this way</u>. If a variable is measured more than once, such as *visual* and *visual 2* (see Fig 1.3) it will be entered as two variables with slightly different names.

	gender	faed	maed	alg1	alg2	geo	trig	calc	mathgr	grades	mathach	mosaic	visual	visual2	salm	ethnic	religion
									calculus in h.s								
1	1	10	10	0	0	0	0	0	0	4	9.00	31.0	8.75	7.00	500	2	1
2	1	2	2	0	0	0	0	0	0	5	10.33	56.0	4.75	4.00	460	3	2
3	1	2	2	0	0	0	0	0	1	6	7.67	25.0	4.75	3.00	420	2	2
4	0	3	3	1	0	0	0	0	0	3	5.00	22.0	1.00	1.00	400	1	1
5	1		3	0	0	0	0	0	0	3	-1.67	17.5	2.25	2.00	450	2	1
6	1	3	2	0	0	0	0	0	1	5	1.00	23.5	1.00	.00	250	3	2
7	0	9	6	1	1	1	0	0	0	6	12.00	28.5	2.50	2.00	480	1	2
8	1	5	3	1	0	0	0	0	0	4	8.00	29.5	3.50	3.00	430	1	3
9	1	3	3	1	0	0	0	0	1	7	13.00	28.0	3.50	2.00	490	1	98
10	0	8	2	0	0	0	0	0	0	5	3.67	27.5	3.75	3.00	300	2	1
11	0	3	4	1	1	1	1	1	0	6	21.00	27.0	11.00	9.50	500	4	99

Fig. 1.3. Part of the hsbdata data view in the SPSS data editor.

Note that in Fig. 1.3 most of the values are single digits, but *mathach, mosaic,* and *visual* include some decimals and even negative numbers. Notice also that some cells, like *father's education* for participant 5, are blank because a datum is missing. Perhaps participant 5 did not know her father's education. Blank is the system missing value that can be used for any missing data in an SPSS data file. We suggest that you leave missing data blank; however, you may run across "user defined" missing data codes like -1, 9, 98, or 99 in other researchers' data (see *religion,* subjects 9 and 11).

Research Questions for the Modified HSB Study [7]

In this book, we will generate a large number of research questions from the modified HSB data set. In this section, we will list some research questions to be answered with the HSB data in order to give you an idea of the range of types of questions that one might have in a typical research project like a thesis or dissertation. In addition to the **difference** and **associational questions** that are commonly seen in a research report, we have asked **descriptive questions** and questions about assumptions in the early assignments. Templates for writing the research problem and research questions or hypotheses are given in Appendix B, which should help you write questions for your own research.

1) Often, we start with basic **descriptive questions** about the demographics of the sample. Thus, we could answer, with the results in Chapter 4, the following basic descriptive question: "What is the average educational level of the fathers of the students in this sample?" "What percentage of the students are male and what percentage are female?"

2) In the assignment for Chapter 4, we also will examine whether the continuous variables (those that might be used to answer associational questions) are distributed normally, an **assumption** of many statistics. One question is, "Are the frequency distributions of the math achievement scores markedly skewed; i.e., different from the normal curve distribution?"

---

[7] The High School and Beyond (HSB) study was conducted by the National Opinion Research Center (1980). The example discussed here and throughout the book is based on 13 variables obtained from a random sample of 75 out of 28,240 high school seniors. These variables include achievement scores, grades, and demographics. The raw data for the 13 variables were slightly modified from data in an appendix in Hinkle, Wiersma, and Jurs (1994). That file had no missing data, which is unusual in behavioral science research so we made some.

3) Tables crosstabulating two categorical variables (ones with a few values or categories) will be computed in Chapter 7. Crosstabulation and the chi-square statistic can answer research questions such as "Is there a relationship between gender and math grades (high or low)?

4) In Chapter 8, we will answer **basic associational research questions** (using Pearson product-moment correlation coefficients) such as, "Is there a positive association/ relationship between grades in high school and math achievement?" This assignment also will produce a correlation matrix of all the correlations among several key variables including math achievement. Similar matrixes will provide the basis for computing multiple regression. In Chapter 8, correlation is also be used to assess reliability.

5) Chapter 8 also poses a **complex associational question** such as "Is there a combination of variables that predicts math achievement?" in order to introduce you to multiple regression.

6) Several basic **difference questions** answered with an independent samples *t* test will be asked in Chapter 9. For example, "Do males and females differ on math achievement?" Basic difference questions in which the independent variable has three or more values will be asked in Chapter 10. For example, "Are there differences among the three father's education groups in regard to average scores on math achievement?" This question will be answered with a one-way or single factor analysis of variance (ANOVA).

7) **Complex difference questions** will also be asked in Chapter 10. One *set* of three questions is as follows: (1) "Is there a difference between students who have fathers with no college, some college, and a BS or more with respect to the student's math achievement?" (2) "Is there a difference between students who had a B or better math grade average and those with less than a B average on a math achievement test at the end of high school?" and (3) "Is there an interaction between a father's education and math grades with respect to math achievement?" This set of three questions will be answered with a factorial ANOVA, introduced briefly here.

This introduction to the research problem and questions raised by the HSB data set should help make the assignments meaningful, and it should provide a guide and examples for your own research.

Interpretation Questions

1.1   Compare the terms *active independent variable* and *attribute independent variable*. What are the similarities and differences?

1.2   What kind of independent variable (active or attribute) is necessary to infer cause? Can one *always* infer cause from this type of independent variable? If so, why? If not, when can one infer cause and when might causal inferences be more questionable?

1.3   What is the difference between the independent variable and the dependent variable?

1.4   Compare and contrast associational, difference, and descriptive types of research questions.

1.5   Write a research question *and* a corresponding hypothesis regarding variables of interest to you but not in the HSBdata set. Is it an associational, difference, or descriptive question?

1.6   Using one or more of the following HSB variables, *religion, mosaic pattern test,* and *visualization score:*
a) Write an associational question.
b) Write a difference question.
c) Write a descriptive question.

CHAPTER 2

Data Coding, Entry, and Checking

This chapter begins with a very brief overview of the initial steps in a research project. After this introduction, the chapter will focus on: 1) getting your data ready to enter into SPSS or a spreadsheet, 2) defining and labeling variables, 3) entering the data appropriately, and 4) checking to be sure that data entry was done correctly without errors.

Plan the Study, Pilot Test, and Collect Data

Plan the study. As discussed in Chapter 1, the research starts with identification of a research problem and research questions or hypotheses. It is also necessary to plan the research design before you select the data collection instrument(s) and begin to collect data. Most research methods books discuss this part of the research process extensively (e.g., see Gliner and Morgan, 2000).

Select or develop the instrument(s). If there is an appropriate instrument available and it has been used with a population similar to yours, it is usually desirable to use it. However, sometimes it is necessary to modify an existing instrument or develop your own. For this chapter we have developed a short questionnaire to be given to students at the end of a course. Remember that questionnaires or surveys are only one way to collect quantitative data. You could also use structured interviews, observations, tests, standardized inventories, or some other type of data collection method. Research methods and measurement books have one or more chapters devoted to the selection and development of data collection instruments. A useful book on the development of questionnaires is Salant and Dillman (1994).

Pilot test and refine instruments. It is always desirable to try out your instrument and directions with, at the very least, a few colleagues or friends. When possible, you also should conduct a **pilot study** with a sample similar to the one you plan to use later. This is especially important if you developed the instrument or it is going to be used with a population different from the one(s) that it was developed for and has been used with in the past.

Pilot participants should be asked about the clarity of the items and whether they think any items should be added or deleted. Then, use the feedback to make modifications in the instrument before beginning data collection. **Content validity** can also be checked by asking experts to judge whether your items cover all aspects of the domain you intended to measure and whether they are in appropriate proportions relative to that domain.

Collect the data. The next step in the research process is to collect the data. There are several ways to collect questionnaire or survey data (such as telephone, mail, or e-mail). We will not discuss them here because that is not the purpose of this book. The Salant and Dillman (1994) book, *How to Conduct Your Own Survey*, provides considerable detail on the various methods for collecting survey data.

You should check your raw data after you collect it even before it is entered into the computer. Make sure that the participants marked their score sheets or questionnaires appropriately; check to see if there are double answers to a question (when only one is expected) or answers that are marked between two rating points. If this happens, you need to have a rule (e.g., "use the average") that you can apply consistently. Thus, you should "clean up" your data, making sure they are clear, consistent, and readable, before entering them into a data file.

Let's assume that the completed questionnaires shown in Fig. 2.1 and 2.2 were given to a small class of 12 students and that they filled them out and turned them in at the end of the class. The researcher numbered the forms from 1 to 12 as shown opposite ID.

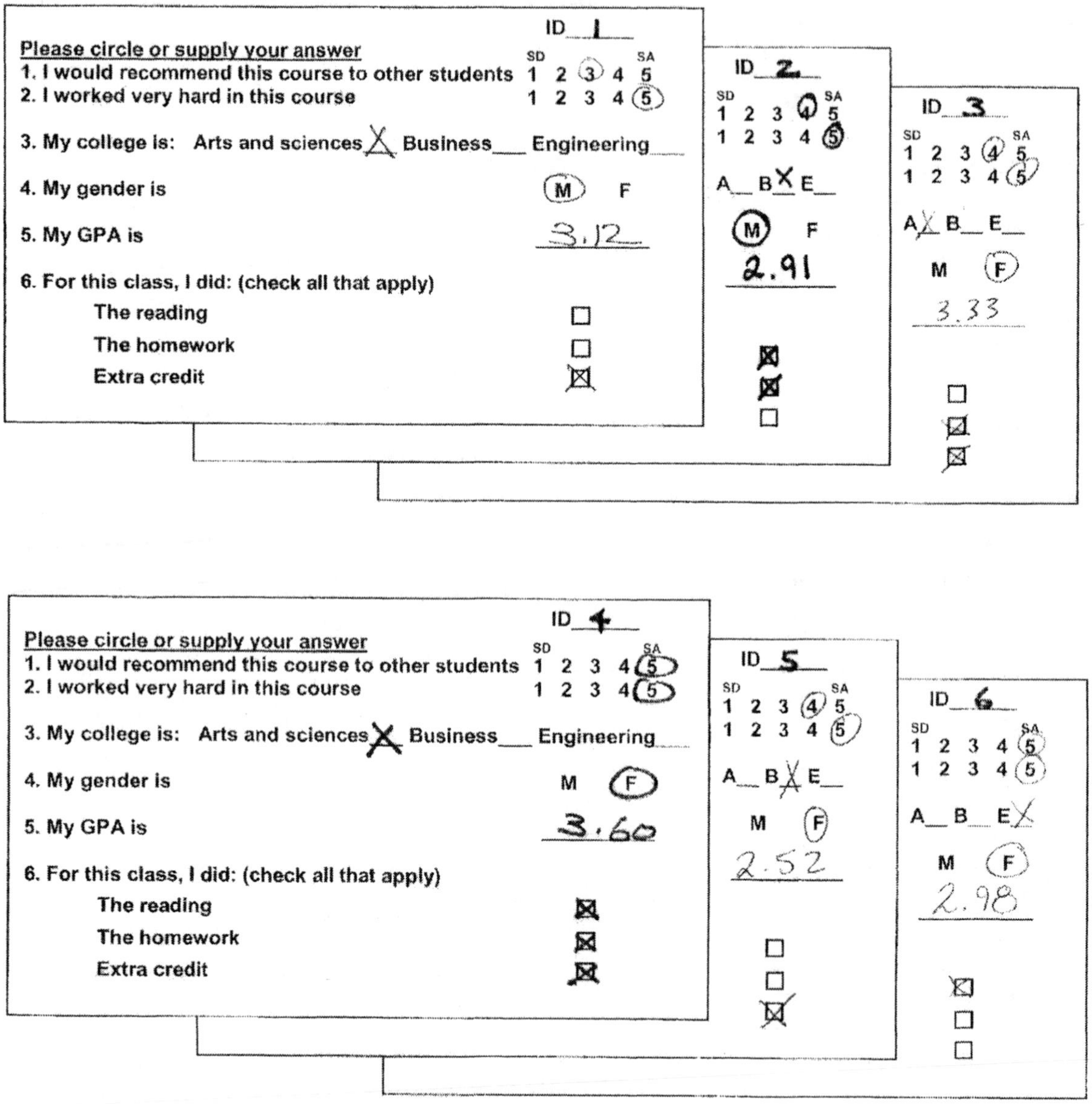

Fig. 2.1. Completed questionnaires for participant 1 through 6.

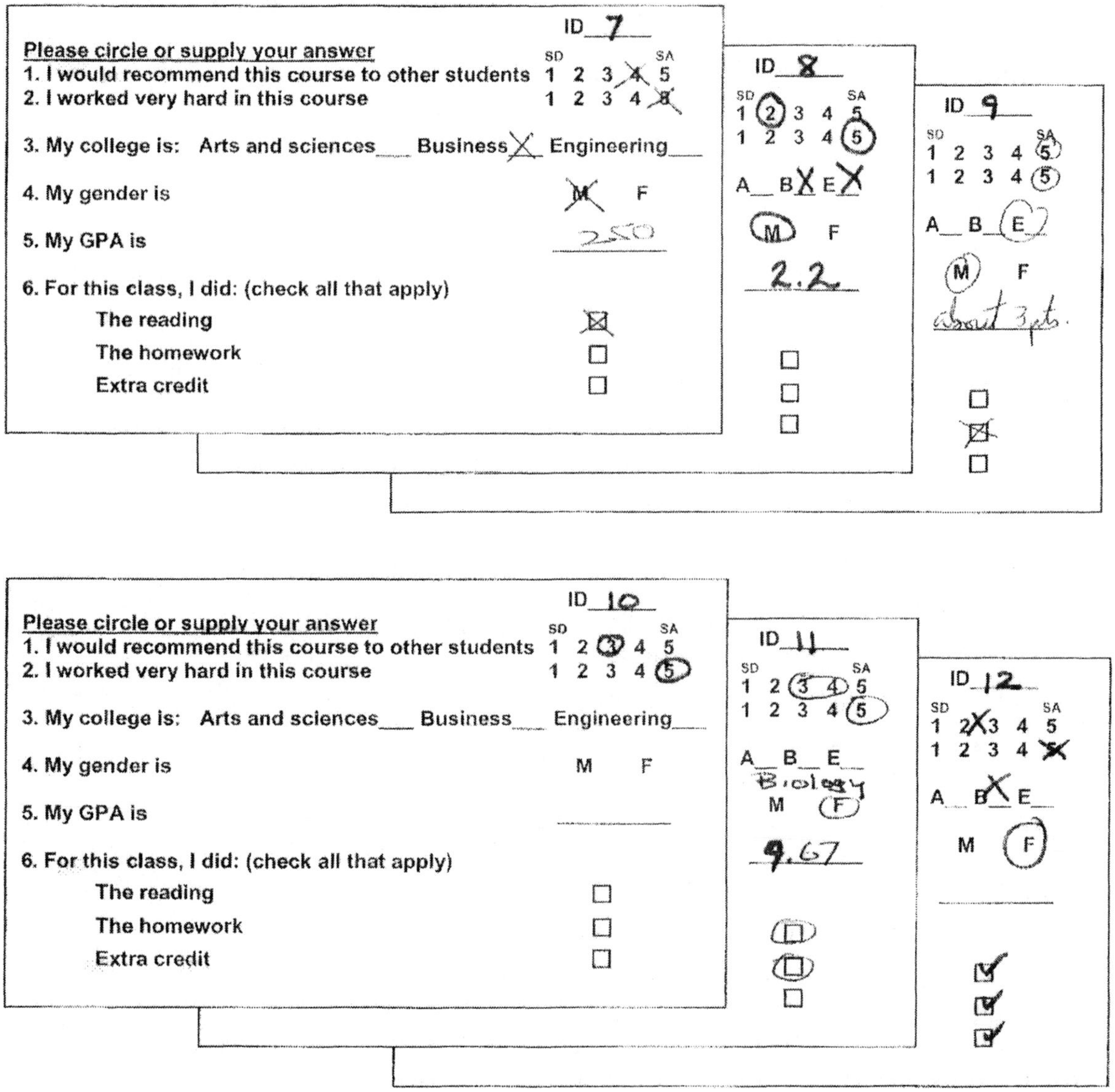
ID 7
Please circle or supply your answer
SD SA
1. I would recommend this course to other students 1 2 3 4 5
2. I worked very hard in this course 1 2 3 4 5
3. My college is: Arts and sciences___ Business___ Engineering___
4. My gender is M F
5. My GPA is
6. For this class, I did: (check all that apply)
The reading
The homework
Extra credit

ID 10
Please circle or supply your answer
SD SA
1. I would recommend this course to other students 1 2 3 4 5
2. I worked very hard in this course 1 2 3 4 5
3. My college is: Arts and sciences___ Business___ Engineering___
4. My gender is M F
5. My GPA is
6. For this class, I did: (check all that apply)
The reading
The homework
Extra credit

Fig. 2.2. Completed questionnaires for participants 7 through 12.

After the questionnaires were turned in and numbered, the researcher was ready to begin the coding process, which we will describe in the next section.

Code Data for Data Entry

Rules for Data Coding

Coding is the process of assigning numbers to the values or levels of each variable. Before starting the coding process we want to present some broad suggestions or rules to keep in mind as you proceed. These suggestions are adapted from rules proposed in Newton and Rudestam's (1999) useful book entitled *Your Statistical Consultant.* We believe that our suggestions are appropriate, but some researchers might propose alternatives, especially for "rules" 1, 2, 4, 5, and 7.

1. *All data should be numeric.* Even though it is possible to use letters or words (string variables) as data, it is not desirable to do so with SPSS. For example, we could code gender as M for male and F for female, but in order to do most statistics with SPSS you would have to convert the letters or words to numbers. It is easier to do this conversion before entering the data into the computer. As you will see in Fig. 2.3, we decided to code females as 1 and males as 0. This is called **dummy coding**. In essence, the 0 means "not female." We could, of course, code males as 1 and females as 0, or we could code one gender as 1 and the other as 2. However, it is crucial that you be consistent in your coding (e.g., for this study all males are coded 0 and females 1) and have a way to remind yourself and others of how you did the coding. Later in this chapter we will show how you can provide such a record called a **codebook**.

2. *Each variable for each case or participant must occupy the same column in the SPSS Data Editor.* With SPSS it is important that data from each participant occupies only one line (row), and each column must contain data on the same variable for all the participants. The SPSS data editor, into which you will enter data, facilitates this by putting the short variable names that you choose at the top of each column, as you saw in Chapter 1, Fig. 1.3. If a variable is measured more than once (e.g., pretest and posttest), it will be entered in two columns with somewhat different names like *mathpre* and *mathpost*.

3. *All values (codes) for a variable must be mutually exclusive.* That is, only one value or number can be recorded for each variable. Some items, like our item 6 in Fig. 2.3, allow for participants to check more than one response. In that case the item should be divided into a separate variable for each possible response choice, with one value of each variable corresponding to yes (checked) and the other to no (not checked). For example, item 6 becomes variables 6, 7, and 8 (see Fig. 2.3). Usually, items should be phrased so that persons would logically choose only one of the provided options, and all possible options are provided. A final category labeled "other" may be provided in cases where all possible options cannot be listed but these "other" responses are usually quite diverse and, thus, usually not very useful for statistical purposes.

4. *Each variable should be coded to obtain maximum information.* Do not collapse categories or values when you set up the codes for them. If needed, let the computer do it later. In general, it is desirable to code and enter data in as detailed a form as available. Thus, enter actual test scores, ages, GPAs, etc. if you know them. It is good to practice to ask participants to provide information that is quite specific. However, you should be careful not to ask questions that are so specific that the respondent may not know the answer or may not feel comfortable providing it. For example, you will obtain more information by asking participants to state their GPA to two decimals (as in Fig. 2.1 and 2.2), than if you asked them to select from a few broad categories (e.g., less than 2.0, 2.0-2.49, 2.50-2.99, etc). However, if students don't know their GPA or don't want to reveal it precisely, they may leave the question blank or write in a difficult to interpret answer.

These issues might lead you to provide a number of categories, each with a relatively narrow range of values, for variables such as age, weight, and income. Never collapse such categories before you enter the data into SPSS. For example, if you had age categories for university undergraduates 16-18, 18-20, 21-23, etc. and you realize that there are only a few students in the below 18 group, keep the codes as is for now. Later you can make a new category of 20 or under by using an SPSS function, **Transform => Recode**. If you collapse categories before you enter the data, the information is gone.

5. ***For each participant, there must be a code or value for each variable.*** These codes should be numbers, except for variables for which the data are missing. We recommend using blanks when data are missing or unusable, because SPSS is designed to handle blanks as missing values. However, sometimes you may have more than one type of missing data, such as items left blank *and* those that had an answer that was not appropriate or usable. In this case you may assign numeric codes such as 98 and 99 to them, but you must tell SPSS that these codes are for missing values, or SPSS will treat them as actual data.

6. ***Apply any coding rules consistently for all participants.*** This means that if you decide to treat a certain type of response as, say, missing for one person, you must do the same for all other participants.

7. ***Use high numbers (value or codes) for the "agree," "good," or "positive" end of a variable that is ordered.*** Sometimes you will see questionnaires that use 1 for "strongly agree," and 5 for "strongly disagree." This is not wrong as long as you are clear and consistent. However, you are less likely to get confused when interpreting your results if high values have positive meaning.

Make a Coding Form
Now you need to make some decisions about how to code the data provided in Fig. 2.1 and 2.2, especially data that are not already in numerical form. When the responses provided by participants are numbers, the variable is said to be "self coding". You can just enter the number that was circled or checked. On the other hand, variables such as *gender* or *college* have no intrinsic value associated with them. See Fig. 2.3 for the decisions we made about how to number the variables, code the values, and name the eight variables. Don't forget to number each of the questionnaires so that you can later check the entered data against the questionnaires.

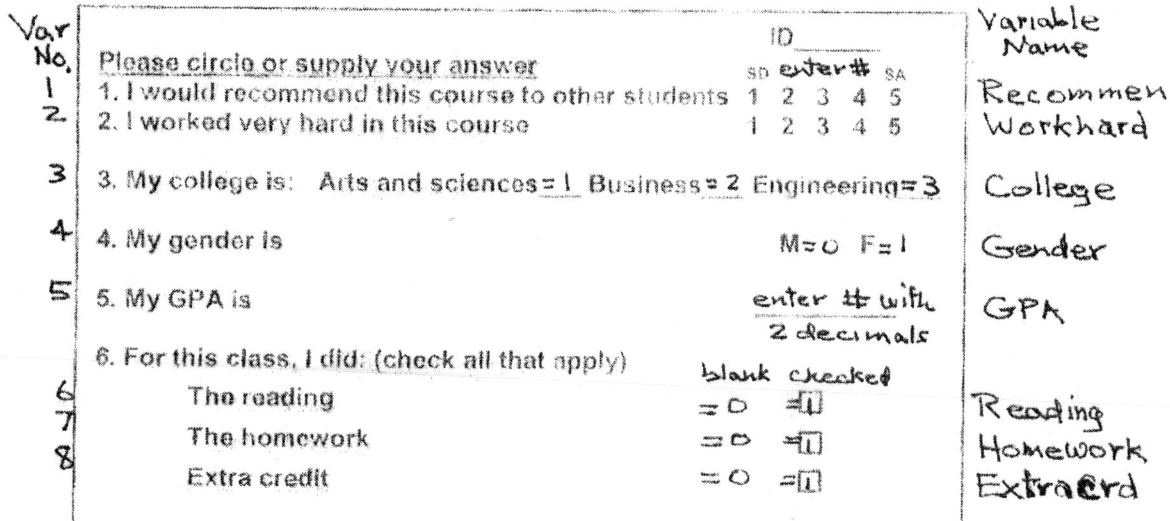
Var No.
ID ____ enter #
Please circle or supply your answer
SD SA
1 1. I would recommend this course to other students 1 2 3 4 5
2 2. I worked very hard in this course 1 2 3 4 5
3 3. My college is: Arts and sciences = 1 Business = 2 Engineering = 3
4 4. My gender is M = 0 F = 1
5 5. My GPA is enter # with 2 decimals
6. For this class, I did: (check all that apply) blank checked
6 The reading = 0 = 1
7 The homework = 0 = 1
8 Extra credit = 0 = 1
Variable Name
Recommen
Workhard
College
Gender
GPA
Reading
Homework
Extracrd

Fig. 2.3. A blank survey showing how to code the data.

Problem 2.1: Check the Completed Questionnaires

Now examine Fig. 2.1 and 2.2 for incomplete, unclear, or double answers. **Stop** and do this now, before proceeding. What issues did you see? The researcher needs to make rules about how to handle these problems and note them on the questionnaires or on a master "coding instructions" sheet so that the same rules are used for all cases.

We have identified at least 11 responses on 6 of the 12 questionnaires that need to be clarified. Can you find them all? How would you resolve them? <u>Write on Fig. 2.1 and 2.2 how you would handle each issue</u> that you see.

Make Rules About How to Handle These Problems
For each type of incomplete, blank, unclear, or double answer, you need to make a rule for what to do. As much as possible, you should make these rules before data collection, but there may well be some unanticipated issues. It is important that you apply the rules consistently for all similar problems so as not to bias your results.

Interpretation of Problem 2.1 and Fig. 2.4.
Now, we will discuss each of the issues and how we decided to handle them. Of course, some reasonable choices could have been different from ours. We think that the data for participants 1 – 6 are quite clear and ready to enter into SPSS with the help of Fig. 2.3. However, the questionnaires for participants 7 – 12 pose a number of minor and more serious problems for the person entering the data. We have written our decision in numbered callout boxes on Fig. 2.4, which are the surveys and responses for subjects 7 – 12.

1. For participant 7, the *GPA* appears to be written as 250. It seems reasonable to assume that he meant to include a decimal after the 2, and so we would enter 2.50. We could instead have said that this was an invalid response and coded it as missing. However, missing data create problems in later data analysis, especially for complex statistics. Thus, we want to use as much of the data provided as is reasonable. The important thing here is that you *must* treat all other similar problems the same way.

2. For subject 8, two colleges were checked. We could have developed a new legitimate response value (4 = other). Because this fictitious university requires that students be identified with one and only one of its three colleges, we have developed two missing value codes (as we did for ethnic group and religion in the HSB data set). Thus, for this variable only, we have used 98, for multiple checked colleges or other written-in responses that do not fit clearly into one of the colleges (e.g., business engineering or history and business). We treat such responses as missing because they seem to be invalid and /or because we would not have enough of any given response to form a reasonable size group for analysis. We used 99 as the code for cases where nothing was checked or written on the form. Having two codes enables us to distinguish between these two types of missing data, if we ever wanted to later. Other researchers (e.g., Newton and Rudestam, 1999) recommend using 8 and 9 in this case, but we think that it is best to use a code that is very different form the "valid" codes so that they stand out if you forget to tell SPSS that they are missing values.

3. Also, subject 8 wrote 2.2. for his *GPA*. It seems reasonable to enter 2.20 as the *GPA*. Actually, in this case if we enter 2.2, SPSS will treat it as 2.20 because we will tell SPSS to use two decimal places.

4. We decided to enter 3.00 for participant 9's *GPA*. Of course, the actual *GPA* could be higher or, more likely, lower, but 3.00 seems to be the best choice given the information provided by the student.

5. Participant number 10 only answered the first two questions, so there are lots of missing data. It appears that he or she decided not to complete the questionnaire. We made a rule that if 3 out of the first 5 items were blank or invalid; we would throw out that whole questionnaire as invalid. In your research report, you should state how many questionnaires were thrown out and for what reason(s). Usually you would not enter any data from that questionnaire, so you would only have 11 subjects or cases to enter. To show you how you would code someone's *college* if they left it blank, we have not deleted this subject.

6. For subject 11, there are several problems. First, she circled both 3 and 4 for the first item; a reasonable decision is to enter the average or midpoint, 3.50.

7. Participant 11 has written in "biology" for *college*. Although there is no biology college at this university; it seems reasonable to enter 1 = arts and sciences in this case and in other cases (e.g., history = 1, marketing = 2, civil = 3) where the actual college is clear. See the discussion of issue 2, above, for how to handle unclear examples.

8. Participant 11 also entered 9.67 for the *GPA*, which is an invalid response because this university has a 4-point grading system (4.00 is the maximum possible *GPA*). To show you one method of checking the entered data for errors, we will go ahead and enter 9.67. If you examine the completed questionnaires carefully, you should be able to spot errors like this in the data and not enter them.

9. Enter 1 (checked) for reading and homework for participant 11. Also enter 0 for extra credit (not checked) as you would for all the boxes left unchecked by other participants (except number 10). Even though this person circled the boxes rather than putting X's or checks in them, her intent is clear.

10. As in point 6 above, we decided to enter 2.5 for participant 12's X between 2 and 3.

11. Participant 12 also left *GPA* blank so, using the SPSS general (system) missing value code, we left it blank.

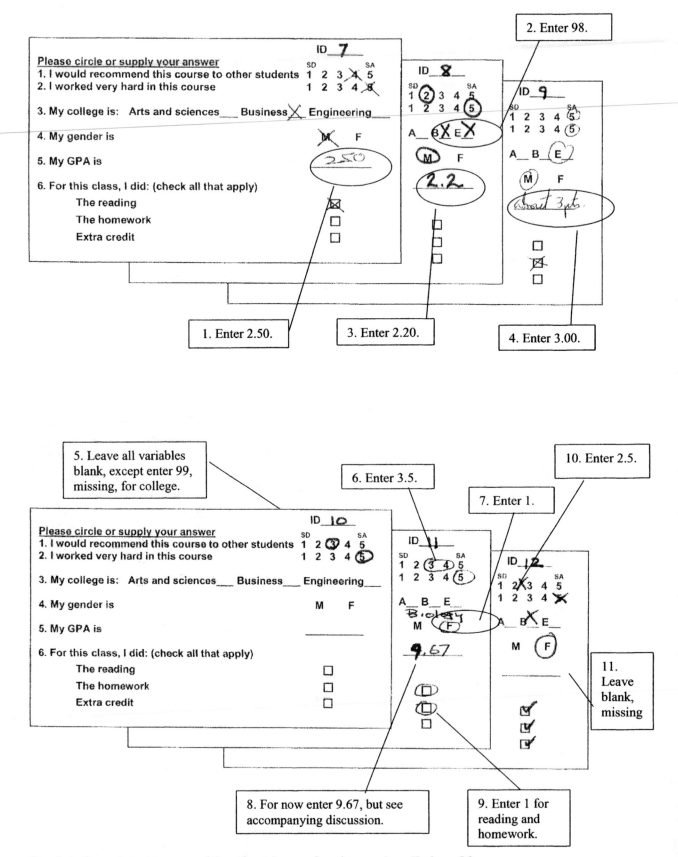

Fig. 2.4. Completed survey with callout boxes showing we handled problem responses.

Clean Up Completed Questionnaires

Now that you have made your rules and decided how to handle each problem, you need to make these rules clear to whoever will enter the data. As mentioned above, we put our decisions in callout boxes on Fig. 2.4; a common procedure would be to write your decisions on the questionnaires, perhaps in a different color.

Problem 2.2: Define and Label the Variables

The next step is to create an SPSS data file into which you will enter the data. If you do not have SPSS open, you need to logon. When you see the SPSS startup window, click the **Type in data** button; then you should see a blank **SPSS Data Editor** that will look something like Fig. 2.5. Also be sure that **Display Commands in the Log** is checked (see Appendix C). See Appendix C if you need more help

This section will help you name and label the variables. Next, we will show you how to enter data. First, let's define and label the first two variables, which are two five-point Likert ratings. To do this we need to use the **Variable View** screen. Look at the bottom left corner of the **SPSS Data Editor** to see whether you are in the **Data View** or **Variable View** screen by noting which tab is white. If you are in **Data View,** to get to **Variable View** do the following:

- Click on the **Variable View** tab at the bottom left of your screen. This will bring up a screen similar to Fig. 2.5. (Or, *double* click on **var** above the blank column to the far left side of the **Data View.**)

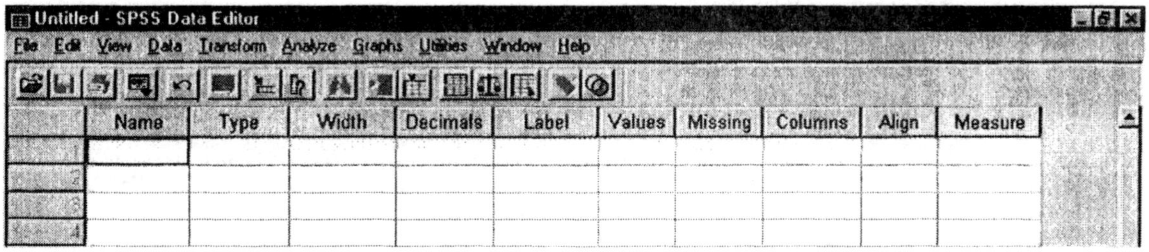

Fig. 2.5. Blank variable view screen in the data editor.

In this window, you will see 10 columns that will allow you to input the variable name, type, width, decimals, label, values, missing (data values), columns, align (data left or right), and measurement type.

Important: This was new to SPSS 10. If you have SPSS 7-9, you will not have the **Variable View** screen option and will have to enter the variable information differently. Please refer to your SPSS **Help** menu.

Define and Label Two Likert-Type Variables

We will now begin to enter information to name, label, and define the characteristics of the variables used in this chapter.
- Click in the blank box directly under **Name** in Fig. 2.5.

- Type *recommen* in this box. Notice the number 1 to the left of this box. This indicates that you are entering your first variable[1].
- Press enter. This will move your cursor to the next box, under **Type**, and pop up some information for **Type**, **Width**, etc.

Note that the **Type** is numeric, **Width** = 8, **Decimals** = 2, **Labels** = (blank), **Values** = None, **Missing** = None, **Columns** = 8, **Align** = right, **Measure** = scale. These are the default values that show up automatically when you enter a variable **Name**, but they can be changed.

For this assignment we will keep the default values for **Type**, **Width**, **Columns**, and **Align**. On the **Variable View** screen, you will notice that the default for **Type** is **Numeric**. This refers to the type of variable you are entering. Usually, you will only use the **Numeric** option. Numeric means the data are numbers. **String** would be used if you input words or letters such as "M" for males and "F" for females. However, it is best not to enter words or letters because you wouldn't be able to do many statistics without recoding them as numbers. In this book, we will always keep the **Type** as **Numeric**.

We recommend keeping the **Width** at eight. This means you *can* have an 8-digit number. Keeping the **Columns** at eight allows our variable names to be included at the top of each column of data. We will always **Align** the numbers to the right. Sometimes, we will change the settings for the other columns.

Now, let's define and label the *recommen* variable.
- For this variable leave the decimals at 2.
- Type *I recommend course* in the **Label** box. This longer label will show in appropriate SPSS windows and on your printouts. The labels can be up to 40 characters but it is best to keep them about 20 or less or your outputs may be difficult to read.

In the **Values** column do the following:
- Double click on **Values**. You will see the word "None" and a small gray box with three dots.
- Click on the three dots. You will then see a screen like Fig. 2.6. (We will add **value labels** for the ends of the Likert scale to help us interpret the data.).
- Type 1 in the **Value** box in Fig. 2.6.
- Type *strongly disagree* in the **Value Label** box. Press **Add**.
- Type *5* and *strongly agree* in the **Values** and **Value Labels** boxes. Your window should look like Fig. 2.6 just before you click on **Add** for the second time.
- Click on **Add.**

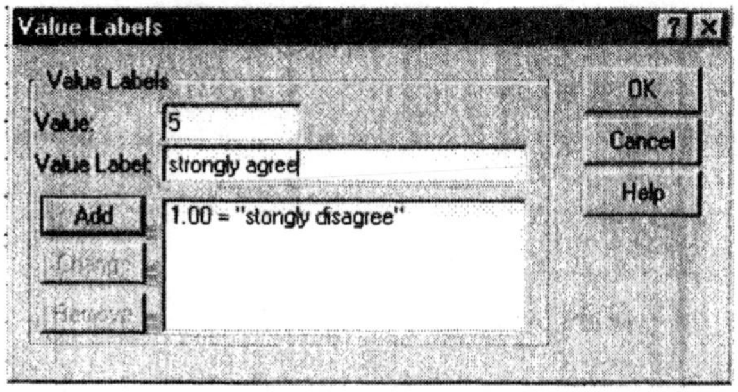

Fig. 2.6 Value labels window.

---

[1] It is no longer necessary in SPSS to keep variable names at 8 characters or less, but we have in this chapter. Other rules about variable names still apply (see footnote 4 in Chapter 1). Note also that bullets are used to indicate that instructions about SPSS actions (e.g., click, highlight) will follow, and key terms shown in SPSS windows (e.g., **Name**) are shown in bold.

Leave the cells for the **Missing** to **Measure** Columns as they currently appear.

Now let's define and label the next variable.
- Click on the next blank box under **Name** (opposite 2) to enter the name of the next variable.
- Type *workhard* in the **Name** column.
- Type *I worked hard* in the **Label** column.
- Insert the highest and lowest **Values** for this variable the same way you did for *recommen* (1 = *strongly disagree* and 5 = *strongly agree*).

Keep all the other columns as they are.

Define and Label College and Gender
- Now, select the cell under **Name** and opposite the 3.
- Call this third variable *college* by typing that in the box.
- Click on the 3rd box under **Decimals**. For this variable, there is no reason to have any decimal places because people were asked to choose only one of the three colleges. You will notice that when you select the box under **Decimals**, up and down arrows appear on the right side of the box. You can either click the arrows to raise or lower the number of decimals, or you can double click on the box and manually type in the desired number.
- For the purposes of this variable, select or type 0 as the number of **decimals.**
- Next, click the box under **Label** to type in the variable label *college*.
- Under **Values**, click on the small gray box with three dots.
- In the **Value Labels** window, type 1 in the **Value** box, type *arts and sciences* in the **Value Label** box.
- Then click **Add**. Do the same for 2=*business*, 3=*engineering*, 98 = *other, multiple ans,* 99 = *blank*.

The **Value Labels** window should resemble Fig. 2.7 just before you click **Add** for the last time.

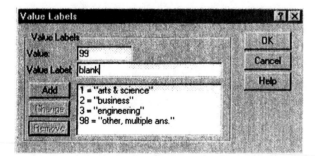

Fig. 2.7. Value labels window.

- Under **Measure,** click the box that reads **Scale**.
- Click the down arrow and choose **Nominal** because for this variable the categories are unordered.

Your screen should look like Fig. 2.8 just after you click on nominal.

Fig. 2.8. Measurement selection.

- Under **Missing**, click on **Discrete Missing Values** and enter 98 and 99 in the first two boxes. (See Fig. 2.9.) This step is essential if you have more than one missing value code. If you leave the **Missing** cell at **None,** SPSS will not know that 98 and 99s should be considered missing. **None** in this column is somewhat misleading. None means no special missing values (i.e., only blanks are considered missing).

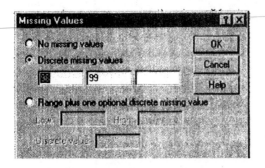

Fig. 2.9. Missing values.

Your **SPSS Data Editor** should now look like Fig. 2.10.

	Name	Type	Width	Decimals	Label	Values	Missing	Columns	Align	Measure
1	recommen	Numeric	8	2	I recommend c	{1.00, stongly	None	8	Right	Scale
2	workhard	Numeric	8	2	I worked hard	{1.00, strongly	None	8	Right	Scale
3	college	Numeric	8	0	college	{1, arts & scie	98, 99	8	Right	Nominal

Fig. 2.10. Completed variable view for first three variables.

Now define and label *gender* similarly to how you did this for *college.*
- First, type the variable **Name** *gender* in the next blank row.
- Click on **Decimals** to change the decimal places to 0 (zero).
- Now click on **Labels** and label the variable *gender.*
- Next you will label the values or levels of the *gender* variable. You need to be sure your coding matches your labels. We arbitrarily decided to code *male* as zero and *female* as 1.
- Click on the **Values** cell.
- Then, click on the gray three-dot box to get a window like Fig. 2.7 again. Remember, this is the same process you conducted when entering the labels for the values of the first three variables.
- Now, type 0 to the right of **Value.**
- To the right of **Value Label** type *male.* Click on **Add.**
- Repeat this process for 1 = *female.* Click on **Add.**
- Click **OK.**
- Finally, click on **Scale** under **Measure** to change the level of measurement to **Nominal** because this is an unordered, dichotomous variable.

Once again, realize that the researcher has made a series of decisions that another researcher could have done differently. For example, you could have used 1 and 2 as the values for gender, and you might have given males the higher number. We have chosen, in this case, to do what is called dummy coding. In essence, 1 is female and 0 is not female. This type of coding is useful for interpreting gender when used in statistical analysis. Let's continue further.

Define and Label Grade Point Average

You should now have enough practice to define and label the *gpa* variable. After naming the variable *gpa,* do the following:

- For **Decimals** leave the decimals at 2.
- Now click on **Label** and label it *grade point average*.
- Click on **Values.** Type 0 = *All F's* and 4 = *All A's*. (Note that for this variable, we have used actual GPA to 2 decimals, rather than dividing it into ordered groups such as a C average, B average, A average.)
- Under **Measure**, leave it as **Scale** because this variable has many ordered values and is likely to be normally distributed in the population.

Define and Label the Last Three Variables

Now you should define the three variables related to the parts of the class that a student completed. Remember we said the **Names** of these variables would be: *reading, homework,* and *extracrd.* The variable **Labels** will be *I did the reading, I did the homework, I did extra credit.* The **Value** labels are: 0 = not checked/blank and 1 = checked. These variables should have no decimals, and the **Measure** should be changed to **Nominal.** Your complete **Variable View** should look like Fig. 2.11.

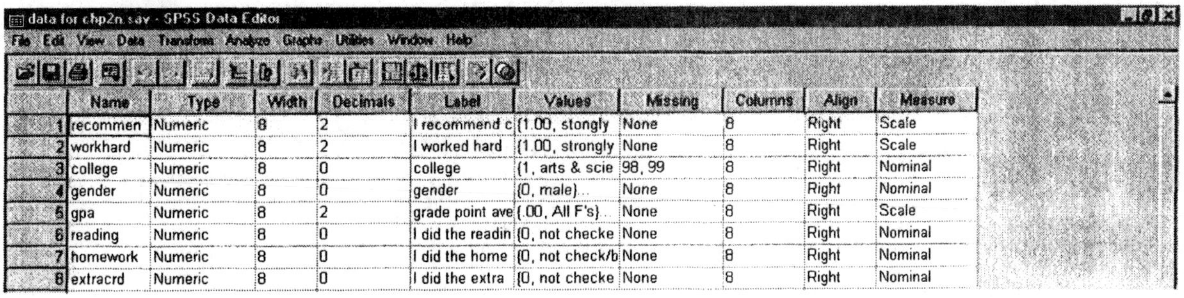

	Name	Type	Width	Decimals	Label	Values	Missing	Columns	Align	Measure
1	recommen	Numeric	8	2	I recommend c	{1.00, stongly	None	8	Right	Scale
2	workhard	Numeric	8	2	I worked hard	{1.00, strongly	None	8	Right	Scale
3	college	Numeric	8	0	college	{1, arts & scie	98, 99	8	Right	Nominal
4	gender	Numeric	8	0	gender	{0, male}	None	8	Right	Nominal
5	gpa	Numeric	8	2	grade point ave	{.00, All F's}	None	8	Right	Scale
6	reading	Numeric	8	0	I did the readin	{0, not checke	None	8	Right	Nominal
7	homework	Numeric	8	0	I did the home	{0, not check/b	None	8	Right	Nominal
8	extracrd	Numeric	8	0	I did the extra	{0, not checke	None	8	Right	Nominal

Fig. 2.11. Completed variable view.

Problem 2.3: Display Your Dictionary or Codebook

Now that you have defined and labeled your variables, you can print a codebook or dictionary of your variables. It is a very useful record of what you have done. Notice that the information in the codebook is essentially the same as that in the variable view (Fig. 2.11) so you do not really have to have both, but the codebook makes a more complete printed record of your labels and values.

- Select **File => Display Data File Information => Working File.** Your **Codebook** should look like Output 2.1, without the callout boxes.

Output 2.1: Codebook

```
DISPLAY DICTIONARY.
```

File Information

```
List of variables on the working file
```

```
Name (Position) Label
```
                                                    ┌──────────────────────┐
                                                    │ Variable number   │
```
recommen (1) I recommend course
```                                                  └──────────────────────┘
```
     Measurement Level: Scale                       ┌──────────────────────┐
     Column Width: 8  Alignment: Right              │  Variable label      │
     Print Format: F8.2                             └──────────────────────┘
     Write Format: F8.2
```
                                                    ┌──┐
```
     Value     Label                                │ This mean the data for this variable can be up │
     1.00      strongly disagree                    │ to 8 digits including 2 decimal places.    │
     5.00      strongly agree                        └──────────────────────────────────────────┘
```
                                                    ┌──────────────────────┐
```
workhard (2) I worked hard                          │  Short variable name │
```                                                  └──────────────────────┘
```
     Measurement Level: Scale
     Column Width: 8  Alignment: Right
     Print Format: F8.2
     Write Format: F8.2
```
                                                    ┌──────────────────────┐
```
     Value     Label                                │ This variable has three │
                                                    │ unordered values so it is │
     1.00      strongly disagree                    │ called nominal.      │
     5.00      strongly agree                        └──────────────────────┘
```

```
college (3) college
     Measurement Level: Nominal
     Column Width: 8  Alignment: Right               ┌──────────────────────────────────┐
     Print Format: F8                                │ These are missing values for this │
     Write Format: F8                                │ variable. Most variables use      │
     Missing Values: 98, 99                          │ blanks, which are the SPSS system │
                                                     │ missing value. However, here we   │
                                                     │ need two missing value codes.     │
     Value     Label                                 └──────────────────────────────────┘

     1         arts and sciences
     2         business                              ┌──────────────────────────────────┐
     3         engineering                           │ The M after 98 and 99 shows that SPSS │
     98 M      other, multiple ans                   │ considers these numbers to be missing data. │
     99 M      blank                                 └──────────────────────────────────┘
```

```
gender (4) gender                                    ┌──────────────────────────────────┐
     Measurement Level: Nominal                      │ We call dichotomous (2 level)     │
     Column Width: 8  Alignment: Right               │ variables nominal, but they are a │
     Print Format: F8                                │ special case as discussed in      │
     Write Format: F8                                │ Chapter 3.                        │
                                                     └──────────────────────────────────┘

     Value     Label                                 ┌──────────────────────────────────┐
                                                     │ These are the values or           │
     0         male                                  │ levels of the gender              │
     1         female                                │ variable and their labels.        │
                                                     └──────────────────────────────────┘
```

```
gpa (5) grade point average
     Measurement Level: Scale
     Column Width: 8  Alignment: Right
     Print Format: F8.2
     Write Format: F8.2                              ┌──────────────────────────────────┐
                                                     │ This variable has many ordered    │
     Value     Label                                 │ values; the possible valus are    │
                                                     │ equally spaced and probably       │
     .00       All F's                               │ normally distributed so we called │
     4.00      All A's                               │ it scale.                         │
                                                     └──────────────────────────────────┘
```

```
reading (6) I did the reading
     Measurement Level: Nominal
     Column Width: 8  Alignment: Right
     Print Format: F8
     Write Format: F8

     Value     Label

     0         not checked/blank
     1         checked
```

```
homework (7) I did the homework
     Measurement Level: Nominal
     Column Width: 8  Alignment: Right
     Print Format: F8
     Write Format: F8

          Value     Label

              0     not checked, balnk
              1     checked


extracrd (8) I did the extra credit
     Measurement Level: Nominal
     Column Width: 8  Alignment: Right
     Print Format: F8
     Write Format: F8

          Value     Label

              0     not checked, blank
              1     checked
```

You may not be able to see all of the file information/codebook on your computer screen. However, you will be able to print the entire codebook.

Problem 2.4: Enter Data

Close the codebook, and then click on **Untitled - SPSS Data Editor** or on the **Data View** tab on the bottom of the screen to return you to the data editor. Note that the SPSS spreadsheet has numbers down the left-hand side (see Fig. 2.13). These numbers represent each subject in the study. The data for each participant's questionnaire go on one and only one line across the page with each column representing a variable from our questionnaire. Therefore, the first column will be *recommen*, the second will be *workhard*, the third will be *college*, etc.

After defining and labeling the variables, your next task is to enter the data directly from the questionnaires or from a data entry form.

Sometimes researchers transfer the data from the questionnaires to a **data entry form** (like Table 2.1) by hand before entering the data into SPSS. This is helpful if the questionnaires or answer sheet are not easily readable, if the responses are to be entered in a different order than on the questionnaire, or if additional coding or recoding is required before data entry. In these situations, you could make mistakes entering the data directly from the questionnaires. On the other hand, if you use a data entry form, you could make copying mistakes, and it takes time to transfer the data from questionnaires to the data entry form. Thus, there are advantages and disadvantages of using a data entry form as an intermediate step between the questionnaire and the SPSS data editor. Our cleaned up questionnaires should be easy enough to use so that you could enter the data directly from Fig. 2.1 and Fig. 2.4 into the SPSS data editor. Try to do that using the directions below. If you have difficulty, you may use Table 2.1, but remember that it took an extra step to produce.

In Table 2.1 the data are shown as they would look if we copied the cleaned up data from the questionnaires to a data entry sheet, except that the data entry form would probably be hand written on ruled paper.

Table 2.1 A Data Entry Form:
Responses Copied from the Questionnaires

	recommen	workhard	college	gender	gpa	reading	homework	extracrd
1	3	5	1	0	3.12	0	0	1
2	4	5	2	0	2.91	1	1	0
3	4	5	1	1	3.33	0	1	1
4	5	5	1	1	3.60	1	1	1
5	4	5	2	1	2.52	0	0	1
6	5	5	3	1	2.98	1	0	0
7	4	5	2	0	2.50	1	0	0
8	2	5	98	0	2.20	0	0	0
9	5	5	3	0	3.00	0	1	0
10			99					
11	3.5	5	1	1	9.67	1	1	0
12	2.5	5	2	1		1	1	1

To enter the data, ensure that your **SPSS Data Editor** is showing.
- If it is not already highlighted, click on the far left column, which should say *recommen*
- To enter the data into this highlighted column, simply type the number and press the **right arrow**. For example, first type 3 (the number will show up in the blank space above of the row of variable names) and then press the **right arrow**; the number will be entered into the highlighted box.

In Fig. 2.12, all the data for the first two participants have been entered.

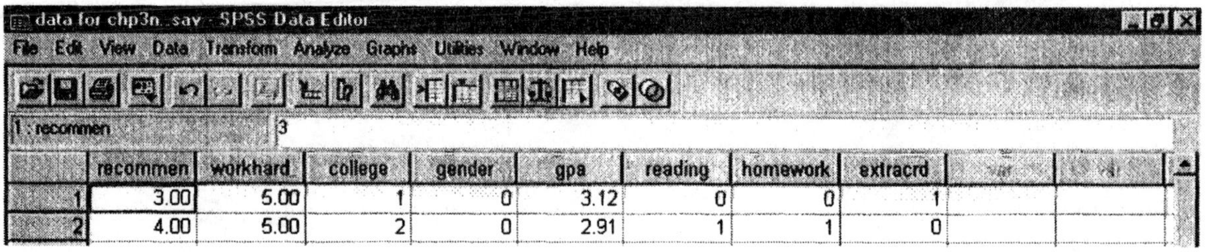

Fig. 2.12. SPSS Data Editor with two participants entered.

- Now enter from your cleaned up questionnaires the data in Fig. 2.1 and Fig. 2.4. If you make a mistake when entering data, correct it by clicking on the cell (the cell will be highlighted), type the correct score, and press enter or the arrow key.

Before you do any analysis, compare the data on your questionnaires with the data in the **SPSS Data Editor.** If you have lots of data, a sample can be checked, but it is preferable to check all of the data. If you find errors in your sample, you should check all the entries.

Problem 2.5: Run Descriptives and Check the Data

In order to get a better "feel" for the data and to check for other types of errors or problems on the questionnaires, we recommend that you run the SPSS program called **Descriptives.** To compute basic descriptive statistics for all your subjects you will need to do these steps:

- Select **Analyze** => **Descriptive Statistics** => **Descriptives** (see Fig. 2.13).[2]

Note: If you are using SPSS 9 or lower, you will find the statistics selections under **Statistics** on your toolbar instead of **Analyze.**

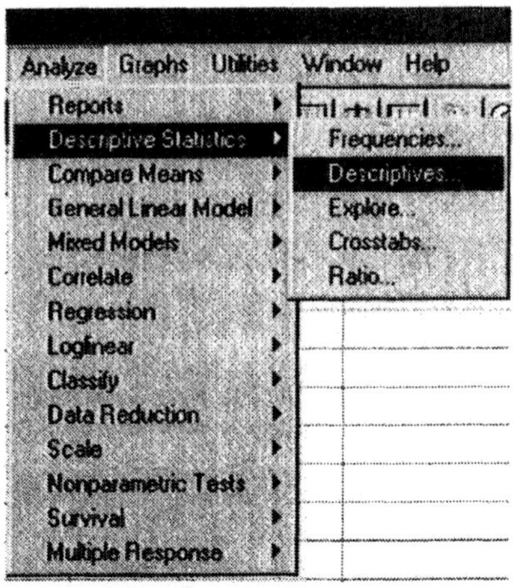

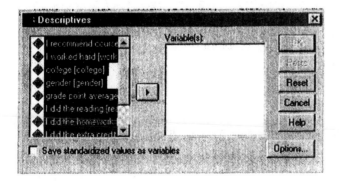

Fig. 2.13 Analyze menu.

After selecting **Descriptives**, you will be ready to compute the mean, minimum, and maximum values for all participants or cases on all variables in order to examine the data.
- Now highlight all of the variables. To highlight, begin at the top of the left box and hold the left mouse button down while you scroll downward until *all* of the variables listed turn blue (see Fig. 2.14a).
- Click on the **arrow** button pointing right. When you finish, the **Descriptives** dialog box should look like Fig. 2.14b.

Fig. 2.14a. Descriptives-before moving variables.

---

[2] This is how we indicate, in this and the following chapters, that you first pull down the **Analyze** menu, then select **Descriptive Statistics** from the first flyout menu, and finally select **Descriptives** from the last flyout menu.

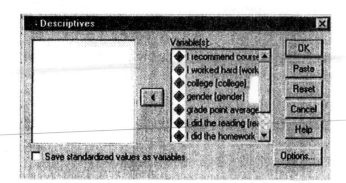

Fig. 2.14b. Descriptives- after moving variables.

- Be sure that *all* of the variables have moved out of the left window. If your screen looks like Fig. 2.14b, then click on **Options.** You will get Fig. 2.15.

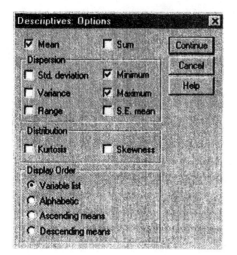

Fig. 2.15. Descriptives: Options

Follow these steps:

- Notice that the **Mean, Std. deviation, Minimum** and **Maximum** were already checked. Click off **Std. deviation**. At this time, we will not request more descriptive statistics. We will do them in Chapter 4.
- Ensure that the **Variable list** bubble is checked in the **Display Order** section. Note: You can also click on **Ascending or Descending means** if you want your variables listed in order of the means. If you wanted the variables listed alphabetically, you would check **Alphabetic.**
- Click on **Continue**, which will bring you back to the main **Descriptives** dialog box (Fig. 2.14b).
- Then click on **OK** to run the program.

You should get an output like Fig. 2.16. If it looks similar, you have done the steps correctly.

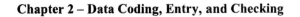

DESCRIPTIVES
    VARIABLES=recommen workhard college gender gpa reading homework extracrd
    /STATISTICS=MEAN MIN MAX .

→ **Descriptives**   This is called the SPSS syntax or log. It is useful for checking what you requested SPSS to do and for running or rerunning advanced statistics. If the syntax does not appear in your Output, consult Appendix A.

Descriptive Statistics

	N	Minimum	Maximum	Mean
I recommend course	11	2.00	5.00	3.8182
I worked hard	11	5.00	5.00	5.0000
college	10	1	3	1.80
gender	11	0	1	.55
grade point average	10	2.20	9.67	3.5830
I did the reading	11	0	1	.55
I did the homework	11	0	1	.55
I did the extra credit	11	0	1	.45
Valid N (listwise)	9			

Fig. 2.16. SPSS output viewer for Descriptives.

The left side of Fig. 2.16 lists the various parts of your output. You can click on any item on the left (e.g., **Title, Notes,** or **Descriptive Statistics**) to activate the output for that item, and then you can edit it. For example you can click on **Title** and then expand the title or add information such as your name and the date. (See also Appendix A for more on editing outputs.)

- Double click on the large, bold word **Descriptives** in Fig. 2.16. Type your name in the box that appears so it will appear on your output when you print it later. Also type "Output 2.2" at the top so you and /or your instructor will know what it is later.

If you haven't yet checked to see if the data in the **SPSS Data Editor** match those on the questionnaires, compare entered data with completed surveys.

Then, for each variable, compare the minimum and maximum scores in Fig. 2.16 with the highest and lowest appropriate values in the codebook (Output 2.1) This checking of data before doing any more statistics is highly recommended.

Note that after each output we have provided a brief interpretation in a box. On the output itself, we have pointed out some of the key things by circling them and making some comments in boxes, which are known as **callout boxes**. Of course, these circles and information boxes will not show up on your printout.

Output 2.2 Descriptives

```
DESCRIPTIVES
  VARIABLES=recommen workhard college gender gpa reading homework extracrd
  /STATISTICS=MEAN MIN MAX.
```

Descriptive Statistics

	N	Minimum	Maximum	Mean
I recommend course	11	2.00	5.00	3.8182
I worked hard	11	5.00	5.00	5.0000
college	10	1	3	1.80
gender	11	0	1	.55
grade point average	10	2.20	9.67	3.5830
I did the reading	11	0	1	.55
I did the homework	11	0	1	.55
I did the extra credit	11	0	1	.45
Valid N (listwise)	9			

Highest and lowest

Average college is not meaningful.

Average GPA.

The number of people with no missing data.

Interpretation of Output 2.2

This output shows, for each of the eight variables, the number (**N**) of participants with no missing data on that variable. The **Valid N, (listwise)** is the number (9) who have no missing data on any variable. The table also shows the **Minimum** and **Maximum** score that any participants had on that variable. For example, no one circled a 1, but one or more persons circled a 2 for the *I recommend course* variable, and at least one person circled 5. Notice that for *I worked hard,* 5 is both the minimum and maximum. This item is, therefore, really a constant and not a variable; it will not be useful in statistical analyses.

The table also provides the **Mean** or average score for each variable. Notice the mean for *I worked hard* is 5 because everyone circled 5. The mean of 1.80 for *college,* a nominal (unordered) variable, is nonsense, so ignore it. However, the means of .55 for the dichotomous variables *gender, I did the reading,* and *I did the homework* indicate that in each case 55% chose the answers that corresponded to 1 (female gender and "yes" for doing the reading and homework). The mean *grade point average* was 3.58, which is probably an error because it is too high for the overall *GPA* for most groups of undergrads. Note also that there has to be an error in *GPA* because the maximum *GPA* of 9.67 is not possible at this university, which has a 4.00 maximum (see codebook). Thus the 9.67 for participant 11 is an invalid response. The questionnaires should be checked again to be sure there wasn't a data entry error. If as in this case, the survey says 9.48, it should be changed to blank, the missing value code.

34

Interpretation Questions

1.   What steps or actions should be taken after you collect data and before you run any analyses?

2.   Are there any other rules of data coding that you think should be added? Are there any of our "rules" that you think should be modified? Which ones? How?

3.   Why would you print a codebook?

4.   If you identified other problems with the completed questionnaires, what were they? How did your decisions about how to handle the problems differ from ours?

5.   Why and why not would you use a data entry form?

6.   a) Why is it important to check your raw (questionnaire) data before entering it into SPSS?
   b) What are ways to check it?

Extra SPSS Problems

Using your College Student data file, do the following problems. Print your outputs and circle the key parts that you discuss.

1.   Compute the N, minimum, maximum, and mean, for all the variables in the college student data file. How many students have complete data? Identify any statistics on the output that are not meaningful. Explain.

2.   What is the mean height of the students? What about the average height of the same sex parent? What percentage of students are males? What percentage have children?

CHAPTER 3

Measurement and Descriptive Statistics

Frequency Distributions

Frequency distributions are critical to understanding our use of measurement terms. We begin this chapter with a discussion of frequency distributions and two examples. Frequency tables and distributions can be used whether the variable involved has ordered or unordered levels (SPSS calls them values). In this section, we will only consider variables with many ordered values.

A **frequency distribution** is a tally or count of the <u>number of times each score on a single variable occurs</u>. For example, the frequency distribution of final grades in a class of 50 students might be 7 A's, 20 B's, 18 C's, and 5 D's. Note that in this frequency distribution most students have B's or C's (grades in the middle) and similar smaller numbers have A's and D's (high and low grades). When there are a small number of scores for the low and high values and most scores are for the middle values, the distribution is said to be **approximately normally distributed.** We will discuss the normal curve in more detail later in this chapter.

When the variable is continuous or has many ordered levels (or values), the frequency distribution usually is based on ranges of values for the variable. For example, the frequencies (number of students), shown by the bars in Fig 3.1, are for a range of points (in this case SPSS selected a range of 50: 250-299, 300-349, 350-399, etc). Notice that the largest number of students (about 20) has scores in the middle two bars of the range (between 450-550). Similar small numbers of students have very low and very high scores. The bars in the histogram form a distribution (pattern or curve) that is quite similar to the normal, bell shaped curve shown by the line that is superimposed on the histogram. Thus the frequency distribution of the *SAT math* scores is said to be **approximately normal**.

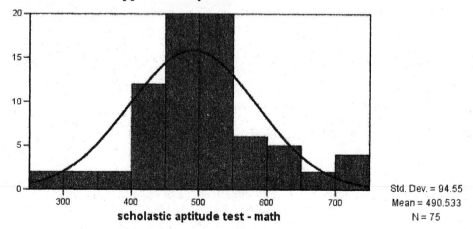

Std. Dev. = 94.55
Mean = 490.533
N = 75

Fig. 3.1. A grouped frequency distribution for SAT Math scores.

Figure 3.2 shows the frequency distribution for the *competence scale*. Notice that the bars form a pattern very different from the normal curve line. This distribution can be said to be **not normally distributed**. As we will see later in the chapter, the distribution is **negatively skewed**.

That is, the tail of the curve or the extreme scores are on the low end or left side. Note how much this differs from the *SAT math* score frequency distribution. As you will see in the Levels of Measurement section (below), we call the *competence scale* variable **ordinal.**

You can create these figures yourself using the hsbdata.sav file.[1] Select:
- **Graphs => Histogram**
- Then move *scholastic aptitude test – math* (or *competence scale*) into the **Variable** box.
- Then check **Display normal curve.**
- Click **OK.**

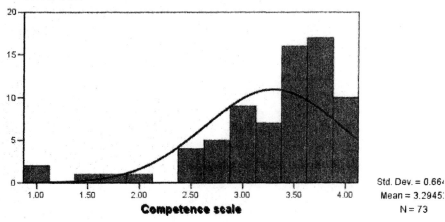

Std. Dev. = 0.66‹
Mean = 3.2945:
N = 73

Fig 3.2. A grouped frequency distribution for the competence scale.

Levels of Measurement

Measurement is the assignment of numbers or symbols to the different characteristics (values) of variables according to rules. In order to understand your variables, it is important to know their level of measurement. Depending on the level of measurement of a variable, the data can mean different things. For example, the number 2 might indicate a score of two; it might indicate that the subject was a male; or it might indicate that the subject was ranked second in the class. To help understand these differences, types or levels of variables have been identified. It is common and traditional to discuss four levels or scales of measurement: **nominal, ordinal, interval, and ratio,** which vary from the unordered (nominal) to the highest level (ratio).[2] These four traditional terms are not the same as those used in SPSS, and we think that they are not always the most useful for determining what statistics to use.

SPSS uses three terms (**nominal, ordinal, and scale**) for the levels of types of measurement. How these correspond to the traditional terms is shown in Table 3.1. When you name and label

---

[1] In this chapter we will not phrase the creation of the SPSS outputs as "problems" for you to answer. However, we will describe with bullets and arrows (as we did in Chapter 2) how to create the figures shown in this chapter. You may want to use SPSS to see how to create these figures and tables.

[2] Unfortunately, the terms "level" and "scale" are used several ways in research. Levels refer to the categories or values of a variable (e.g., male or female or 1, 2, or 3); level, can also refer to the three or four different types of measurement (nominal, ordinal, etc). These several types of measurement have also been called "scales of measurement," but SPSS uses scale specifically for the highest type or level of measurement. Scale is also used to describe questionnaire items that are rated from strongly disagree to strongly agree (Likert scale) and for the sum of such items (summated scale). We wish there weren't so many uses of these terms; the best we can do is try to be clear about our usage.

variables in SPSS, you have the opportunity to select one of these three types of measurement as was demonstrated in Chapter 2 (see Fig 2.10). Although what you choose does *not* affect what SPSS does in most cases, an appropriate choice indicates that you understand your data and may help guide your selection of statistics.

We believe that the terms **nominal, dichotomous, ordinal**, and **approximately normal** (for normally distributed) are usually more useful than the traditional or SPSS measurement terms for the selection and interpretation of statistics. In part this is because statisticians disagree about the usefulness of the traditional levels of measurement in determining appropriate selection of statistics. Furthermore, our experience is that the traditional terms are frequently misunderstood and applied inappropriately by students. Hopefully, our terms, as discussed below, are clear and useful.

Table 3.1 compares the three sets of terms and provides a summary description of our definitions of them. Professors differ in the terminology they prefer and on how much importance to place on levels or scales of measurement so you will see all of these terms and the others mentioned below in textbooks and articles.

Table 3.1. *Similar Traditional, SPSS, and Our Measurement Terms*

Traditional Term	Traditional Definition	SPSS Term	Our Term	Our Definitions
Nominal	Two or more <u>unordered</u> categories	Nominal	Nominal	Three or more <u>unordered</u> categories.
NA	NA	NA	Dichotomous	Two categories, either ordered or unordered.
Ordinal	<u>Ordered</u> levels, in which the difference in magnitude between levels is not equal	Ordinal	Ordinal	Three or more <u>ordered</u> levels, but the frequency distribution of the scores is <u>not</u> normally distributed.
Interval & Ratio	**Interval:** <u>ordered</u> levels, in which the difference between levels is equal, but no true zero. **Ratio:** <u>ordered</u> levels; the difference between levels is equal, and a true zero.	Scale	Approximately Normal	Many (at least 5) <u>ordered</u> levels or scores, with the frequency distribution of the scores being approximately normal.

Nominal Variables

This is the most basic or lowest level of measurement, in which the numerals assigned to each category stand for the <u>name</u> of the category, but they have no implied order or value. For example, in the HSB study, the values for the *religion* variable are 1= *protestant*, 2 =*catholic*, 3 = *no religion*. This does not mean that that two protestants equal one catholic or any of the typical mathematical uses of the numerals. The same reasoning applies to many other true nominal variables, such as ethnic group, type of disability, or section number in a class schedule. In each of these cases, the categories are distinct and non-overlapping, but not ordered. Each category or group in the modified HSB variable *ethnicity* is different from each other but there is no order to the categories. Thus, the categories could be numbered 1 for *Asian American*, 2 for *Latino American*, 3 for *African American*, and 4 for *European American* or the reverse or any combination of assigning one number to each category.

What this implies is that you must *not* treat the numbers used for identifying nominal categories as if they were numbers that could be used in a formula, added together, subtracted from one another, or used to compute an average. Average ethnic group makes no sense. However, if you ask SPSS to compute the average ethnic group, it will do so and give you meaningless information. The important aspect of nominal measurement is to have clearly defined, non-overlapping or mutually exclusive categories that can be coded reliably by observers or by self-report.

Using nominal measurement does dramatically reduce the statistics that can be used with your data, but it does not altogether eliminate the possible use of statistics to summarize your data and make inferences. Therefore, even when the data are unordered or nominal categories, your research may benefit from the use of appropriate statistics. Later we will discuss the types of statistics, both descriptive and inferential, that are appropriate for nominal data.

Other terms for nominal variables. Unfortunately, the literature is full of similar, but not identical terms to describe the measurement aspects of variables. **Categorical, qualitative,** and **discrete** are terms sometimes used interchangeably with nominal, but we think that nominal is better because it is possible to have ordered, discrete categories (e.g., low, medium, and high IQ, which we and other researchers would consider an ordinal variable). "Qualitative" is also used to discuss a different approach to doing research, with important differences in philosophy, assumptions, and approach to conducting research.

Dichotomous Variables
Dichotomous variables always have only two levels or categories. In some cases, they may have an implied order (e.g., *math grades* in high school are coded 0 for *less than an A or B* average and 1 for *mostly A or B*). Other dichotomous variables do not have any order to the categories (e.g., *male* or *female*). For many purposes, it is best to use the same statistics for dichotomous and nominal variables. However, a statistic such as the mean or average, which would be meaningless for a three or more category nominal variable (e.g., *ethnicity*), does have meaning when there are only two categories. For example, in the HSB data the average *gender* is .55 (with *males* = 0 and *females* = 1). This means that 55% of the participants were *females*, the higher code. Furthermore, we will see with multiple regression that dichotomous variables, called *dummy variables*, can be used as independent variables along with other variables that are normally distributed.

Other terms for dichotomous variables. In the SPSS **Variable View** (e.g., see Fig 2.11), we label dichotomous variables "nominal," and this is common in textbooks. However, please remember that dichotomous variables are really a special case and for some purposes they can be treated <u>as if</u> they were scale or normal. Dichotomous data have two discrete categories and are sometimes called **discrete variables** or **categorical variables** or **dummy variables**.

Ordinal Variables

In ordinal measurement, there are not only mutually exclusive categories as in nominal scales, but the categories are <u>ordered</u> from low to high, such that ranks could be assigned (e.g., 1st, 2nd, 3rd). Thus in an ordinal scale one knows which participant is highest or most preferred on a dimension but the intervals between the various categories are not equal. Our definition of ordinal focuses on whether the frequency counts for each category or value are distributed like the bell shaped, normal curve with more responses in the middle categories and fewer in the lowest and highest categories. If not approximately normal, we would call the variable ordinal. Ordered variables with only a few categories (say 2-4) would also be called ordinal. As indicated in Table 3.1, however, the traditional definition of ordinal focuses on whether the differences between pairs of levels are equal.

Other terms for ordinal variables. Some authors use the term **ranks** interchangeably with ordinal. However, most analyses that are designed for use with ordinal data (nonparametric tests) rank the data as a part of the procedure, assuming that the data you are entering are not already ranked. Moreover, the process of ranking changes the distribution of data such that it can be used in many analyses usually requiring normally distributed data. Ordinal data is often be **categorical** (e.g., good, better, best are three ordered categories) so that term is sometimes used to include both nominal and ordinal data.

Approximately Normal (or Scale) Variables

Approximately normally distributed variables not only have levels or scores that are *ordered* from low to high, but also, as stated in Table 3.1, the frequencies of the scores are approximately normally distributed. That is, most scores are somewhere in the middle with similar smaller numbers of low and high scores. Thus a Likert scale, such as strongly agree to strongly disagree, would be considered normal if the frequency distribution was approximately normal. We think normality, because it is an assumption of many statistics, should be the focus of this highest level of measurement. Many normal variables are continuous; (i.e., they have an infinite number of possible values within some range). If not continuous, we suggest that there be at least five ordered values or levels and that they have an implicit, underlying continuous nature. For example, a five-point Likert scale has only five response categories but, in theory, a person's rating could fall anywhere between 1 and 5 (e.g., half way between 3 and 4).

Other terms for approximately normal variables. **Continuous, dimensional,** and **quantitative** are some terms that you will see in the literature for variables that vary from low to high, and are assumed to be normally distributed. SPSS uses **scale,** as previously noted. Traditional measurement terminology uses the terms interval and ratio. SPSS does not use these terms, but because they are common in the literature and overlapping with the term *scale,* we will describe them briefly. **Interval** variables have ordered categories that are equally spaced (i.e., have equal intervals between them). Most physical measurements (*length, weight, temperature,* etc.) have equal intervals between them. Many physical measurements (*length* and *weight*), in fact, not only have equal intervals between the levels or scores, but also a true zero, which means in the above examples, zero length or weight. Such variables are called **ratio** variables. Our Fahrenheit temperature scale and almost all psychological scales do *not* have a true zero and thus even if they are very well constructed equal interval scales, it is not possible to say that zero degrees Fahrenheit involves the absence of something or that one has no intelligence or no extroversion or no attitude of a certain type. The differences between interval and ratio scales are not important for us because we can do all of the types of statistics that we have available with interval data. SPSS terminology supports this non-distinction by using the term **scale** for both interval and ratio data. In fact, the more important thing, because it is an assumption of most parametric statistics, is that the variables be approximately normally distributed, not whether they have equal intervals.

How to Distinguish Between the Types of Measurement

Distinguishing between nominal and ordered variables. When you label variables in SPSS, the **Measure** column (see Fig. 2.12) provides only three choices: nominal, ordinal, or scale. How do you decide? We suggest that *if the variable* has only two levels, you call it nominal even though it is often hard to tell whether such a *dichotomous* variable, (e.g., Yes or No, Pass or Fail), is unordered or ordered. Although some such dichotomous variables are clearly nominal (e.g., *gender*) and others are clearly ordered (e.g., *math grades*--high and low), all dichotomous variables form a special case, as previously discussed.

If there are three or more categories, it is usually fairly easy to tell whether the categories are ordered or not, so students and researchers should be able to distinguish between nominal and ordinal data. That is good because this distinction makes a lot of difference in choosing appropriate statistics.

Distinguishing between ordinal and normal variables. Is a 5-point Likert scale ordinal or approximately normal? Using our definitions, there is a way to test variables to see whether it is more reasonable to treat them as *normal* variables or *ordinal* variables. Unfortunately, you will not know for sure until after the data have been collected and preliminary analyses are done. One of the assumptions of most of the statistics (e.g., *t* test) that you will compute with SPSS is that the dependent variable must be at least approximately normally distributed.

Table 3.2. provides a summary of the characteristics and examples of our four types of measurement. It should provide a good review of the concept of type of measurement of a variable.

Table 3.2. *Characteristics and Examples of the Four Types of Measurement*

	Nominal	**Dichotomous**	**Ordinal**	**Normal**
Characteristics	3+ levels Not ordered True categories Names, labels	2 levels Ordered or not	3+ levels Ordered levels Unequal intervals between levels Not normally distributed	5+ levels Ordered levels Approximately normally distributed Equal intervals between levels
Examples	Ethnicity Religion Curriculum type Hair color	Gender Math grades (high vs. low)	Competence Scale Mother's education	SAT math Math achievement Height

Remember that in SPSS, there are only three measurement types or levels, and the researcher is the one who determines if the variable is called as nominal, ordinal, or scale (see Fig. 2.9 again). We have called dichotomous variables nominal in our hsbdata file.

Descriptive Statistics and Plots

Frequency Tables

Now, we will expand our discussion of frequency distributions to include frequency tables, which are constructed in very similar ways for all four types of measurement. A difference is that with **nominal** data the order in which the categories are listed is arbitrary. In Fig. 3.3, we have listed *protestant, catholic,* and then *no religion*. However, *protestant* could be put after or between *catholic* and *no religion* because the categories are not ordered. In ordinal and approximately normal data, the order can not vary (e.g., medium is always between low and high).

religion

		Frequency	Percent	Valid Percent	Cumulative Percent
Valid	protestant	30	40.0	44.8	44.8
	catholic	23	30.7	34.3	79.1
	no religion	14	18.7	20.9	100.0
	Total	67	89.3	100.0	
Missing	other religion	4	5.3		
	blank	4	5.3		
	Total	8	10.7		
Total		75	100.0		

Fig 3.3. A frequency table for religion.

Fig. 3.3. is a table that shows religious affiliation from the hsbdata that we are using in this book. In this example, there is a **Frequency** column that shows the numbers of students who checked each type of religion (e.g., 30 said *protestant* and 4 left it *blank*). Notice that there is a total (67) for the three responses considered **Valid** and a total (8) for the two types of response considered to be **Missing** as well as an overall total (75). The **Percent** column indicates that 40.0% are *protestant*, 30.7% are *catholic*, 18.7% said they had *no religion*, 5.3% had one of several *other religions*, and 5.3% left the question *blank*. The **Valid Percentage** column excludes the eight missing cases and is often the column that you would use. Given this dataset it would be accurate to say that <u>of those not coded as missing</u>, 44.8% were *protestant* and 34.3 % *catholic*, and 20.9% had *no religion*.

To get Fig. 3.3, select:
- **Analyze => Descriptive Statistics => Frequencies =>** *religion* **=> OK** (make sure that the **Display frequency tables** box is checked

When the variable has ordered levels (i.e., is **ordinal** or **approximately normal**), the procedure is the same and the frequency table has the same structure. However, when the variable is ordinal or approximately normal, the **Cumulative Percent** column is useful. With a nominal variable, it is not useful. From Fig. 3.4, we can say that 22.7% of the students had grades that were *mostly C's* <u>or less</u> and that 64% had *mostly B's* <u>or less</u>.

To create Fig. 3.4, select:
- **Analyze => Descriptive Statistics => Frequencies =>** *grades in h.s.* **=> OK.**

grades in h.s.

		Frequency	Percent	Valid Percent	Cumulative Percent
Valid	mostly D	1	1.3	1.3	1.3
	half CD	8	10.7	10.7	12.0
	mostly C	8	10.7	10.7	22.7
	half BC	16	21.3	21.3	44.0
	mostly B	15	20.0	20.0	64.0
	half AB	18	24.0	24.0	88.0
	mostly A	9	12.0	12.0	100.0
	Total	75	100.0	100.0	

Fig. 3.4 A frequency table for an ordered variable: grades in h.s.

As mentioned above, frequency distributions indicate how many participants are in each category, and whether they are ordered or unordered categories. If one wants to make a diagram of a frequency distribution there are several choices, four of which are bar charts, frequency polygons, histograms, and box and whisker plots.

Bar Charts
With **nominal** data, you should not use a graphic that connects adjacent categories because with nominal data there is no necessary ordering of the categories or levels. Thus, it is better to make a bar graph or chart of the frequency distribution of variables like *religion, ethnic group,* or other nominal variables; the points that happen to be adjacent in your frequency distribution are not by necessity adjacent.

Fig. 3.5 is a bar chart created by selecting:
- **Analyze => Descriptive Statistics => Frequencies =>** *religion* **=> Charts => Bar charts => Continue => OK.**

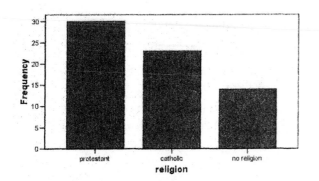

Fig. 3.5. Sample frequency distribution bar chart for the nominal variable of religion.

Histograms

As we can see if we compare Fig. 3.1 and 3.2 to Fig. 3.5, histograms look much like bar charts except in histograms there is no space between the boxes, indicating that there is a continuous variable theoretically underlying the scores (i.e., scores could theoretically be any point on a continuum from the lowest to highest score). Histograms can be used even if data, as measured, are not continuous, if the underlying variable is conceptualized as continuous. For example, the *competence scale* items were rated on a 4-point scale, but one could, theoretically, have any amount of competence.

Frequency Polygons

Figure 3.6, is a frequency polygon; it connects the points between the categories, and is best used with **approximately normal** data, but it can be used with ordinal data.

To create Fig. 3.6, select:
- **Graphs => Line** (be sure that **Simple** and **Summaries for groups of cases** are checked) => **Define** =>*motivation scale* to **Category Axis** box => **OK.**

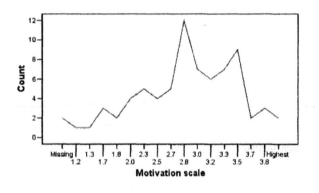

Fig. 3.6. Sample frequency polygon showing approximately normal data.

Box and Whiskers Plot

For **ordinal** and **normal** data, the box and whiskers plot is useful; it should not be used with nominal data because then there is no necessary ordering of the response categories. The box and whisker plot is a graphical representation of the distribution of scores and is helpful in distinguishing between ordinal and normally distributed data, as we will see.

Using our hsbdata set, you can see how useful this graphic analysis technique is for examining frequency distributions. Fig. 3.7 compares genders on scores from the math section of the SAT.

This box and whiskers plot was created by selecting:
- **Analyze => Descriptive Statistics => Explore =>** *SATM* to **Dependent List** box => *gender* to **Factor List => Display Plots => OK.**

Fig. 3.7 shows two box plots, one for males and one for females. The box represents the middle 50% of the cases (i.e., those between the 25th and 75th percentiles). The whiskers indicate the expected range of scores. Scores outside of this range are considered unusually high or low. Such scores, called **outliers**, are shown above and/or below the whiskers with circles or asterisks (for very extreme scores) and the SPSS **Data View** line number for that participant. Note there are no outliers for the 34 males, but there is one low (#63) and one high (#54) female outlier. (Note, this number will not be the participant's ID unless you specify that SPSS should report this by ID number or the ID numbers correspond exactly to the line number).

We will come back to Fig. 3.7 in several later sections of this chapter.

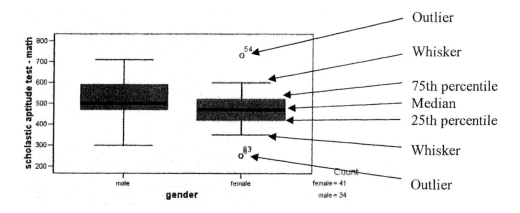

Fig. 3.7. A box and whisker plot for ordinal or normal data.

Measures of Central Tendency

Three measures of the center of a distribution are commonly used: **mean, median,** and **mode**. Any of them can be used with normally distributed data; however, with ordinal data, the mean of the raw scores is usually *not* appropriate. Although, if one is computing certain statistics, the mean of the *ranked* scores provides useful information. With nominal data the mode is the only appropriate measure.

Mean. The arithmetic average or mean takes into account all of the available information in computing the central tendency of a frequency distribution. Thus, it is usually the statistic of choice, assuming that the data are normally distributed data. The mean is computed by adding up all the raw scores and dividing by the number of scores ($M=\Sigma X/N$).

Median. The middle score or median is the appropriate measure of central tendency for ordinal level raw data. The median is a better measure of central tendency than the mean when the frequency distribution is skewed. For example, the median income of 100 mid-level workers and one millionaire reflects the central tendency of the group better (and is substantially lower) than the mean income. The average or mean would be inflated in this example by the income of the one millionaire. For normally distributed data, the median is in the center of the **box and whisker plot**. Notice that in Fig. 3.7 the median for males is not in the center of the box.

Mode. The most common category, or mode can be used with any kind of data but generally provides the least precise information about central tendency. Moreover, if one's data are continuous, there often are multiple modes, none of which truly represents the "typical" score. In fact if there are multiple modes, SPSS provides only the lowest one. One would use the mode as the measure of central tendency if the variable is nominal or you want a quick non-calculated measure. The mode is the tallest bar in a bar graph or histogram (e.g., in Fig. 3.5, *protestant*, category 1, is the mode).

You also can compute the **Mean, Median,** and **Mode,** plus other descriptive statistics with SPSS by using the Frequencies command.

To get Fig 3.8, select:
- **Analyze => Descriptives => Frequencies =>** *scholastic aptitude test – math* **=> Statistics => Mean, Median, and Mode => Continue => OK.**

Note in Fig. 3.8 that the mean and median are very similar, which is in agreement with our conclusion from Fig. 3.1 that *SATM* is approximately normally distributed. Note that the mode is 500, as shown in Fig. 3.1 by the highest bars.

Statistics

scholastic aptitude test - math

N	Valid	75
	Missing	0
Mean		490.53
Median		490.00
Mode		500

Fig. 3.8. Central Tendency Measures using the SPSS Frequencies command.

Measures of Variability

Variability tells us about the spread or dispersion of the scores. At one extreme, if all of the scores in a distribution are the same, there is no variability. If the scores are all different and widely spaced apart, the variability will be high. The **range** (highest minus lowest score) is the crudest measure of variability but does give an indication of the spread in scores if they are ordered.

Standard Deviation. This common measure of variability, is most appropriate when one has normally distributed data, although the mean of <u>ranked</u> ordinal data may be useful in some cases. The standard deviation is based on the deviation (x) of each score from the mean of all the scores. Those deviation scores are squared and then summed (Σx^2). This sum is divided by N-1, and, finally, the square root is taken (SD = $\sqrt{\Sigma x^2/N\text{-}1}$).

We can use the SPSS **Descriptives** command to get measures of central tendency and variability. Figure 3.9 is a printout from the hsbdata set for the *scholastic aptitude test - math* scores. We can easily see that of the 75 people in the data set, the **Minimum** (low) score was 250, the **Maximum** high score was 730. The **Range** is 480 (730-250). (Remember the two female outliers in Fig. 3.7, the box and whisker plot.) The **mean** score was 490.53 and **std** (standard deviation) 94.55. A rough estimate of the standard deviation is the range divided by 5 (e.g., 480/5=96).

To get Fig. 3.9, select:
- **Analyze => Descriptives Statistics => Descriptive =>** *SAT math* **=> Options => Mean, Std Deviation, Range, Minimum, Maximum,** and **Skewness => Continue => OK.**

We will discuss **Skewness** later in the chapter.

Descriptive Statistics

	N	Range	Minimum	Maximum	Mean	Std.	Skewness	
	Statistic	Statistic	Statistic	Statistic	Statistic	Statistic	Statistic	Std. Error
scholastic aptitude test - math	75	480	250	730	490.53	94.553	.128	.277
Valid N (listwise)	75							

Fig. 3.9. Descriptive statistics for the scholastic aptitude test – math (SATM).

Interquartile range. For ordinal data, the interquartile range, seen in the **box plot** (Fig. 3.7) as the distance between the top and bottom of the box, is an useful measure of variability. Note that the whiskers indicate the expected range, and scores outside that range are shown as outliers.

With nominal data none of the above variability measures (range, standard deviation, or interquartile range are appropriate). Instead, for nominal data, one would need to ask how many different categories there are and what are the percentages or frequency counts are in each category to get some idea of variability. Minimum and maximum frequency may provide some indication of distribution as well.

Measurement and Descriptive Statistics
Table 3.3 summarizes much of the above information about the appropriate use of various kinds of descriptive statistics given nominal, dichotomous, ordinal, or normal data.

Table 3.3. *Selection of Appropriate Descriptive Statistics and Plots*

	Nominal	Dichotomous	Ordinal	Normal
Frequency Distribution	Yes[a]	Yes	Yes	OK[b]
Bar Chart	Yes	Yes	Yes	OK
Histogram	No[c]	No	OK	Yes
Frequency Polygon	No	No	OK	Yes
Box and Whiskers Plot	No	No	Yes	Yes
Central Tendency				
Mean	No	OK	Of ranks, OK	Yes
Median	No	OK=Mode	Yes	OK
Mode	Yes	Yes	OK	OK
Variability				
Range	No	Always 1	Yes	Yes
Standard Deviation	No	No	Of ranks, OK	Yes
Interquartile range	No	No	OK	OK
How many categories	Yes	Always 2	OK	Not if truly continuous
Shape				
Skewness	No	No	Yes	Yes

[a]Yes means a good choice with this level of measurement.
[b]OK means OK to use, but not the best choice at this level of measurement.
[c]No means not appropriate at this level of measurement.

Conclusions About Measurement and the Use of Statistics

Statistics based on means and standard deviation are valid for normally distributed or **normal** data. Typically, these data are used in the most powerful tests called **parametric** statistics. However, if the data are ordered but grossly non-normal (i.e., **ordinal**), means and standard deviations may not give meaningful answers. Then the median and a **nonparametric** test would be preferred. Nonparametric tests typically have somewhat less **power** than parametric tests (they are less able to demonstrate truly significant effects), but they sacrifice in power for nonparametric tests based on ranks usually is relatively minor. If the data are **nominal**, one would have to use the mode or counts. In this case, there would be a major sacrifice in power.

The Normal Curve

Figure 3.10 is an example of a normal curve. The frequency distributions of many of the variables used in the behavioral sciences are distributed approximately as a normal curve. Examples of such variables that approximately fit a normal curve are height, weight, intelligence and many personality variables. Notice that for each of these examples, most people would fall toward the middle of the curve, with fewer people at the extremes. If the average height of men in the United States were 5'10", then this height would be in the middle of the curve. The heights of men who are taller than 5'10" would be to the right of the middle on the curve, and those of men who are shorter than 5'10" would be to the left of the middle on the curve, with only a few men 7' or 5' tall.

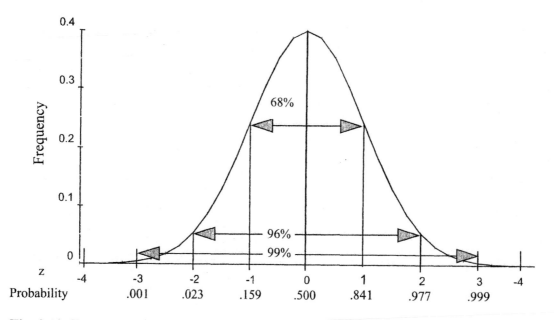

Fig. 3.10. Frequency distribution and probability distribution for the normal curve.

The normal curve can be thought of as derived from a frequency distribution. It is theoretically formed from counting an "infinite" number of occurrences of a variable. Usually when the normal curve is depicted, only the X axis (horizontal) is shown. To determine how a frequency distribution is obtained, you could take a fair coin, and flip it 10 times, and record the number of heads on this first set or trial. Then flip it another 10 times and record the number of heads. If you had nothing better to do, you could do 100 trials. After performing this task, you could plot the number of times that the coin turned up heads out of each trial of 10. What would you expect? Of course, the largest number of trials probably would show 5 heads out of 10. There would be very few, if any trials, where 0, 1, 9, or 10 heads occur. It could happen, but the probability is quite low, which brings us to a probability distribution. If we performed this experiment 100 times, or 1,000 times, or 1,000,000 times, the frequency distribution would "fill in" and look more and more like a normal curve.

Properties of the Normal Curve
The normal curve has five properties that are always present.
1. The normal curve is unimodal. It has one "hump", and this hump is in the middle of the distribution. The most frequent value is in the middle.
2. The mean, median, and mode are equal.
3. The curve is symmetric. If you fold the normal curve in half, the right side would fit perfectly with the left side; that is, it is not **skewed**.
4. The range is infinite. This means that the extremes approach but never touch the X axis.
5. The curve is neither too peaked nor too flat and its tails are neither too short nor too long; it has no **kurtosis.** Its proportions are like those in Fig 3.10.

Non-Normally Shaped Distributions
Skewness. If one tail of a frequency distribution is longer than the other, and if the mean and median are different, the curve is skewed. Because most common inferential statistics (e.g., *t* test) assume that the dependent variable is normally distributed (the data are normal) it is important that we know if our variables are highly skewed.

Figure 3.2 showed a frequency distribution that is skewed to the left. This is called a negative skew. A perfectly normal curve has a skewness of zero (0.0). The curve in Fig. 3.2, for the *competence* scale, has a skewness statistic of -1.63, which indicates that the curve is quite different from a normal curve. We will use a somewhat arbitrary guideline that if the skewness is more than +1.0 or less than -1.0, the distribution is markedly skewed and it would be prudent to use a nonparametric (ordinal type) statistic. However, some parametric statistics, such as the two-tailed t test and ANOVA, are quite robust so even a skewness of more than +/-1 may not change the results much. We will provide more examples and discuss this more in Chapter 4.

Kurtosis. If a frequency distribution is more peaked than the normal curve shown in Fig. 3.10, it is said to have positive kurtosis and is called leptokurtic. Note in Fig 3.1 that the *SAT-math* histogram is peaked (i.e., the bar for 500 extends above the normal curve line), and thus there is some positive kurtosis. If a frequency distribution is relatively flat with heavy tails, it has negative kurtosis and is called platykurtic. Although SPSS can easily compute a kurtosis value for any variable using an option in the Frequencies command, usually we will not do so because kurtosis does not seem to affect the results of most statistical analyses very much.

Areas Under the Normal Curve
The normal curve is also a probability distribution. Visualize that the area under the normal curve is equal to 1.0. Therefore, portions of this curve could be expressed as fractions of 1.0. For example, if we assume that 5'10" is the average height of men in the United States, then the probability of a man being 5'10" or taller is .5. The probability of a man being over 6'3" or less than 5'5" is considerably smaller. It is important to be able to conceptualize the normal curve as a probability distribution because statistical convention sets acceptable probability levels for rejecting the null hypothesis at .05 or .01. As we shall see, when events or outcomes happen very infrequently, that is, only 5 times in 100 or 1 time in 100 (way out in the left or right tail of the

curve), we wonder if they belong to that distribution or perhaps to a different distribution. We will come back to this point later in the book.

All normal curves, regardless of whether they are narrow or spread out, can be divided into areas or units in terms of the standard deviation. Approximately 34% of the area under the normal curve is between the mean and one standard deviation above or below the mean (see Fig 3.10 again). If we include both the area to the right *and* to the left of the mean, 68% of the area under the normal curve is within one standard deviation from the mean. Another approximately 13.5% of the area under the normal curve is accounted for by adding a second standard deviation to the first standard deviation. In other words, two standard deviations to the right of the mean accounts for an area of approximately 47.5%, and two standard deviations to the left *and* right of the mean make up an area of approximately 95% of the normal curve. If we were to subtract 95% from 100% the remaining 5% relates to that ever present probability or *p* value of 0.05 needed for statistical significance. Values not falling within two standard deviations of the mean are seen as relatively rare events.

The Standard Normal Curve
All normal curves can be converted into standard normal curves by setting the mean equal to zero and the standard deviation equal to one. Since all normal curves have the same proportion of the curve within one standard deviation, two standard deviations, etc. of the mean, this conversion allows comparisons among normal curves with different means and standard deviations. Figure 3.10, the normal distribution, has the standard normal distribution units underneath. These units are referred to as *z* **scores.** If you examine the normal curve table in any statistics book, you can find the areas under the curve for one standard deviation ($z=1$), two standard deviations ($z=2$), etc. As described in Appendix A, the Quick Reference Guide, it is easy for SPSS to convert raw scores into *standard scores*. This is often done when one wants to aggregate or add together several scores that have quite different means and standard deviations.

Interpretation Questions

3.1   If you have categorical, ordered data (such as low income, middle income, high income) what type of measurement would you have? Why?

3.2   a) What are the differences between nominal, dichotomous, ordinal, and normal variables? b) In social science research, why isn't it important to distinguish between interval and ratio variables?

3.3   What percent of the area under the standard normal curve is between the mean and one standard deviation above the mean?

3.4   a) How do *z* scores relate to the normal curve? b) How would you interpret a *z* score of −3.0? c) What percentage is between a *z* of -2 and a *z* of +2?

3.5   Why should you not use a frequency polygon if you have nominal data? What would be better to use to display nominal data?

CHAPTER 4

Understanding Your Data and Checking Assumptions

Before computing any inferential statistics, it is important to do exploratory data analysis (EDA) as outlined below. This chapter will help you understand your data, help you to see if there are any errors, and help you to know if your data meet basic assumptions for statistics that you will compute.

In the process of understanding your data, different types of analyses and plots will be generated depending on what level of measurement you have. Therefore, it is important to identify whether each of your variables is **nominal, dichotomous, ordinal,** or **normal** (SPSS uses the term **scale**). Keep in mind that there are times when whether you call a variable ordinal or scale might change based on your EDA. For example, a variable that you considered to be ordinal may be normally distributed, and, thus, better to be labeled as scale. Recall from Chapters 2 and 3 that making the appropriate choice indicates that you understand your data and should help guide your selection of a statistic.

Exploratory Data Analysis (EDA)

What is EDA?
After the data are entered into SPSS, the first step to complete (before running any inferential statistics) is EDA, which involves computing various descriptive statistics and graphs. **Exploratory Data Analysis** is used to <u>examine and get to know your data</u>. Chapters 2, 3, and especially this chapter, focus on ways to do exploratory data analysis with SPSS. EDA is important to do for several reasons:

1. To see if there are problems in the data such as outliers, non-normal distributions, problems with coding, missing values, and/or errors inputting the data.

2. To examine the extent to which the assumptions of the statistics that you plan to use are met.

In addition to these two reasons, which are discussed in this chapter, one could also do EDA for other purposes such as:

3. To get basic information regarding the demographics of subjects to report in the Method or Results section.

4. To examine relationships between variables to determine how to conduct the hypothesis-testing analyses. For example, correlations can be used to see if two or more variables are so highly related that they should be combined for further analyses and/or if only one of them should be included in the central analyses. We create *parents' education*, in Chapter 5, by combining *father's* and *mother's education*, because they are quite highly correlated.

How to Do EDA
There are two general methods used for EDA: generating plots of the data and generating numbers from your data. Both are important and can be very helpful methods of investigating the data. Descriptives Statistics (including the minimum, maximum, mean, standard deviation, and skewness), frequency distribution tables, boxplots, histograms, and stem and leaf plots are a few procedures used in EDA.

After collecting data and inputting them into SPSS, many students jump immediately to doing inferential statistics (e.g., *t* tests and ANOVA's). <u>Don't do this!</u> Many times there are errors or problems with the data that need to be located and either fixed or at least noted before doing any inferential statistics.

At this point, you are probably asking "Why?" or "I'll do that boring descriptive stuff later while I am writing the methods section." Wait! Being patient can alleviate many problems down the road.

In the next two sections we discuss checking for errors and checking assumptions. Some of this discussion reviews material presented in Chapters 2 and 3, but it is so important that it is worth repeating.

Check for Errors
There are many ways to check for errors; for example:
1. Look over the raw data (questionnaires, interviews, or observation forms) to see if there are inconsistencies, double coding, obvious errors, etc. Do this before entering the data into the computer.
2. Check some, or preferably, all of the raw data (e.g., questionnaires) against the data in your **SPSS Data Editor** file to be sure that errors were not made in the data entry.
3. Compare the minimum and maximum values for each variable in your Descriptives output with the allowable range of values in your codebook.
4. Examine the means and standard deviations to see if they look reasonable, given what you know about the variables.
5. Examine the *N* column to see if any variables have a lot of missing data, which can be a problem when you do statistics with two or more variables. Missing data could also indicate that there was a problem in data entry.
6. Look for outliers in the data.

Statistical Assumptions
Every statistical test has assumptions. Statistical assumptions are much like the directions for appropriate use of a product found in an owner's manual. **Assumptions** <u>explain when it is and isn't reasonable to perform a specific statistical test</u>. When the *t* test was developed, for example, the person who developed it needed to make certain assumptions about the distribution of scores, etc., in order to be able to calculate the statistic accurately. If these assumptions are not met, the value that SPSS calculates, which tells the researcher whether or not the results are statistically significant, will not be completely accurate and may even lead the researcher to draw the wrong conclusion about the results. In each chapter, the appropriate inferential statistics and their assumptions are described.

Parametric tests. These include most of the familiar ones (e.g., *t* test, analysis of variance, correlation). They usually have more assumptions than nonparametric tests. Parametric tests were designed for data that have certain characteristics, including approximately normal distributions.

Some parametric statistics have been found to be "robust" to one or more of their assumptions. **Robust** means that the assumptions can be violated quite a lot without damaging the validity of the statistic. For example, one assumption of the *t* test and ANOVA is that the dependent variable is normally distributed for each group. Statisticians who have studied these statistics have found that even when data are not normally distributed (e.g., skewed a lot), they still can be used under many circumstances.

Nonparametric tests. These tests (e.g., chi-square, Mann-Whitney U, Spearman rho) have fewer assumptions and often can be used when the assumptions of a parametric test are violated. For example, they do not require normal distributions of variables or homogeneity of variances.

Check Assumptions

Homogeneity of variances. Both the *t* test and ANOVA may be affected quite a lot if the variances (standard deviation squared) of the groups to be compared are substantially different. Thus, this is a critical assumption to meet or correct for. Fortunately, SPSS provides the Levene test to check this assumption and ways to adjust the results if the variances are significantly different.

Normality. As mentioned above, many parametric statistics assume that certain variables are distributed approximately normally. That is, the frequency distribution would look like a symmetrical bell-shaped or normal curve, with most subjects having values in the mid range and with similar small numbers of participants with both high and low scores. A distribution that is asymmetrical with more high than low scores (or vice versa) is **skewed**. Thus, it is important to check skewness. There are also several other ways to check for normality, some of which were presented in Chapter 3. In this chapter we will look in detail at one graphical method, boxplots. However, remember that *t* (if 2-tailed) and ANOVA are quite robust to violations of normality.

Check other assumptions of the specific statistic. In later chapters, we will discuss other assumptions as they are relevant to the problem posed.

The type of variable you are exploring (whether it is nominal, ordinal, dichotomous, or normal/ scale) influences the type of exploratory data analysis (EDA) you will want to do. Thus, we have divided the problems in this chapter by the measurement levels of the variable because, for some types of variables, certain descriptive statistics will not make sense (e.g., a mean for a nominal variable, or a boxplot for a dichotomous variable). Remember that the researcher has labeled the type of measurement as either nominal, ordinal or scale when completing the **SPSS Data Editor Variable View.** Remember also that <u>we decided to label dichotomous variables **nominal**,</u> and <u>variables that we assumed were normally distributed were labeled **scale**.</u>

For all the problems in Chapter 4 you will be using the HSB data file.

- Retrieve **hsbdata.sav** from the CD in the back of the book. It is desirable to make a working copy of this file. See Appendix C for instructions if you need help with this or getting started with SPSS. Appendix C also shows how to set your computer to print the SPSS syntax.

Problem 4.1: Descriptive Statistics for the Ordinal and Scale Variables

In this problem we will use all of the HSB Variables that were labeled as ordinal or scale in the **SPSS Variable View.** With those types of variables, it is important to see if the means make sense (are they close to what you expected?), to examine the range of the data, and to check the shape of the distribution (i.e., skewness value).

4.1 Examine the data to get a good understanding of the central tendency, variability, range of scores and the shape of the distribution for each of the ordinal and scale variables. Are the variables normally distributed?

This problem includes descriptive statistics and ways to examine your data to see if the variables are approximately normally distributed, an assumption of most of the parametric inferential statistics that we will use. Remember that **skewness** is an important statistic for understanding if a variable is normally distributed; it is an index that helps determine how much a variable's distribution deviates from the distribution of the normal curve. Skewness refers to the lack of symmetry in a frequency distribution. Distributions with a long "tail" to the right have a **positive skew** and those with a long tail on the left have a **negative skew**. If a frequency distribution of a variable has a large (plus or minus) skewness, that variable is said to deviate from normality. In this assignment, we examine this assumption for several key variables. However, some of the parametric inferential statistics that we will use later in the book are robust or quite insensitive to violations of normality. Thus, we will assume that it is okay to use parametric statistics to answer most of our research questions as long as the variables are not extremely skewed.

We will answer Problem 4.1 by using the **Descriptives** command, which will make a compact, space efficient output. You could instead run the **Frequencies** program because you can get the same statistics with that command. We will use the Frequencies command later in the chapter. When using the Descriptives command to compute the basic descriptive statistics for all of the ordinal and scale variables, you should use these steps:

- Select **Analyze ⇒ Descriptive Statistics ⇒ Descriptives**

After selecting **Descriptives**, you will be ready to compute the mean, standard deviation, skewness, minimum, and maximum for all participants or cases on all the variables that were called ordinal or scale under measure in the **SPSS Data Editor Variable View.** We will not include the nominal variables (*ethnicity* and *religion*) and do not include *gender, algebra1, algebra2, geometry, trigonometry, calculus,* and *math grades,* which are dichotomous variables. We will use them in a later problem.

Highlight (in the left box) all of the variables that were called **ordinal**. These include: *father's education, mother's education, grades in h.s.,* and all the item variables (*item 01* through *item 11 reversed).*

- Click on the **arrow** button pointing right to produce Fig. 4.1.
- Be sure that all of the requested variables have moved out of the left window.

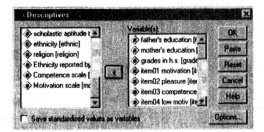

Fig. 4.1. Descriptives.

- Click on **Options.** The Options window (Fig. 4.2) will open.
- Select **Mean.**
- Under **Dispersion,** select **Std. Deviation, Variance, Range, Minimum,** and **Maximum.**
- Under **Distribution,** check **Skewness.**

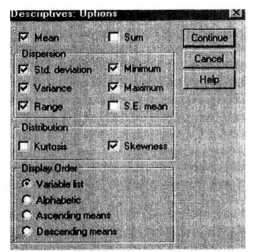

Fig. 4.2. Descriptives: Options.

- Click on **Continue** to get back to Fig. 4.1.
- Click on **OK** to produce Output 4.1a.

Next, we will repeat these steps for the variables that were labeled **scale** in the **SPSS Data Editor.**
- Click on **Reset** in Fig 4.1 to move the ordinal variable back to the left.
- Highlight *math achievement, mosaic, visualization, visualization retest, scholastic aptitude test-math, competence,* and *motivation.*
- Repeat the steps used above to create **Descriptive Statistics** for the scale variables.

Compare your syntax output to Outputs 4.1a and 4.1b. If they look the same you have done the steps correctly. If the syntax is not showing in your output, consult the Appendix C to see how to set your computer so that the syntax is displayed.

Output 4.1a: Descriptives for the Ordinal Variables

```
DESCRIPTIVES
  VARIABLES=faed maed grades item01 item02 item03 item04 item05 item06 item07
  item08 item09 item10 item11 item12 item13 item14 item04r item05r item08r
  item11r
  /STATISTICS=MEAN STDDEV VARIANCE RANGE MIN MAX .
```

Syntax or log file shows the variables and statistics that you requested.

Descriptives

Descriptive Statistics

	N	Range	Minimum	Maximum	Mean	Std.	Variance	Skewness	
	Statistic	Statistic	Statistic	Statistic	Statistic	Statistic	Statistic	Statistic	Std. Error
father's education	73	8	2	10	4.73	2.830	8.007	.684	.281
mother's education	75	8	2	10	4.11	2.240	5.015	1.124	.277
grades in h.s.	75	6	2	8	5.68	1.570	2.464	-.332	.277
item01 motivation	74	3	1	4	2.96	.928	.861	-.763	.279
item02 pleasure	75	3	1	4	3.52	.906	.821	-1.910	.277
item03 competence	74	3	1	4	2.82	.897	.804	-.579	.279
item04 low motiv	74	3	1	4	2.16	.922	.850	.422	.279
item05 low comp	75	3	1	4	1.61	.971	.943	1.581	.277
item06 low pleas	75	3	1	4	2.43	.975	.951	-.058	.277
item07 motivation	75	3	1	4	2.76	1.051	1.104	-.433	.277
item08 low motiv	75	3	1	4	1.95	.914	.835	.653	.277
item09 competence	74	3	1	4	3.32	.760	.578	-1.204	.279
item10 low pleas	75	3	1	4	1.41	.737	.543	1.869	.277
item11 low comp	75	3	1	4	1.36	.747	.558	2.497	.277
item12 motivation	75	3	1	4	3.00	.822	.676	-.600	.277
item13 motivation	75	3	1	4	2.67	.794	.631	-.320	.277
item14 pleasure	75	3	1	4	2.84	.717	.515	-.429	.277
item04 reversed	74	3	1	4	2.84	.922	.850	-.422	.279
item05 reversed	75	3	1	4	3.39	.971	.943	-1.581	.277
item08 reversed	75	3	1	4	3.05	.914	.835	-.653	.277
item11 reversed	75	3	1	4	3.64	.747	.558	-2.497	.277
Valid N (listwise)	69								

Output 4.1b Descriptives for Variables Labeled as Scale

```
DESCRIPTIVES
  VARIABLES=mathach mosaic visual visual2 satm competence motivation
  /STATISTICS=MEAN STDDEV VARIANCE RANGE MIN MAX .
```

Descriptives

Descriptive Statistics

	N	Range	Minimum	Maximum	Mean	Std.	Variance	Skewness	
	Statistic	Statistic	Statistic	Statistic	Statistic	Statistic	Statistic	Statistic	Std. Error
math achievement t	75	25.33	-1.67	23.67	12.5645	6.67031	44.493	.044	.277
mosaic, pattern test	75	60.0	-4.0	56.0	27.413	9.5738	91.658	.529	.277
visualization test	75	15.00	-.25	14.75	5.2433	3.91203	15.304	.536	.277
visualization retest	75	9.50	.00	9.50	4.5467	3.01816	9.109	.235	.277
scholastic aptitude test - math	75	480	250	730	490.53	94.553	8940.252	.128	.277
Competence scale	73	3.00	1.00	4.00	3.2945	.66450	.442	-1.634	.281
Motivation scale	73	2.83	1.17	4.00	2.8744	.63815	.407	-.570	.281
Valid N (listwise)	71								

Interpretation of Output 4.1a and 4.1b.

These Outputs provide descriptive statistics for all of the variables labeled as **ordinal** (4.1a) and **scale** (4.1b). Notice that the variables are listed down the left column of the outputs and the requested descriptive statistics are listed across the top row. The descriptive statistics included in the output are the number of subjects (**N**), the **Range, Minimum** (lowest), and **Maximum** (highest) scores, and the **Mean** (or average) for each variable. In addition, the std (the standard deviation), the **Variance**, the **Skewness** statistic and the **std error** of the skewness. Note, from the bottom line of the Outputs, that the **Valid N (listwise)** is 69 for Output 4.1a and 71 for 4.1b rather than 75, which is the number of participants in the data file. This is because the **listwise** *N* only includes the persons with *no* missing data on any variable requested in the output. Notice that several variables (e.g., *father's education, item01, motivation,* and *competence*) each have a few participants missing.

Using your output to check your data for errors. For both the ordinal and scale variables, check to make sure that all **Means** seem reasonable. That is, you should check your means to see if they are within the ranges you expected (given the information in your codebook) and if the means are close to what you might expect (given your understanding of the variable). Next, check the output to see that the **Minimum** and **Maximum** are within the appropriate (codebook) range for each variable. If the minimum is smaller or the maximum is bigger than you expected (e.g., 100 for a variable that has 1 – 50 for possible values), then you should suspect that there was an error somewhere. Finally, you should check the *N* column to see if the *N*s are what you were expecting. If it happens that you have more participants missing than you expected, check the original data to see if some were entered incorrectly. Notice that *competence scale* and *motivation scale* each have a few participants missing.

Using the output to check assumptions. The main assumption that we can check from this output is normality. We won't pay much attention to the skewness for *item 01* to *item 11 reversed* that have only four levels (1-4). These ordinal variables have fewer than five levels, so they will not be considered to be scale even though some of the "item" variables are not very skewed. We will not use them as individual variables because we will be combining them to create summated variables (the *motivation* and *competence* and *pleasure* scales) before using inferential statistics. From Output 4.1a, we can see that two of the variables that we called **ordinal** (*father's education* and *grades in h.s.*) are approximately normally distributed. These ordinal variables, with five or more levels, have skewness values between –1 and 1. Thus, we can assume that they are more like scale variables, and we can use inferential statistics that have the assumption of normality. To better understand these variables, it may be helpful to change the **Measure** column in the **Variable View** so that these two variables will be labeled as scale.

For the variables that were labeled as scale, we hope that they are normally distributed. Look at the **Skewness Statistic** in Output 4.1b to see if it is between –1 and 1. From the output we see that most of these variables have skewness values between –1 and 1, but two (*mother's education* and *competence*) do not. Most statistics books do not provide advice about how to decide whether a variable is at least approximately normal. SPSS recommends that you divide the skewness by its standard error. If the result is less than 2.5 (which is approximately the $p = .01$ level) then skewness is *not* significantly different from normal. A problem with this method, aside from having to use a calculator, is that the standard error depends on the sample size, so with large samples most variables would be found to be non normal. A simpler guideline is that if the skewness is less than plus or minus one ($< +/- 1.0$) the variable is at least approximately normal.

There are several ways to check this assumption in addition to checking the skewness value. If the mean, median, and mode, which can be obtained with the Frequencies command, are approximately equal, then you can assume that the distribution is approximately normally distributed. For example, remember from Chapter 3 (Fig. 3.8) that the mean (490.53), median (490.00), and mode (500) for *scholastic aptitude test- math* were very similar values, and the skewness value is .128 (see Output 4.1). Thus, we can assume that *SAT-math* is approximately normally distributed.

Problem 4.2: Box Plots for One Variable and Multiple Variables

In addition to numerical methods for understanding your data there are several graphical methods. In Chapter 3, we demonstrated the use of histograms with the normal curve superimposed and also frequency polygons (line graphs) to roughly assess normality. The trouble is that visual inspection of histograms can be deceiving because some approximately normal distributions don't look very much like a normal curve.

In this problem we will use **Boxplots** to examine some HSB variables. Boxplots are a method of graphically representing ordinal and scale data. They can be made with many different combinations of variables and groups. Using boxplots for one, two, or more variables or groups in the same plot can be useful in helping you understand your data.

4.2a. Create a boxplot for *math achievement test*.

There are several commands in SPSS that will compute boxplots; we will show one way here. To create a boxplot follow these steps:

- Select **Graphs ⇒ Boxplots...** The **Boxplot** window should appear.
- Select **Simple** and **Summaries of separate variables.** Your window should look like Fig. 4.3.
- Click on **Define.** The **Define Simple Boxplot: Summaries of Separate Variables** window will appear.

Fig. 4.3. Boxplot.

- Highlight the variable that you are interested in (in this case it is *math achievement test*). Click on the arrow to move it into the **Boxes Represent** box. When you finish, the dialog box should look like Fig. 4.4.
- Click on **OK.**

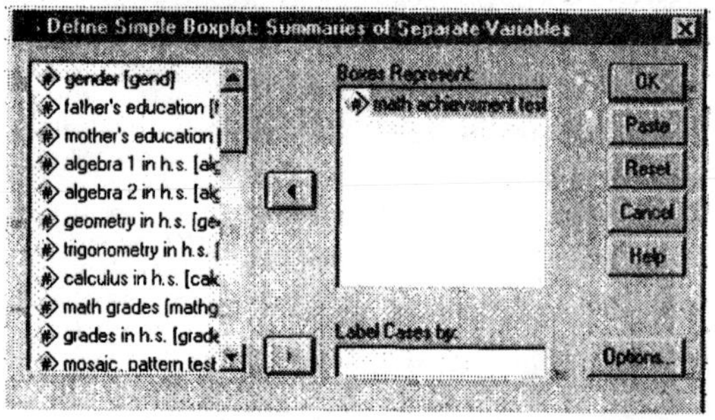

Fig. 4.4. Define Simple Boxplot: Summaries of separate variables.

Output 4.2a: Boxplot of Math Achievement Test

```
EXAMINE
  VARIABLES=mathach /COMPARE VARIABLE/PLOT=BOXPLOT/STATISTICS=NONE/NOTOTAL
  /MISSING=LISTWISE.
```

Explore

Case Processing Summary

	Cases					
	Valid		Missing		Total	
	N	Percent	N	Percent	N	Percent
math achievement test	75	100.0%	0	.0%	75	100.0%

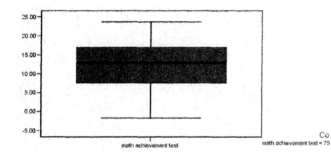

```
EXAMINE
  VARIABLES=competence motivation /COMPARE VARIABLE/PLOT=BOXPLOT/STATISTICS=NONE
  /NOTOTAL
  /MISSING=LISTWISE.
```

To create a boxplot with more than one variable in the same plot, follow these commands.
4.2b. Compare the boxplots of competence and motivation to each other.
To create more than one boxplot on the same graph follow these commands:

- Select **Graphs** ⇒ **Boxplots**… The **Boxplot** window should appear.
- Select **Simple** and **Summaries of separate variables**. Your window should again look like Fig. 4.3.
- Click on **Define**. The **Define Simple Boxplot**: **Summaries of Separate Variables** window will appear.
- Highlight both of the variables that you are interested in (in this case they would be *competence* and *motivation*). Click on the arrow to move them into the **Boxes Represent** box.
- Click on **OK**.

Output 4.2b: Boxplots of Competence and Motivation Scales

Explore

Case Processing Summary

	Cases					
	Valid		Missing		Total	
	N	Percent	N	Percent	N	Percent
Competence scale	71	94.7%	4	5.3%	75	100.0%
Motivation scale	71	94.7%	4	5.3%	75	100.0%

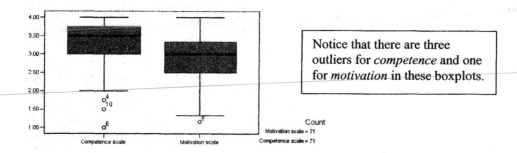

Notice that there are three outliers for *competence* and one for *motivation* in these boxplots.

Interpretation of Outputs 4.2a and 4.2b

Outputs 4.2a and 4.2b include a **Case Processing Summary** table and boxplots. The **Valid** *N*, **Missing** cases and **Total** cases are shown in the case processing summary table. In Output 4.2a, for *math achievement*, the valid *N* is 75, and there are no missing cases. The plot in Output 4.2a includes only one boxplot for our requested variable of *math achievement*. Each "box" represents the middle 50% of the cases and the "whiskers" at the top and bottom of the box indicate the "expected" top and bottom 25%. If there were **outliers** there would be "O"s and if there were really extreme scores they would be shown with asterisks, above or below the end of the whiskers. Notice that there are not any Os or *s in the boxplot in Output 4.2a.

The **Case Processing** table for Output 4.2b indicates that there are 71 valid cases, with 4 cases having missing data on one or both variables. Each of the requested variables is listed separately in the case processing summary table. For the boxplot, you can see there are two separate boxplots. As indicated by the Os at the bottom of the whiskers, the boxplot for *competence* shows there are three outliers, and the boxplot for *motivation* indicates there is one outlier.

Using your output to check your data for errors. If there are "O"s or asterisks, then you need to check the raw data or score sheet to be sure there was not an error. The numbers next to the "Os" indicate which participants these scores belong to. This can be helpful when you want to check to see if these are errors or if they are the actual scores of the subject. We decided not to make a variable called something like subject number because SPSS automatically numbers each case in the left hand column of the data editor. You can, however, make a variable that numbers each subject in some that you find useful. If you wish to label outliers using such an ID number, which you have entered as a variable, you must indicate that variable in the dialog box in Fig. 4.4 where it says **Label Cases by.**

Using the output to check your data for assumptions. Boxplots can be useful for identifying variables with extreme scores, which can make the distribution skewed (i.e., non normal). Also if there are few outliers, if the whiskers are approximately the same length, and if the line in the box is approximately in the middle of the box, then you can assume that the variable is approximately normally distributed. Thus, *math achievement* (output 4.2a) is near normal, *motivation* (4.2b) is approximately normal, but *competence* (4.2b) is quite skewed and not normal.

Problem 4.3: Boxplots Split by A Dichotomous Variable

Now let's make a boxplot comparing males and females on *math achievement*. This is similar to what we did in Chapter 3, but here we will request statistics and **stem-and-leaf** plots.

4.3. Create a boxplot for *math achievement* split by *gender*.

Use these commands:
- **Analyze => Descriptive Statistics => Explore.**
- The **Explore** window (Fig. 4.5) will appear.
- Click on *math achievement* and move it to the **Dependent List**.
- Next, click on *gender* and move it to the **Factor** (or independent variable) **List**.
- Click on **Both** under **Display.** This will produce both a table of descriptive statistics and two kinds of plots: **stem-and-leaf** and **Box-and-whiskers.**

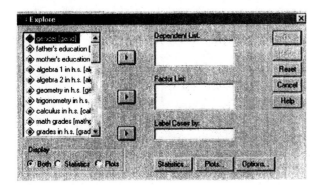

Fig. 4.5. Explore.

- Click on OK.

You will get an output file complete with syntax, statistics, stem-and-leaf plots, and boxplots. See Output 4.3 and compare it to your own output and syntax. As with most SPSS subprograms, we could have requested a wide variety of other statistics, if we had clicked on Statistics and/or Plots in Fig 4.5.

Output 4.3: Boxplots Split by Gender with Statistics and Stem–and–Leaf Plots

```
EXAMINE
  VARIABLES=mathach BY gend
  /PLOT BOXPLOT STEMLEAF
  /COMPARE GROUP
  /STATISTICS DESCRIPTIVES
  /CINTERVAL 95
  /MISSING LISTWISE
  /NOTOTAL.
```

Explore

gender

Case Processing Summary

		Cases					
		Valid		Missing		Total	
	gender	N	Percent	N	Percent	N	Percent
math achievement test	male	34	100.0%	0	.0%	34	100.0%
	female	41	100.0%	0	.0%	41	100.0%

Descriptives

gender			Statistic	Std. Error
math achievement test	male	Mean	14.7550	1.03440
		95% Confidence Interval for Mean Lower Bound	12.6505	
		Upper Bound	16.8595	
		5% Trimmed Mean	14.8454	
		Median	14.3330	
		Variance	36.379	
		Std. Deviation	6.03154	
		Minimum	3.67	
		Maximum	23.7	
		Range	20.0	
		Interquartile Range	10.0005	
		Skewness	-.156	.403
		Kurtosis	-.963	.788
	female	Mean	10.7479	1.04576
		95% Confidence Interval for Mean Lower Bound	8.6344	
		Upper Bound	12.8615	
		5% Trimmed Mean	10.6454	
		Median	10.3330	
		Variance	44.838	
		Std. Deviation	6.69612	
		Minimum	-1.7	
		Maximum	23.7	
		Range	25.3	
		Interquartile Range	10.5000	
		Skewness	.331	.369
		Kurtosis	-.698	.724

Note that we have circled, for males and for females, three key statistics: mean, variance, and skewness.

Stem-and-Leaf Plots

```
math achievement test Stem-and-Leaf Plot for
GEND= male

Frequency    Stem &  Leaf

    1.00       0 .  3
    7.00       0 .  5557799
   11.00       1 .  01123444444
    7.00       1 .  5578899
    8.00       2 .  11123333

Stem width:  10.0
Each leaf:      1 case(s)
```

11 persons (Frequency) had stems of 1 (scores between 10 and14). One had 10, 2 had 11, etc.

```
math achievement test Stem-and-Leaf Plot for
GEND= female

Frequency    Stem &  Leaf

    1.00      -0 .  1
    7.00       0 .  1123344
   12.00       0 .  555666778999
   11.00       1 .  00002334444
    5.00       1 .  77779
    5.00       2 .  02233

Stem width:  10.0
Each leaf:      1 case(s)
```

1 person had a negative score (stem − 0) of -1.

62

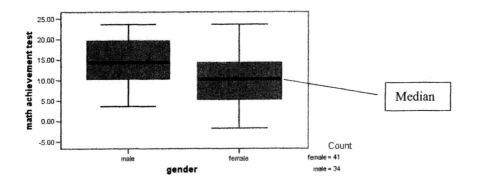

Interpretation of Output 4.3
The first table under **Explore** provides descriptive statistics about the number of males and females with **Valid** and **Missing** data. Note that we have 34 males and 41 females with valid *math achievement test* scores.

The **Descriptives** table contains many different statistics for males and females separately. Several of them are beyond what we will cover in this book. Note that the average *math achievement test* score is 14.76 for the males and 10.75 for females. We will discuss the variances and skewness below under assumptions.

The **Stem-and-Leaf Plot** for each gender separately are next. These plots are sort of like a histogram or frequency distributions turned on the side. They give a visual impression of the distribution, and they show *each* person's score on the dependent variable (*math achievement*). Note that the legend indicates that **Stem width** equals 10 and **Each leaf** equals one case. This means that entries that have 0 for the stem are less than 10, those with 1 as the stem range from 10 to 19, etc. Each number in the **Leaf** column represents the last digit of one person's *math achievement* score. The numbers in the **Frequency** column indicate how many participants had scores in the range represented by that stem. Thus, in the male plot, one student had a **Stem** of 0 and a **Leaf** of 3; i.e. a score of 03. The Frequency of students with **Leafs** between 05 and 09 is 7, and there were three scores of 05, two of 07, and two of 09. Eleven had a **Stem** of 1 and **Leaf** of 0 (a score of 10); two had scores of 11, etc.

Boxplots are the last part of the output. This boxplot has two boxes (one for males and one for females). By inspecting the plots, we can see that the median score for males is quite a bit higher than that for females, although there is some overlap of the boxes. We need to be careful in concluding that males score higher than females, especially based on a small sample of students. In Chapter 10, we will show how an inferential statistic (the *t* test) can help us know how likely it is that this apparent difference could have occurred by chance.

Using the output to check your data for errors. Checking the box and stem-and-leaf plots plots can help identify outliers that might be data entry errors. In this case there aren't any.

Using the output to check your data for assumptions. As noted in the interpretation of Outputs 4.2a and 4.2b, you can tell if a variable is grossly non normal by looking at the boxplots. The stem-and-leaf plots provide similar information. You can also examine the skewness values for each gender separately in the table of **Descriptives** (see the circled skewness values). Note that for both males and females the skewness values are less than one, which indicates that <u>math achievement is approximately normal for both genders</u>. This is

---

an assumption of the *t* test.

The **Descriptives** table also provides the variances for males and females. A key assumption of the *t* test is that the variances are approximately equal (i.e., the assumption of homogeneity of variances). Note that the variance is 36.38 for males and 44.84 for females. These do not seem grossly different, and we find out in Chapter 10 that they are, in fact, not significantly different. Thus, the assumption of homogenous variances is *not* violated.

Problem 4.4: Descriptives for Dichotomous Variables

Now, let's explore the dichotomous variables. To do this, we will do the **Descriptives** command for each of the dichotomous variables. Once again, we could have done **Frequencies,** with or without frequency tables, but we chose **Descriptives.** This time we will select fewer statistics because the standard deviation, variance, and skewness values are not very meaningful with dichotomous variables.

4.4.   Examine the data to get a good understanding of each of the dichotomous variables.

When using the **Descriptives** command to compute the basic descriptive statistics for the dichotomous variables you will need to do these steps:

* Select **Analyze $\Rightarrow$ Descriptive Statistics $\Rightarrow$ Descriptives** .

After selecting **Descriptives,** you will be ready to compute the *N*, minimum, maximum, and mean for all participants or cases on all selected variables in order to examine the data.

* Before starting this problem, press Reset (see Fig. 4.1) to clear the **Variable** box.
* Now *highlight all* of the **dichotomous** variables in the left box. These variables have only two levels. They are: *gender, algebra 1, algebra 2, geometry, trigonometry, calculus, and math grades.*
* Click on the **arrow** button pointing right.
* Be sure that all of these variables have moved out of the left window.
* Click on **Options.** The **Options** window will open.
* Select **Mean, Minimum, and Maximum.**
* Unclick **Std. Deviation.**
* Click on **Continue.**
* Click on **OK**.

Compare your output to Output 4.4. If it looks the same you have done the steps correctly.

Output 4.4 Descriptives for Dichotomous Variables

```
DESCRIPTIVES
  VARIABLES=gender alg1 alg2 geo trig calc mathgr
/STATISTICS= MEAN MIN MAX .
```

Descriptives

Descriptive Statistics

	N	Minimum	Maximum	Mean
gender	75	0	1	.55
algebra 1 in h.s.	75	0	1	.79
algebra 2 in h.s.	75	0	1	.47
geometry in h.s.	75	0	1	.48
trigonometry in h.s.	75	0	1	.27
calculus in h.s.	75	0	1	.11
math grades	75	0	1	.41
Valid N (listwise)	75			

> *Interpretation of Output 4.4*
>
> Output 4.4 includes only one table of **Descriptive Statistics**. Across the top row are the requested statistics of *N*, **Minimum, Maximum, and Mean.** We could have requested other statistics, but they would not be very meaningful for dichotomous variables. Down the left column are the variable labels. The *N* column indicates that all the variables have complete data. The **Valid *N* (listwise)** is 75, which also indicates that all the participants had data for each of our requested variables.
>
> The most helpful column is the **Mean** column. You can use the mean to understand what percentage of participants fall into each of the two groups. For example, the mean of *gender* is .55, which indicates that that 55% of the participants were coded as 1 (female), thus 45% were coded 0 (male). Because the mean is greater than .50, there are more females than males. If the mean is close to 1 or 0 (e.g., algebra 1 and calculus), then splitting the data on that dichotomous variable might not be useful because there will be many participants in one group and very few participants in the other.
>
> *Checking for errors*. The **Minimum** column shows that all the dichotomous variables had "0" for a minimum and the **Maximum** column indicates that all the variables have "1" for a maximum. This is good because it agrees with the codebook.

Problem 4.5: Frequency Tables for a Few Variables

Displaying Frequency tables for variables can help you understand how many participants are in each level of a variable and how much missing data of various types you have. For nominal variables, most descriptive statistics are meaningless. Thus, having a frequency table is usually the best way to understand your nominal variables. We created a frequency table for the nominal variable, *religion,* in Chapter 3 so we will not redo it here.

4.5.   Examine the data to get a good understanding of the frequencies of scores for one nominal variable plus one scale/normal, one ordinal, and one dichotomous variable.
Use the following commands:

- Select **Analyze** ⇒ **Descriptive Statistics** ⇒ **Frequencies**.
- Click on **Reset** if any variables are in the **Variables** box.
- Now *highlight* a **nominal** variable, *ethnicity,* in the left box.
- Click on the **arrow** button pointing right.

- Highlight and move over one **scale** variable (we chose *visualization retest*), one **ordinal** variable (we chose *father's education*), and one **dichotomous** variable (we used *gender*).
- Be sure **Display frequency table** is checked.
- Do not click on **Statistics** because we do not want to select any this time.
- Click on **OK.**

Compare your output to Output 4.5. If it looks the same you have done the steps correctly.

Output 4.5 Frequency Tables for Four Variables

```
FREQUENCIES
  VARIABLES=ethnic visual2 faed gend
  /ORDER=  ANALYSIS .
```

Frequencies

Statistics

		ethnicity	visualization retest	father's education	gender
N	Valid	73	75	73	75
	Missing	2	0	2	0

Frequency Table

See the Interpretation section for how to discuss these numbers.

ethnicity

		Frequency	Percent	Valid Percent	Cumulative Percent
Valid	Euro-Amer	41	54.7	56.2	56.2
	African-Amer	15	20.0	20.5	76.7
	Latino-Amer	10	13.3	13.7	90.4
	Asian-Amer	7	9.3	9.6	100.0
	Total	73	97.3	100.0	
Missing	multi ethnic	1	1.3		
	blank	1	1.3		
	Total	2	2.7		
Total		75	100.0		

visualization retest

		Frequency	Percent	Valid Percent	Cumulative Percent
Valid	Lowest	7	9.3	9.3	9.3
	1.00	7	9.3	9.3	18.7
	2.00	7	9.3	9.3	28.0
	3.00	10	13.3	13.3	41.3
	4.00	10	13.3	13.3	54.7
	5.00	8	10.7	10.7	65.3
	6.00	4	5.3	5.3	70.7
	7.00	5	6.7	6.7	77.3
	8.00	7	9.3	9.3	86.7
	highest	10	13.3	13.3	100.0
	Total	75	100.0	100.0	

father's education

		Frequency	Percent	Valid Percent	Cumulative Percent
Valid	< h.s. grad	22	29.3	30.1	30.1
	h.s. grad	16	21.3	21.9	52.1
	< 2 yrs voc	3	4.0	4.1	56.2
	2 yrs voc	8	10.7	11.0	67.1
	< 2 yrs coll	4	5.3	5.5	72.6
	> 2 yrs coll	1	1.3	1.4	(74.0)
	coll grad	7	9.3	9.6	83.6
	master's	6	8.0	8.2	91.8
	MD/PhD	6	8.0	8.2	100.0
	Total	73	97.3	100.0	
Missing	System	2	2.7		
Total		75	100.0		

74% of fathers have 2 years or less of college.

gender

		Frequency	Percent	Valid Percent	Cumulative Percent
Valid	male	34	45.3	45.3	45.3
	female	41	54.7	54.7	100.0
	Total	75	100.0	100.0	

Interpretation of Output 4.5.
The first table, titled **Statistics**, provides, in this case, only the number of participants for whom we have **Valid** data and the number with **Missing** data. We did not request any other statistics because almost all of them (e.g., skewness, standard deviation) are not appropriate to use with the nominal and dichotomous data, and we have such statistics for the ordinal and normal/scale variables.

The other four tables are labeled **Frequency Table**; there is one for *ethnicity*, one for *visualization test*, one for *father's education*, and one for *gender*. The left-hand column shows the **Valid** categories (or levels or values), **Missing** values, and **Total** number of participants.

The **Frequency** column gives the number of participants who had each value. The **Percent** column is the percent who had each value, including missing values. For example, in the ethnicity table, 54.7% of all participants were *Euro-American*, 20.0% were *African-American*, 13.3% were *Latino-American*, and 9.3% were *Asian-American*. There also were a total of 2.7% missing: 1.3% were *multiethnic*, and 1.3 were left *blank*. The **valid percent** shows the percent of those with *nonmissing* data at each value; e.g., 56.2% of the 73 students with a single listed ethnic group were *Euro-Americans*. Finally, **Cumulative Percent** is the percent of subjects in a category *plus* the categories listed above it.

As mentioned in Chapter 3, this last column is not very useful with nominal data, but can be quite informative for frequency distributions with several ordered categories. For example, in the distribution of father's education, 74% of the fathers had less than a bachelor's degree (i.e., they had not graduated from college).

Interpretation Questions

4.1. Using Output 4.1a and 4.1b: a) What is the mean *visualization test* score? b) What range for *grades in h.s.?* c) What is the minimum score for *mosaic pattern test?* How can that be?

4.2. Using Output 4.1b: a) For which variables that we called scale, is the skewness statistic more than +/- 1.00? b) Why is the answer important? c) Does this agree with the boxplots in Problem 2?

4.3. Using Output 4.2b: a) How many participants have missing data? b) What percent of students have a valid (non-missing) *motivation* or *competence* score? Can you tell from Output 4.1 and 4.2b how many are missing both *motivation* and *competence* scores?

4.4. Using Output 4.4: a) Can you interpret the means? Explain. b) How many participants are there all together? c) How many have complete data (nothing missing)? d) What percent are *male*? e) What percent took *algebra 1*?

4.5. Using Output 4.5: a) 9.6% of what group are *Asian Americans?* b) What percent of students have *visualization retest* scores of 6? c) What percent had such scores of 6 or less?

Extra SPSS Problems

Using the College Student data file, do the following problems. Print your outputs and circle the key parts of the output that you use discuss.

4.1 For the variables with five or more ordered levels, compute the skewness. Describe the results. Which variables in the data set are approximately normally distributed/scale? Which ones are ordered but not normal?

4.2 Do a stem-and-leaf plot for same sex parent's height split by gender. Discuss the plots.

4.3 Which variables are nominal? Run Frequencies for the nominal variables and other variables with fewer than five levels. Comment on the results.

4.4. Do boxplots for student height and for hours of study. Compare the two plots.

CHAPTER 5

Data File Management

In this assignment, you will do several data transformations to get your data in the form needed to answer the research questions. This aspect of data analysis is sometimes called file management and can be quite time consuming. That is especially true if you have a lot of questions/items that combined to compute the summated or composite variables that you want to use in later analyses. For example, in this chapter you will revise two of the math pleasure items and then compute the average of the four pleasure items to make the pleasure scale score. This is a somewhat mundane and tedious aspect of research, but it is important to do it carefully so you do not introduce errors into your data.

In this chapter, you will learn four useful data transformation techniques: **Count, Recode,** and two ways to **Compute** a new variable, that is the sum or average of several initial variables. From these operations we will produce seven new variables. In the last problem you will produce, for the five of the new variables, several of the descriptive statistics that we produced in the last chapter, and we will use them to check for errors and assumptions.

- Get/retrieve **hsbdata** from your disk. (See the **Get Data** step in Appendix A for reference).

Problem 5.1: Count Math Courses Taken

Sometimes you want to know how many items the subjects have taken, bought, done, etc. One time this happens is when the question was "check all that apply." In Chapter 2, we could have counted how many aspects of the class assignments (reading, homework, and extra credit) the students checked by asking the computer to **count** the number of items checked. In this problem, we will count the number of *math courses* coded as 1, which means "taken."

5.1   How many math courses (*algebra 1, algebra 2, geometry, trigonometry,* and *calculus*) did each of the 75 participants take in high school? **Label** your new variable.

If the hsbdata file is not showing, click on the hsbdata bar at the bottom of your screen until you see your data showing. Now, let's count the number of math courses (*mathcrs*) that each of the 75 participants took in high school.
- Select **Transform => Count**. You will see a window like Fig. 5.1 below.
- Now, type *mathcrs* in the **Target Variable** box. This is the SPSS name for your new variable.
- Next, type *math courses taken* in the **Target Label** box.
- Then, highlight *algebra 1, algebra 2, geometry, trigonometry, and calculus* and click on the **arrow** button to move them over to the **Numeric Variables** box. Your **Count** window should look like Fig. 5.1.

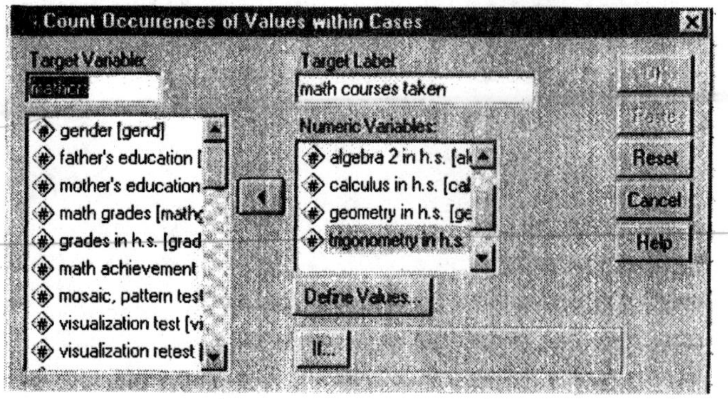

Fig.5.1. Count.

Click on **Define Values.**

- Type **1** in the **Value** box and click on **Add**. This sets up the computer to count how many 1's (or courses taken) each participant had. The window will now look like Fig. 5.2.
- Now click on **Continue** to return to the dialog box in Fig. 5.1.
- Click on **OK**. The first 10 numbers of your new variable, under *mathcrs*, should look like Fig. 5.3. It is the last variable way over to the right side or your **Data Editor.**

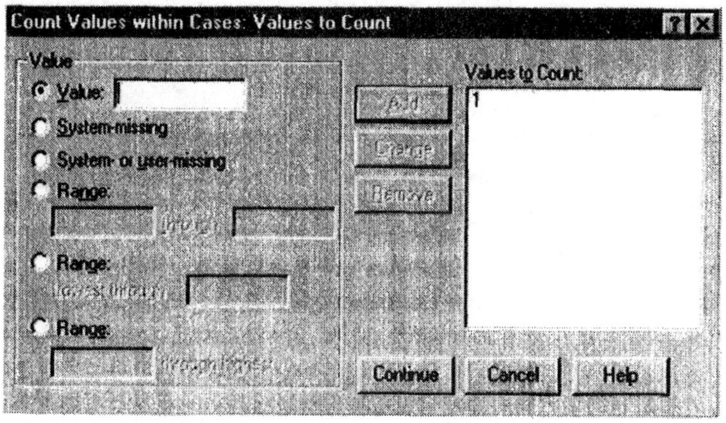

mathcrs
.00
.00
.00
1.00
.00
.00
3.00
1.00
1.00
.00

Fig. 5.2. Count values within cases. 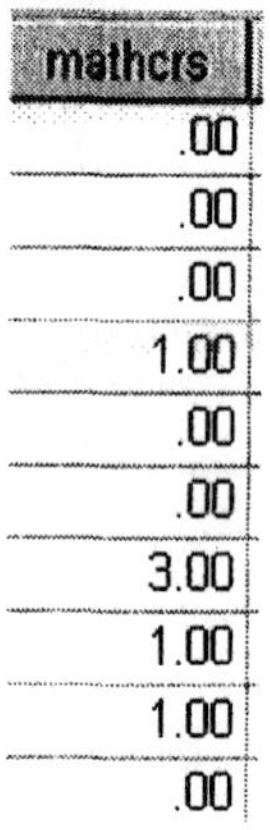   **Fig. 5.3. Data column.**

Your output should look like the syntax in Output 5.1.

If you want to delete the decimal places for your new data:
- Go to the **Variable View**.
- Place the cursor on the last (new) variable, *mathcrs*.
- Click on **Type.**
- Enter 0 in the **Decimal Places** box.
- Then click on **OK**.

Output 5.1: Counting Math Courses Taken

```
COUNT
  mathcrs = alg1 alg2 calc geo trig  (1)  .
VARIABLE LABELS mathcrs 'math courses taken'.
EXECUTE .
```

Interpretation of Output 5.1
Check your syntax and counts. Is the syntax exactly like the syntax above? Another way to check your count statement is by examining your data file. Look at the first participant (top now) and notice that there are zeroes in the *alg1, alg2, geo, trig,* and *calc* columns. The same is true for participants 2 and 3. Thus, they have taken no (0) math courses. They should and do have zeros in the new *mathcrs* column, which is now the last column on right. Also, it would be good to check a few participants who took several math courses just to be sure the count worked correctly.

Notice that there are no tables or figures for this output, just syntax. Remember to set your computer to obtain a listing of the syntax (see Appendix A, **Print Syntax**).

Problem 5.2: Recode and Relabel Mother's and Father's Education

Now, we will **Recode** *mother's education* and *father's education* so that those with no postsecondary education (2s and 3s) have a value of **1**, those with some postsecondary will have **2** and those with a bachelor's degree or more will have a value of **3**.

It is usually *not* desirable to dichotomize (divide into two categories) or trichotomize (divide into three categories) a good, ordered variable. However, we need an independent variable with a few levels or categories to demonstrate certain analyses later, and these variables seem to have a logical problem with the ordering of the categories/values. The problem can be seen in the codebook. A value of 5 is given for students who had a parent with 2 years of vocational college (and presumably an A.S. or A.A. degree), but a 6 is given to a parent with less than 2 years of (a 4-year) college. Thus, we could have a case where a parent who went to a 4-year college for a short time would be rated as having more education than a parent with an associate's degree. This would make the variable not fully ordered.

Recodes also are used to combine two or more small groups or categories of a variable so that group size will be large enough to perform statistical analyses. For example, we have only a few fathers or mothers who have a masters or doctorate so we will combined them with bachelor degrees and call them "B.S. or more."

5.2.   **Recode** *mother's* and *father's education* so that those with no postsecondary education have a value of 1, those with some postsecondary have a value of 2, and those with a bachelor's degree or more have a value of 3. **Label** the new variables and values.

Follow these steps:
- Click on **Transform => Recode => Into Different Variables** and you should get Fig. 5.4.
- Now click on *mother's education* and then the **arrow** button.
- Click on *father's education* and the **arrow** to move them to the **Numeric Variables =>**
  Output box.
- Now highlight *faed* in the **Numeric Variable** box so that it turns blue.
- Click on the **Output Variable Name** box and type *faedRevis*.
- Click on the **Label** box and type *father's educ revised*.
- Click on **Change**. Did you get *faed =>faedRevis* in the **Numeric Variable -> Output**
  Variable box as in Fig. 5.4?

Now repeat these procedures with *maed* in the **Numeric Variable => Output box.**
- Highlight *maed.*
- Click on **Output Variable Name**, type *maedRevis*.

- Click **Label**, type *mother's educ revised*.
- Click **Change**.
- Then click on **Old and New Values** to get Fig. 5.5.

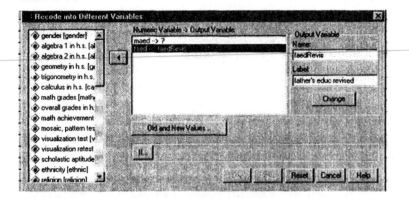

Fig. 5.4. Recode into different variables.

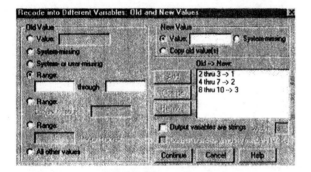

Fig. 5.5. Recode.

- Click on **Range** and type **2** in the first box and **3** in the second box.
- Click on **Value** (part of **New Value** on the right) and type **1**.
- Then click on **Add**.
- Repeat these steps to change old values **4** through **7** to a new **Value** of **2**.
- Then **Range: 8** through **10** to **Value: 3**. Does it look like Fig. 5.5?
- If it does, click on **Continue**.
- Finally, click on **OK**.

Check your **Data View** to see if *faedRevis* and *maedRevis,* with numbers ranging from 1 to 3, have been added on the far right side. To be extra careful, check the data file for a few participants to be sure the recodes were done correctly. For example, the first participant had 10 for *faed* which should be 3 for *faedRevis*. Is it? Check a few more to be sure; or compare your syntax file with the one in Output 5.2 below.

- Now, we will **label** the new (1, 2, 3) values.
- Go to your hsbdata file and click on **Variable View** (it is in the bottom left corner).
- In the *faedRevis* variable row, click on the **Values** cell and then the gray three-dot box.
- Click on the **Value** box and type **1**.
- Type *HS grad or less* where it says **Value Label**.
- Click on **Add**.
- Then click on the **Value** box again and type **2**.
- Click on the **Value Label** box and type *Some College*.

- Click on **Add**.
- Click once more on the **Value** box and type **3**.
- Click on the **Value Label** box and type *BS or More*.
- Again, click on **Add**. Does your window look like Fig. 5.6? If so,
- Click on **OK**.

<u>**Important**</u>: You have only labeled *faedRevis* (*father's educ revised*). You need to repeat these steps for *maedRevis*. Do **Value Labels** for *maedRevis* on your own.

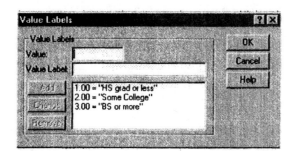

Fig. 5.6. Value labels.

Your output should be only the syntax in Output 5.2

Output 5.2: Recoding Mother's and Father's Education

```
RECODE
   faed maed
   (2 thru 3=1)  (4 thru 7=2)  (8 thru 10=3)  INTO  faedRevis  maedRevis.
VARIABLE LABELS faedRevis "father's educ revised" /maedRevis "mother's educ revised".
EXECUTE .
```

Interpretation of Output 5.2
This syntax shows that you have recoded *father's* and *mother's education* so that 2s and 3s become 1, 4s through 7s become 2 and 8 through 10 become 3. The new variable names are *faedRevis* and *maedRevis*, and the labels are *father's educ revised* and *mother's educ revised*. Again, there is no output other than syntax. Remember it is crucial to check some of your recoded data to be sure that it worked the way you intended.

Problem 5.3: Recode and Compute Pleasure Scale Score

Now let's **Compute** the average "pleasure from math" scale score (*pleasure scale*) from *item02*, *item06* , *item10,* and *item 14* <u>after</u> reversing (**Recoding**) *item06* and *item10* which are negatively worded or low pleasure items (see the codebook in chapter 1). We will keep both the new *item06r* and *item 10r* and old (*item06* and *item10*) variables to check the recodes and to play it safe. Then, we will **Label** the new computed variable as *pleasure scale*.

5.3. **Compute** the average *pleasure scale* from *item02, item06, item10* and *item 14* <u>after</u> reversing (use the **Recode** command) *item06* and *item10*. Name the new computed variable *pleasure* and label its highest and lowest values.

- Click on **Transform => Recode => Into Different Variables**.

- Click on **Reset** to clear the window of old information as a precaution.
- Click on *item06*.
- Click on the **arrow** button.
- Click on **Output Variable Name** and type *item06r*.
- Click on **Label** and type *item06 reversed*.
- Finally click on **Change**.
- Now repeat these steps for ***item10***. Does it look like Fig. 5.7?

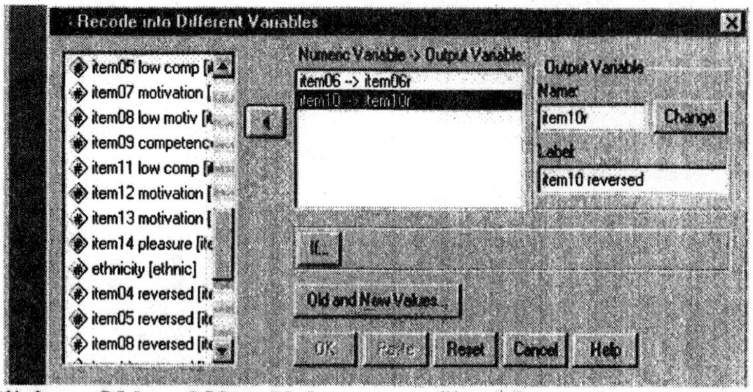

Fig. 5.7. Recode into different variables.

Click on **Old and New Values** to get Fig. 5.8.

- Now click on the **Value** box (under **Old Value**) and type **4**.
- Click on the **Value** box for the **New Value** and type **1**.
- Click on **Add**.

This is the first step in recoding. You have told the computer to change values of 4 to 1. Now do these steps over to recode the values **3** to **2**, **2** to **3**, and **1** to **4**. If you did it right, the screen will look like Fig. 5.8 in the **Old => New** box. Check your box carefully to be sure the recodes are exactly like Fig. 5.8.

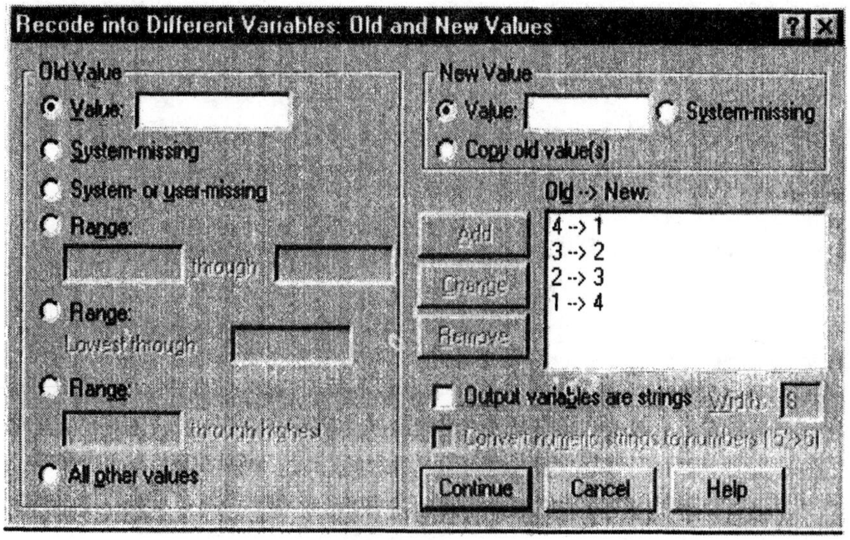

Fig. 5.8. Recode: Old and new values.

- Click on **Continue** and then **OK**.

Now check your **Data** file to see if there is an *item06r* and an *item10r* in the last two columns with numbers ranging from 1 to 4. To double check the recodes, compare the *item06* and *item10* columns in your data file with the *item06r* and *item10r* columns for a few subjects. Also, you should check your syntax file with Output 5.3a.

Output 5.3a: Recoding Mother's and Father's Education

```
RECODE
  item06 item10
  (4=1)  (3=2)  (2=3)  (1=4)  INTO  item06r  item10r .
VARIABLE LABELS item06r 'item06 reversed' / item10r 'item10 reversed'.
EXECUTE .
```

Now let's compute the average *pleasure scale*.

- Click on **Transform => Compute**.
- In the **Target Variable** box of Fig. 5. 9, type *pleasure*.

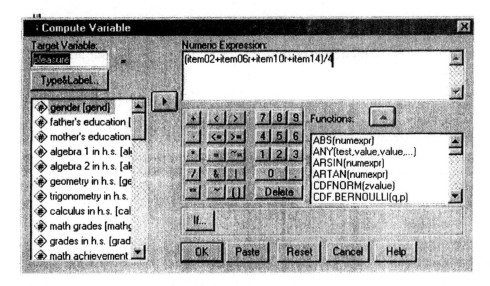

Fig. 5.9. Compute variable.

- Click on **Type & Label** and give it the name *pleasure scale* (see Fig. 5.10).
- Click on **Continue** to return to Fig. 5.9.
- In the **Numeric Expression** box type (item*02+item06r+item10r+item14*)/4. Be sure that what you typed is exactly like this!
- Finally, click on **OK.**

Fig.5.10. Compute variable: Type and label.

- Now provide **Value Labels** for the *pleasure scale* using commands similar to those you did for *father's educ revised.*
- Type 1, then *very low*, and click **Add.**

- Type 4, then very high, and click **Add.** See Fig. 5.6 if you need help.

In the **Compute** method we just used, the computer added items 02, 06r, 10r, and 14 and then divided the sum by four, giving the result a new name, *pleasure*. Be sure your formula is <u>exactly</u> like the one shown. For example, <u>you must have the parentheses, and you must have zero (not the letter O) in front of *item02* and *item06r*.</u>

Because you are less likely to make a mistake than if you type the formula in the **Numeric Expression** box, in Fig. 5.9 it is safer (but slower) to use the key pad. To use the key pad, click on *item 02* and the arrow to move it to the right, then click on +, click *item06r* and move it, click +, etc.

Check your data file to see if *pleasure* has been added. It is also prudent to <u>calculate the pleasure score by hand for a few participants to be sure it was done correctly</u>. The computer will not make calculation mistakes but *sometimes you may not tell it exactly what you intended*. Check your syntax with the one in Output 5.3b.

Output 5.3b: Computation of Pleasure Scale

```
COMPUTE pleasure = (item02 + item06r + item10r + item14 )/ 4 .
EXECUTE .
```

Interpretation of Output 5.3
The method we used to compute summated or composite scales will not compute an average score for a particular participant if he or she is missing data for *any* of the questions. The computed score will be missing. This can result in a sizable decrease in subjects who have composite scores if several participants did not answer even one or a few questions. In this circumstance one might choose to use the **MEAN** function, shown Problem 4 and in the callout box beside Fig. 5.11, because it utilizes all of the available data.

Problem 5.4: Compute Parents Revised Education with the Mean Command

We have decided to combine *father's* and *mother's education* scores because, as we will find out later, they are highly correlated. Thus, for some purposes, it is better to treat them as one variable. We also wanted to demonstrate the use of the **Mean** function, which is an alternative to the **Compute** commands that we used to create the *pleasure scale*. Note that in this problem we will use the original *father's* and *mother's education* variables (not the revised ones). This provides us with a variable that has more range and will be used later on.

5.4. Compute *parents education* using the **Mean** function, an alternative method.

- Click on **Transform** = > **Compute** to get Fig 5.11.
- In the **Target Variable box**, type *parEduc*.
- Click on **Type & Label** and give it the name *parent's education*.
- In the **Function Box** highlight **MEAN** click the up arrow to move it into the **Numeric Expression Box.**
- Enter *faed* and *maed* in the brackets. Either type them or click them over. Note the comma between the variables.

- Also, you should label, at least, the highest and lowest **Values** by clicking on the **None** in the **Values** column of the *parent's education* row of the **Variable View.**
- Type 2, and *less than h.s. grad,* click **Add.**
- Type 10 and *Ph.D./M.D.,* **Add.** (Note you can get values of 2.5 and 3.5 etc. so leave the decimals at 2.)
- Click on **OK.**

Output 5.4: Computation of Parent's Education

```
COMPUTE ParEduc = MEAN(faed,maed) .
VARIABLE LABELS parEduc "parent's education" .
EXECUTE .
```

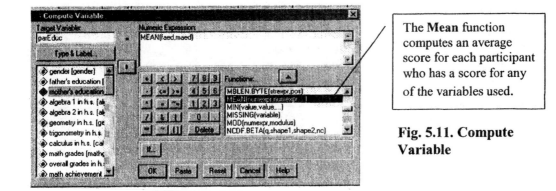

The **Mean** function computes an average score for each participant who has a score for any of the variables used.

Fig. 5.11. Compute Variable

Interpretation of Output 5.4

Note that you have created another new variable (*parEduc*), which is the seventh and last one you will create for the hsbdata set. It can be found as the 45th variable in the **Variable View** and in the far right column of the **Data View**.

You will see when we print the **Descriptives** in Problem 5, that all 75 participants have a *parent's education* value because none of them are missing both *father's* and *mother's education*. It seems reasonable to use only *mother's education* if *father's education* is unknown. This would be even more helpful if we were to compute *parent's education* when there were a lot of cases in which *father's education* was unknown, as is sometimes the case. Because almost all students know *mother's education,* by using the **Mean** function, almost all would have a parent's education score.

On the other hand, the **Mean** function should be used cautiously. For example, using the MEAN function if a student answered only one of the four *pleasure scale* items they would still get an average *pleasure score* based on that one item. If the item was not representative (i.e., usually rated higher or lower than the others), then the *pleasure* score would be misleading.

Problem 5.5: Check for Errors and Normality for the New Variables

5.5.   Run **Descriptives** in order to understand the new variables, check for errors and see if they are distributed normally.

Using chapter 4 (Problem 4.1) as a guide, compute the descriptive statistics (**Minimum, Maximum, Mean, Standard Deviation, Variance,** and **Skewness**) for the new variables: *math courses taken, father's educ revised, mother's educ revised, pleasure,* and *parent's education..*

Output 5.5: Descriptive Statistics

```
DESCRIPTIVES
    VARIABLES=mathcrs faedRevis maedRevis pleasure parEduc
    /STATISTICS=MEAN STDDEV VARIANCE MIN MAX SKEWNESS .
```

Descriptives

Descriptive Statistics

	N	Minimum	Maximum	Mean	Std.	Variance	Skewness	
	Statistic	Statistic	Statistic	Statistic	Statistic	Statistic	Statistic	Std. Error
math courses taken	75	0	5	2.11	1.673	2.799	.325	.277
father's educ revised	73	1.00	3.00	1.7397	.85028	.723	.533	.281
mother's educ revised	75	1.00	3.00	1.4667	.68445	.468	1.162	.277
pleasure scale	75	1.50	4.00	3.1300	.60454	.365	-.682	.277
parent's education	75	2.00	10.00	4.3933	2.31665	5.367	.923	.277
Valid N (listwise)	73							

Interpretation of Output 5.5

The **Descriptives** table provides, as did Output 4.1, the requested statistics and the *N*s for each variable, as well as the listwise *N*.

Check for Errors. It is especially important to check new computed variables for errors. Note that *father's education revised* has an *N* of 73 (2 missing). That is what we would expect given that the original *father's education* variable had *N*=73. However, *parent's education* has no missing data because we used the **Mean** function. Check also the minimum and maximum scores for each variable to see if they lie within the acceptable range of values. For example, because there are five math courses, the number of *math courses taken* has to be between 0 and 5, and it is. Note that although the codebook and **Variable View** say the *pleasure score* can vary between 1.00 and 4.00 actually the lowest score in this group was 1.50. That is okay, but it would be a problem if the lowest score was 3.5 out of 4 or if the highest score was only 1.5. Some variability is necessary for statistical analyses.

Check assumptions. Note that *math courses taken* and the *pleasure scale* have **skewness** scores less than 1.0 so we can consider them to be approximately normally distributed. The skewness for *mother's education revised* is 1.16 so it is moderately skewed, as was *mother's education*. However, we will usually use it as an independent variable in an ANOVA so normality is not required. Note that the skewness for *parent's education* is within our acceptable limits at .92 so that is another reason to use it rather than *mother's* or *father's education.*

Saving the Updated HSB Data file

You should *always* save your **data file** if you entered new data or made any changes. If you forget to **Save,** you will have to do these **Recodes** etc. over again! To save, follow these steps:

- Click on the **SPSS Data Editor** button at the bottom of your screen.
- Then click **File => Save As.**
- Give your data file a new name; i.e., hsbdataB.sav.
- **Select Drive A:** to save on your floppy disk (or use C: or a network drive if you have the capability).

Interpretation Questions

5.1.   Using your initial HSB data file (or the file in chapter 1), compare the original data to your new variables: a) How many math courses did participant number 11 take? b) What should *faedr* be for participants 2, 5, and 8? c) What should the *pleasure scale* score be for participant 1? d) Why is comparing a few initial scores to transformed scores important?

5.2   Why did you recode *father's* and *mother's education*?

5.3   Why did you reverse questions 6 and 10?

5.4   Why did you compute *parent's education*?

5.5.   When would you use the **Mean** function to compute an average? And when would the **Mean** function not be appropriate?

5.6.   In Output 5.5, do the *pleasure scale* scores differ markedly from the normal distribution? How do you know? Is *math courses taken* normally distributed?

Extra SPSS Problems

Using the college student data, solve the following problems:

5.1.   Compute a new variable labeled *average overall* evaluation (*aveEval*) by computing the average score (*evalinst + evalprog + evalphys + evalsocl/4*).

5.2   Compute a similar variable (*meanEval*), using the **Mean** command. Compare the two (5.1 and 5.2) scores. Why do they differ?

5.3   **Count** the number of types of TV shows that each student watches.

5.4   Recode the *student's current gpa* into three categories 1 = 2.00-2.99; 2 = 2.00 – 2.99; 3 = 3.00 – 4.00. Produce a frequency table for the recorded values.

CHAPTER 6

Selecting and Interpreting Inferential Statistics

To understand the information in this chapter, it is necessary to remember or to review the sections in Chapter 1 about **variables** and levels of **measurement** (nominal, dichotomous, ordinal, and normal/scale). It is also necessary to remember the distinction we made between difference and associational research questions and between **descriptive and inferential statistic**. This chapter focuses on inferential statistics, which as the name implies, refers to statistics that make inferences about population values based on the sample data that you have collected and analyzed. What we call **difference inferential statistics** lead to inferences about the differences (usually mean differences) between groups in the populations from which the samples were drawn. **Associational inferential statistics** lead to inferences about the association or relationship between variables in the population. Thus, the purpose of inferential statistics is to enable the researcher to make generalizations beyond the specific sample data. Before we describe how to select statistics, we will introduce design classifications.

General Design Classifications for Difference Questions

Many research questions focus on whether there is a significant difference between two or more groups or conditions. When a group comparison or difference question is asked, the independent variable and design can be classified as between groups or within subjects. Understanding this distinction is one essential aspect of determining the proper statistical analysis for this type of question.

Labeling difference question designs. It is helpful to have a brief descriptive label that identifies the design for other researchers and also guides us toward the proper statistics to use. We do not have design classifications for the descriptive or associational research questions, so this section only applies to difference questions. Designs are usually labeled in terms of (a) the overall type of design (between groups or within subjects), (b) the number of independent variables, and (c) the number of levels within each independent variable.

Between-groups designs. These are designs where each participant in the research is in one and only one condition or group. For example, in a study investigating the "effects" of fathers' education on *math achievement*, there may be three groups (or levels or values) of the independent variable, *father's education*. These levels are: (a) *high school or less*, (b) *some college*, and (c) *BS or more*. In a between groups design, each participant is in only one of the three conditions or levels. If the investigator wished to have 20 participants in each group, then 60 participants would be needed to carry out the research.

Within subjects or repeated measures designs. These designs are conceptually the opposite of between groups designs. In within subjects designs, each participant in the research receives or experiences all of the conditions or levels of the independent variable. These designs also include examples where the participants are matched by the experimenter or in some natural way (e.g., twins, husband and wife, or mother and child). When each participant is assessed more than once, these designs are also referred to as **repeated measures** designs. Repeated measures designs are common in longitudinal research and intervention research. Comparing performance on the same dependent variable assessed before and after intervention (pretest and posttest) is a common example of a repeated measures design. We might call the independent variable in such a study "time of measurement," or "change over time." The HSB study did not really have a within-subjects aspect to the design. However, one of the variables is repeated (*visualization score* with two levels: *visualization* and *visualization retest*) and one is within subjects (*education*, each student has both a *mother's education* and *father's education*). We will use a paired or matched statistic to see if *mother's education* is on the average higher or lower than *father's education*.

Single factor designs. If the design has only one independent variable (either a between groups design or a within subjects design), then it should be described as a basic or single factor or one-way design. **Factor** and **way** are other names for group difference independent variables. For example, a between groups design with one independent variable that has four levels is a single factor or "one-way" between groups design with four levels. If the design was a within subjects design with four levels, then it would be described as a single factor repeated measures design with four levels (e.g., the same test being given four times).

Between groups factorial designs. When there is more than one group difference independent variable, and each level of each factor (independent variable) is possible in combination with each level of the design is called **factorial**. For example, a factorial design could have two independent variables (i.e., factors) *gender* and *ethnicity*, allowing for male and female members of each ethnic group. In these cases, the number of levels of *each* factor (independent variable) becomes important in the description of the design. For example, if *gender* had two levels (*male* and *female*) and *ethnicity* had three levels (Euro-American, African-American, and Latino-American), then this design is a 2 x 3 between groups factorial design. It could also be called a two-way or two factor design because there are two independent variables..

Mixed factorial designs. If the design has a between groups variable and a within subjects independent variable, it is called a **mixed design.** For example, let's say that the two independent variables are gender (a between-groups variable) and "time of measurement" (with pretest and posttest as the two, within-subjects levels); this is a 2 x 2 mixed factorial design with repeated measures on the second factor. The mixed design is common in experimental studies with a pretest and posttest, but the analysis can be complex.

Remember, when describing a design, that each independent variable is described using one number, which is the number of levels for that variable. Thus a design description with two numbers (e.g., 3 x 4) has two independent variables or factors, which have 3 and 4 levels. The dependent variable is not part of the design description, so it was not considered in this section.

Selection of Inferential Statistics

How do you decide which of the many possible inferential statistics to use? Although this section may seem overwhelming at first because many statistical tests are introduced, don't be concerned if you don't now know much about the tests mentioned. You should come back to this chapter later, from time to time, when you have to make a decision about which statistic to use, and by then, the tests will be more familiar. We present eight steps shown in Fig 6.1 to help guide you in the selection of an appropriate statistical test. The steps and tables are our recommendations, but as you will see these are often other appropriate choices.

Remember that **difference questions** <u>compare groups and utilize</u> the statistics, which we call <u>difference inferential statistics</u>. These statistics (e.g., *t* test and analysis of variance) are shown in Tables 6.1 and 6.3.

Associational questions <u>utilize</u> what we call <u>associational inferential statistics</u>. The statistics in this group <u>examine the association or relationship between two or more variables</u> and are shown in Table 6.2 and 6.4.

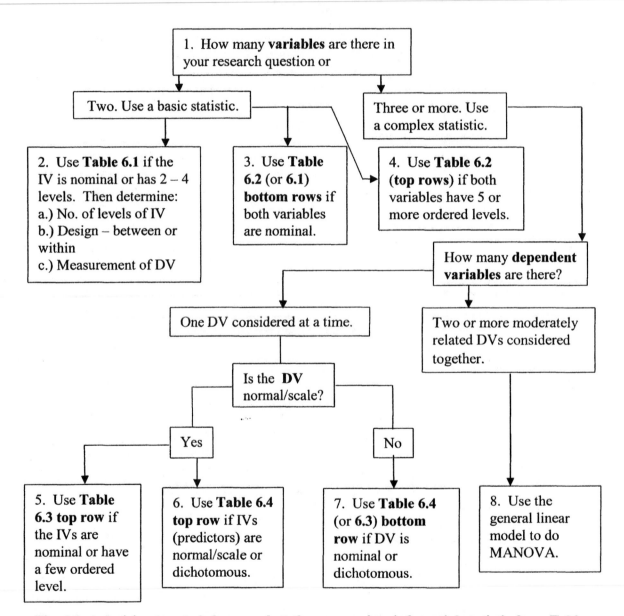

Fig. 6.1. A decision tree to help you select the appropriate inferential statistic from Tables 6.1 to 6.4.

Using Tables 6.1 to 6.4 to Select Inferential Statistics

As with research questions and hypotheses discussed in Chapter 1, we divide inferential statistics into basic and complex. For **basic (or bivariate) statistics** <u>there is *one* independent and *one* dependent variable</u> and you will use Table 6.1 or 6.2. For **complex statistics** <u>there are three or</u>

more variables. We decided to call them **complex** rather than **multivariate**, which is more common in the literature, because there is not unanimity about the definition of multivariate, and several such complex statistics (e.g., factorial ANOVA) are not usually classified as multivariate. For complex statistics, you will use Tables 6.3 or 6.4. Most of the statistics shown in these four tables are discussed in the remaining chapters in this book, and text is provided demonstrating how to compute and interpret them using SPSS 12.

Two of the complex statistics in Tables 6.3 and 6.4 (**Factorial ANOVA** and **multiple regression**) are introduced in this book, but they and other such statistics are discussed in more detail in our *SPSS for Intermediate Statistics* book Leech, Barrett, and Morgan (2004). The statistics are identified with I.B. (intermediate book) in the tables. These four tables include most of the inferential statistics that you will encounter in reading research articles. Note that the boxes in the decision tree are numbered to correspond to the numbers in the text below, which expands somewhat on the decision tree.

1. Decide <u>how many variables</u> there are in your research question or hypothesis. If there are only two variables, use Tables 6.1 or 6.2. If there is *more* than one independent and/or one dependent variable (i.e., three or more variables) to be used in this analysis, use Tables 6.3, 6.4, or 6.5.

Basic (2 Variable) Statistics
2. If the <u>independent variable is nominal</u> (i.e., has unordered levels) **or** <u>has a few (2-4) ordered levels</u>, use Table 6.1. Then, your question is a **basic** two variable **difference question** to compare groups. You must then determine: (a) whether there are <u>two *or* more than two levels</u> (also called categories or groups or samples) of your independent variable, (b) whether the design is <u>between groups or within subjects</u>, and (c) whether the <u>measurement level</u> of the dependent variable is (i) <u>normal/scale</u> and parametric assumptions are not markedly violated *or* (ii) <u>ordinal</u> or (iii) <u>nominal</u> *or* dichotomous (see Chapter 3 if you need help). The answers to these questions lead to a specific box and statistic in Table 6.1.

3. If <u>both variables are nominal or dichotomous</u>, you could ask <u>either a difference question</u> (use the bottom row of Table 6.1; e.g., **chi-square**) <u>or an associational question</u> and use the bottom row of Table 6.2 to select **phi** or **Cramer's** *V.* Note, in the second to bottom row of Table 6.2, we have included **eta**, an associational statistic used with one nominal and one normal or scale variable. We will later see it used as an effect size measure with ANOVAs. There are many other nonparametric associational measures, some of which we will see in the next chapter.

4. If <u>both variables have many (we suggest 5 or more) ordered levels</u>, use Table 6.2 (top two rows). Your research question would be a **basic** two variable (bivariate) **associational question**. Which row you use depends on *both* variables. If both are normal/scale then you would probably select the **Pearson product moment correlation** or **bivariate regression** (top row). Regression should be used if one has a clearly directional hypothesis, with an independent and dependent variable. Correlation is chosen if one is simply interested in how the two variables are related. If one or both variables are ordinal (ranks or grossly skewed) or other assumptions are markedly violated, the second row (**Kendalls' tau** or **Spearman rho**) is a better choice.

Table 6.1. *Selection of an Appropriate Inferential Statistic for Basic, Two Variable, Difference Questions or Hypotheses*[a]

Scale of Measurement of **Dependent Variable** ↓	COMPARE ↓	One Factor or Independent Variable with **2 Levels** or Categories/Groups/Samples		One Independent Variable **3 or more Levels** or Groups	
		Independent Samples or Groups **(Between)**	Repeated Measures or Related Samples **(Within)**	Independent Samples or Groups **(Between)**	Repeated Measures or Related Samples **(Within)**
Dependent Variable Approximates **Normal /Scale** Data and Assumptions Not Markedly Violated	MEANS	INDEPENDENT SAMPLES *t* TEST ch. 10 or ONE-WAY ANOVA Ch. 9	PAIRED SAMPLES *t* TEST Ch. 9	ONE-WAY ANOVA Ch. 10	GLM REPEATED MEASURES ANOVA I.B. [b]
Dependent Variables Clearly **Ordinal** or Parametric Assumptions Markedly Violated	MEAN RANKS	MANN-WHITNEY Ch. 9	WILCOXON Ch. 9	KRUSKAL-WALLIS Ch. 10	FRIEDMAN IB [b]
Dependent Variable **Nominal** or **Dichotomous**	COUNTS	CHI-SQUARE Ch. 7	MCNEMAR	CHI-SQUARE Ch. 7	COCHRAN Q TEST

[a] It is acceptable to use statistics that are in the box(es) below the appropriate statistic, but there is usually some loss of power. It is not acceptable to use statistics in boxes above the appropriate statistic or ones in another column.

[b] IB=Our intermediate book. Leech et al. (2004) *SPSS for Intermediate Statistics: Use and Interpretation.*

Complex (3 or more variable) Questions and Statistics

It is possible to break down a complex research problem or question into a series of basic (bivariate) questions and analyses. However, there are advantages to combining them into one complex analysis; additional information is provided and a more accurate overall picture of the relationships is obtained.

5. If you have one normally distributed (scale) dependent variable and two (or perhaps three or four) independent variables, each of which is nominal or has a few (2-4) ordered levels, you will use the top row of Table 6.3 and one of three types of **factorial ANOVA**. These analysis of variance (ANOVA) statistics answer **complex difference questions**.

Table 6.2. *Selection of an Appropriate Inferential Statistic for Basic, Two Variable, Associational Questions or Hypotheses*

Level (scale) of Measurement of **Both Variables** ⬇	RELATE ⬇	Two Variables or Scores for the Same or Related Subjects
Variables are Both **Normal /Scale** and Assumptions not Markedly Violated	SCORES	PEARSON (r) or BIVARIATE REGRESSION Ch. 8
Both Variables at Least **Ordinal** Data or Assumptions Markedly Violated	RANKS	KENDALL TAU or SPEARMAN (Rho) Ch. 8
One Variable is **Normal /Scale** and One is **Nominal**		ETA Ch. 7
Both Variables are **Nominal** or **Dichotomous**	COUNTS	PHI or CRAMER'S V Ch. 7

Note, in Table 6.3, that there are no complex difference statistics available in SPSS if the dependent variable is ordinal. **Loglinear** analysis is a nonparametric statistic somewhat similar to the between group factorial ANOVA for the case where all the variables are nominal or dichotomous (see Table 6.3).

Table 6.3. *Selection of the Appropriate Complex (Two or More Independent Variables) Statistic to Answer Difference Questions or Hypotheses*

Dependent Variable(s) ↓	Two or More Independent Variables		
	All Between Groups	All Within Subjects	Mixed (Between & Within)
One **Normal/ Scale** Dependent Variable	GLM, Factorial ANOVA or ANCOVA ch. 10 and I.B. [a]	GLM with Repeated Measures on all Factors I.B.	GLM with Repeated Measures on some Factors I.B.
Ordinal Dependent Variable	None Common	None Common	None Common
Dichotomous Dependent Variable	LOG-LINEAR	None Common	None Common

[a] I.B. = Leech et al. (2004) *SPSS for Intermediate Statistics: Use and Interpretation.*

6. The statistics in Table 6.4 are used to answer **complex associational questions**. If you have two or more independent or predictor variables and one normal (scale) dependent variable, the top row of Table 6.4 and **multiple regression** are appropriate.

7. If the dependent variable is dichotomous or nominal, consult the bottom row of Table 6.4, and use **Discriminant Analysis** or **Logistic Regression**, both discussed in Leech et al. (2003).

8. Use a **MANOVA** if you have two or more normal (scale) dependent variables treated simultaneously.

Occasionally you will see a research article in which a dichotomous *dependent variable* was used with a *t* test, or ANOVA, or as either variable in a Pearson correlation. Because of the special nature of dichotomous variables, this is not necessarily wrong, as would be the use of a nominal (three or more unordered levels) dependent variable with these parametric statistics. However, we think that it is usually a better practice to use the same statistics with dichotomous variables that you would use with nominal variables. The exception is that it is appropriate to use dichotomous (dummy) independent variables in multiple and logistic regression (see Table 6.4 again).

Table 6.4. *Selection of the Appropriate Complex Associational Statistic for Predicting a Single Dependent/Outcome Variable from Several Independent Variables*

| One Dependent or Outcome Variable ↓ | Several Independent or Predictor Variables | | |
	Normal or Scale	Some Normal Some Dichotomous (2 category)	All Dichotomous
Normal/Scale (Continuous)	MULTIPLE REGRESSION ch. 8 and I.B. [a]	MULTIPLE REGRESSION ch. 8 and I.B.	MULTIPLE REGRESSION ch. 8 and I.B.
Dichotomous	DISCRIMINANT ANALYSIS I.B.	LOGISTIC REGRESSION I.B.	LOGISTIC REGRESSION I.B.

[a] I.B. = Our intermediate book. Leech et al. (2004) *SPSS for Intermediate Statistics: Use and Interpretation*

The General Linear Model

Whether or not there is a relationship between variables can be answered in two ways. For example, if each of two variables provide approximately normally distributed data with five or more levels, based on Fig. 6.1 and Table 6.2, the statistic to use is either the Pearson correlation or bivariate (simple) regression, and that would be our recommendation. Instead, some researchers choose to divide the independent variable into two or several categories or groups such as low, medium, and high and then do a one-way ANOVA.

Conversely, in a second example, others who start with an independent variable that has only a few (say two through four *ordered* categories) may choose to do a correlation instead of a one-way ANOVA. Although these choices are not necessarily wrong, we do not think they are usually the best practice. In the first example, information is lost by dividing a continuous independent variable into a few categories. In the second example, there would be a restricted range, which tends to decrease the size of the correlation coefficient.

In the above examples we recommended one of the choices, but the fact that there *are* two choices raises a bigger and more complex issue. Statisticians point out, and can prove mathematically, that the distinction between difference and associational statistics is an artificial one and that one-way ANOVA and Pearson correlation are mathematically the same, as are factorial ANOVA and multiple regression. <u>Figure 6.2 shows the equivalencies and that although we have made a distinction between difference and associational inferential statistics, they both serve the purpose of exploring and describing (top box) relationships and both are subsumed by the general linear model (middle box).</u>

Statisticians state that all common parametric statistics are relational. Thus, the full range of methods used to analyze one continuous dependent variable and one or more independent variables, either continuous or categorical, are mathematically similar. The model on which this is based is called the **general linear model**. The idea is that the relationship between the independent and dependent variables can be expressed by an equation with weights for each of the independent/predictor variables plus an error term.

The bottom part of Fig. 6.2 indicates that a *t* test or one-way ANOVA with a nominal or dichotomous independent variable is analogous to eta, a correlation coefficient for a nominal independent variable and a continuous dependent variable. Likewise, a one-way ANOVA with an ordered independent variable is analogous to bivariate regression. Finally, as shown in the lowest boxes in Fig. 6.2, factorial ANOVA (with dichotomous or ordered factors) and multiple regression are analogous mathematically. Note in Fig. 6.1 and Table 6.3 that SPSS uses the GLM program to perform a variety of statistics including factorial ANOVA and MANOVA.

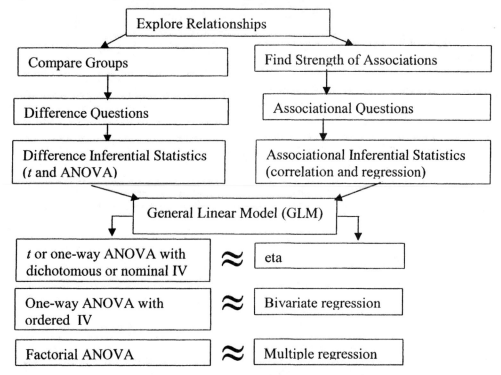

Fig. 6.2 A general linear model diagram of the selection of inferential statistics.

Although we recognize that our distinction between difference and associational parametric statistics is a simplification, we still think it is useful. We hope that this glimpse of an advanced topic is clear and helpful.

Interpreting the Results of a Statistical Test

In the following chapters, we present information about how to check assumptions, do the SPSS commands, interpret the above statistics, and write about them. For each statistic (F, etc.) the SPSS computations produce a number or **calculated value** based on the specific data in your study. SPSS labels them t, F, etc. or sometimes just value.

Statistical Significance

The calculated value is compared to a **critical value** (found in a statistics table or stored in the computer's memory) that takes into account the degrees of freedom, which are usually based on the number of participants. Figure 6.3 shows how to interpret any inferential test once you know the probability level (p or sig.) from the computer or statistics table. In general, if the calculated value of the statistic (t, F, etc.) is relatively large, the probability or p is small, (e.g., .05, .01, .001). If the probability is *less than* the preset alpha level (usually .05), we can say that the results are **statistically significant** or that they are significant at the .05 level or that $p < .05$. We can also reject the null hypothesis of no difference or no relationship. Note that, using SPSS computer printouts, it is quite easy to determine statistical significance because the actual significance or probability level (p) is printed so you do not have to look up a critical value in a table. SPSS labels this p value **Sig**. so all of the common inferential statistics have a common metric, the significance level or **Sig**. This level is also the probability of a Type I error or the probability of rejecting the null hypothesis when it is actually true. Thus, regardless of what specific statistic you use, if the sig. or p is small (usually less than .05) the finding is statistically significant, and you can reject the null hypothesis of no difference or no relationship.

Sig.[1]	Meaning	Null Hypothesis	Interpretation
1.00	$p = 1.00$	Don't Reject	Not Statistically Significant (could be due to chance)
.50	$p = .50$		
.06	$p = .06$		
.05	$p \leq .05$	Reject [2]	Statistically Significant[3] (not likely due to chance)
.01	$p = .01$		
.000	$p < .001$		

1. SPSS uses **Sig.** to indicate the significance or probability level (p) of all inferential statistics. These are just a sample of Sig. values, which would be any value from 0 to 1.
2. $p \leq .05$ is the typical alpha level that researchers use to assess whether the null hypothesis should be rejected or not. However, sometimes researchers use more liberal levels. (e.g., .10 in exploratory studies) or more conservative levels (e.g., .01).
3. Statistically significant does *not* mean that the results have practical significance or importance.

Fig. 6.3 Interpreting Inferential Statistics using the SPSS Sig.

Practical Significance versus Statistical Significance
Students, and sometimes researchers, misinterpret statistically significant results as being practically or clinically important. But statistical significance is not the same as practical significance or importance. With large samples you can find statistical significance even when the differences or associations are very small/weak. Thus, in addition to statistical significance, we will examine effect size. We will see that it is quite possible, with a large sample, to have a statistically significant result that is weak (i.e., has a small **effect size.**) Remember that the null hypothesis states that there is *no* difference or *no* association. A statistically significant result with a small effect size means that we can be very confident that there is at least a little difference or association, but it may not be of any practical importance.

Confidence Intervals
One alternative to null hypothesis significance testing (NHST) is to create confidence intervals. These intervals provide more information than NHST and *may* provide more practical information. For example, suppose one knew that an increase in reading scores of 5 points, obtained on a particular instrument, would lead to a functional increase in reading performance. Two different methods of instruction were compared. The result showed that students who used the new method scored statistically significantly higher than those who used the other method. According to NHST, we would reject the null hypothesis of no difference between methods and conclude that our new method is better. If we apply **confidence intervals** to this same study, we can determine an interval that contains the *population mean difference* 95% of the time. If the lower bound of that interval is greater than 5 points, we can conclude that using this method of instruction would lead to a practical or functional increase in reading levels. If however, the confidence interval ranged from say 1 to 11, the result would be statistically significant, but the mean difference in the population could be as little as 1 point, or as big as 11 points. Given these results we could not be confident that there would be a *practical* increase in reading using the new method.

Effect Size
A statistically significant outcome does not give information about the strength or size of the outcome. Therefore, it is important to know, in addition to information on statistical significance, the size of the effect. **Effect size** is defined as the strength of the relationship between the independent variable and the dependent variable, and/or the magnitude of the difference between levels of the independent variable with respect to the dependent variable. Statisticians have proposed many effect size measures that fall mainly into two types or families, the *r* family and the *d* family.

The r family of effect size measures. One method of expressing effect sizes is in terms of strength of association. The most well-known variant of this approach is the **Pearson correlation coefficient, r.** Using Pearson *r*, effect sizes always have an absolute value less than 1.0, varying between -1.0 and $+1.0$ with 0 representing no effect and $+1$ or -1 the maximum effect. This *family* of effect sizes includes many other associational statistics such as rho (r_s), phi (ϕ), eta (η), and the multiple correlation (R).

The d family of effect size measures. The *d* family focuses on magnitude of difference rather than strength of association. If one compares two groups, the effect size (*d*) can be computed by subtracting the mean of the second group (B) from the mean of the first group (A) and dividing by the pooled standard deviation of both groups. The general formula is on the left. If the two groups have equal ns, the pooled SD is the average of the SDs for the two groups. When ns are unequal, the formula on the right is the appropriate one.

$$d = \frac{M_A - M_B}{SD_{pooled}} \qquad\qquad d = \frac{M_A - M_B}{\sqrt{\dfrac{(n_A - 1)SD_A^2 + (n_B - 1)SD_B^2}{n_A + n_B - 2}}}$$

Issues about effect size measures. Unfortunately, as just indicated, there are many different effect size measures and little agreement about which to use. Although d is the most commonly discussed effect size measure, it is not available on SPSS outputs. However, d can be calculated by hand from information in the SPSS printout, using the appropriate formula from above. The correlation coefficient, r, and other measures of the strength of association such as phi (ϕ), eta^2 (η^2), and R^2 *are* available in SPSS.

There are many other formulas for *d* family effect sizes, but they all express effect size in standard deviation units. Thus, a d of .5 means that the groups differ by one half of a pooled standard deviation. Using d, effect sizes usually vary from 0 to + or - 1 but d can be more than 1.

There is disagreement among researchers about whether it is best to express effect size as the unsquared or squared r family statistic (e.g., r or r^2). The squared versions have been used because they indicate the percentage of variance in the dependent variable that can be predicted from the independent variable(s). However, some statisticians argue that these usually small percentages give you an underestimated impression of the strength or importance of the effect. Thus, we (like Cohen, 1988) decided to use the unsquared statistics (r, ϕ, η, and R) as our r family indexes.

Although the 4th edition of the *Publication Manual of the American Psychological Association* (APA, 1994) recommended that researchers report effect sizes, relatively few researchers did so before 1999 when the APA Task Force on Statistical Inference stated that effect sizes should *always* be reported for your primary results (Wilkinson & The Task Force, 1999). The 5th edition (APA, 2001) adopted this recommendation of the Task Force so in the future, most journal articles will discuss the size of the effect as well as whether or not the result was statistically significant.

Interpreting Effect Sizes

Assuming that you have computed an effect size measure, how should it be interpreted? Based on Cohen (1988), Table 6.5 provides guidelines for interpreting the size of the "effect" for five common effect size measures: d, r, ϕ, R and η.

Note that these guidelines are based on the effect sizes usually found in studies in the behavioral sciences and education. Thus, they do not have absolute meaning; large, medium, and small are only relative to typical findings in these areas. For that reason, we suggest using "larger than typical" instead of large, "typical" instead of medium, and "smaller than typical" instead of small. The guidelines will not apply to all subfields in the behavioral sciences, and they definitely will not apply to fields, designs, or contexts where the usually expected effects are either larger or smaller. It is advisable to examine the research literature to see if there is information about typical effect sizes on the topic and adjust the values that are considered typically accordingly.

Table 6.5 *Interpretation of the Strength of a Relationship (Effect Sizes)*

General Interpretation of the Strength of a Relationship	The *d* Family[a]	The *r* Family[b]		
	d	*r* and ϕ	*R*	η (eta)[d]
Much larger than typical	≥ 1.00[c]	$\geq .70$	.70+	.45+
Large or larger than typical	.80	.50	.51	.37
Medium or typical	.50	.30	.36	.24
Small or smaller than typical	.20	.10	.14	.10

[a] *d* values can vary from 0.0 to + or -1.0 infinity, but *d*s greater than one is uncommon.
[b] *r* family values can vary from 0.0 to + or – 1.0, but except for reliability (i.e., same concept measured twice), *r* is rarely above .70. In fact, some of these statistics (e.g., phi) have a restricted range in certain cases; that is, the maximum phi is less then 1.0.
[c] We interpret the numbers in this table as a range of values. For example a *d* greater than .90 (or less than -.90) would be described as "much larger than typical" a *d* between say .70 and .90 would be called "larger than typical," and *d* between say .60 and .70 would be "typical to larger than typical." We interpret the other three columns similarly.
[d] Partial etas from SPSS multivariate tests are equivalent to *R*. Use *R* column.

Cohen (1988) provided research examples of what he labeled small, medium, and large effects to support the suggested *d* and *r* family values. Most researchers would not consider a correlation (*r*) of .5 to be very strong because only 25% of the variance in the dependent variable is predicted. However, Cohen argued that a *d* of .8 (and an *r* of .5, which he shows are mathematically similar) are "grossly perceptible and therefore large differences, as (for example is) the mean difference in height between 13- and 18-year-old girls" (p. 27). Cohen stated that a small effect may be difficult to detect, perhaps because it is in a less well controlled area of research. Cohen's medium size effect is "…visible to the naked eye. That is, in the course of normal experiences, one would become aware of an average difference in IQ between clerical and semi-skilled workers…" (p. 26).

Effect size and practical significance. The effect size indicates the strength of the relationship and, thus, are relevant for practical significance. Although some researchers consider effect size measures to be an index of practical significance, we think that <u>effect size measures are not direct indexes of the importance of a finding</u>. As implied above, what constitutes a large or important effect depends on the specific area studied, the context, and the methods used. Furthermore, practical significance always involves a judgment by the researcher and/or the consumers (e.g., clinicians, clients, teachers, school boards) of research that takes into account such factors as cost and political considerations. A common example is that the effect size of taking daily aspirin its effect on heart attacks is quite small but the practical importance is high because preventing heart attacks is a life or death matter, the cost of aspirin is low, and side effects are uncommon. On the other hand, a curriculum change could have a large effect size but be judged to not be practical because of high costs and/or extensive opposition to its implementation.

Steps in Interpreting Inferential Statistics
When you interpret inferential statistics, we recommend:

<u>First decide whether to reject the null hypothesis.</u> However, that is not enough for a full interpretation. If you find that the outcome is statistically significant, you need to answer at least two *more* questions. Figure 6.4 summarizes the steps described below about how to more fully interpret the results of an inferential statistic.

<u>Second, what is the direction of the effect?</u> Difference inferential statistics compare groups so it is necessary to state which group performed better. We discuss how to do this in Chapters 9 and 10. For associational inferential statistics (e.g., correlation), the sign is very important, so you must indicate whether the association or relationship is positive or negative. We discuss how to interpret correlations in Chapters 7 and 8.

<u>Third, what is the size of the effect?</u> You should include the effect size, confidence intervals, or both in the description of your results. Unfortunately, SPSS does not always provide effect sizes and confidence intervals, so for some statistics we will have to compute or estimate the effect size by hand.

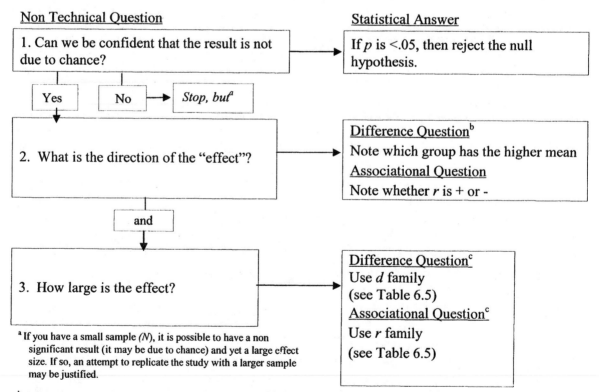

<u>Non Technical Question</u>

| | | <u>Statistical Answer</u> |

1. Can we be confident that the result is not due to chance? → If *p* is <.05, then reject the null hypothesis.

Yes   No → *Stop, but*[a]

2. What is the direction of the "effect"? → <u>Difference Question</u>[b]
Note which group has the higher mean
<u>Associational Question</u>
Note whether *r* is + or -

and

3. How large is the effect? → <u>Difference Question</u>[c]
Use *d* family
(see Table 6.5)
<u>Associational Question</u>[c]
Use *r* family
(see Table 6.5)

[a] If you have a small sample *(N)*, it is possible to have a non significant result (it may be due to chance) and yet a large effect size. If so, an attempt to replicate the study with a larger sample may be justified.

[b] If there are three or more means or a significant interaction a post hoc test (e.g., Tukey) will be necessary for complete interpretation.

[c] Interpretation of effect size is based on Cohen (1988) and Table 6.6. A "large" effect is one that Cohen states is "grossly perceptible." It is larger than typically found but does not necessarily explain a large amount of variance. You might use confidence intervals in addition or instead of effect sizes.

Fig. 6.4. Steps in the interpretation of an inferential statistic.

<u>Fourth</u>, but not shown in the Fig. 6.3, the <u>researcher or the consumer of the research should make a judgment about whether the result has practical or clinical significance or importance.</u> To do so

they need to take into account the effect size, the costs of implementing change, and the probability and severity of any side effects or unintended consequences.

An Example of How to Select and Interpret Inferential Statistics

As a review of what you have read in Chapter 1 and this chapter, we now provide an extended example based on the HSB data. We will walk you through the process of identifying the variables, research questions, and approach, and then show how we selected appropriate statistics and interpreted the results.

Research problem. Suppose your research problem was to investigate *gender* and *math courses* taken and their relationship to *math achievement.*

Identification of the variables and their measurement. The research problem specifies three variables: gender, math courses taken, and math achievement. The latter appears to be the outcome or dependent variable, and gender and math courses taken are the independent or predictor variables because they occurred before the math exam. As such, they are *presumed* to have an effect on math achievement scores.

What is the level of measurement for these three variables? *Gender* is clearly dichotomous (*male* or *female*). *Math courses taken* has six ordered values, from 0 to 5 courses. These are scale data because there should be an approximately normal distribution of scores: most students took some but not all of the *math courses.* Likewise, the *math achievement* test has many levels, with more scores somewhere in the middle than at the high and low ends. It is necessary to confirm that math courses taken and math achievement are at least approximately normally distributed by requesting that SPSS compute the skewness of each.

Research questions. There are a number of possible research questions that could be asked and statistics that could be used with these three variables, including all of the types of questions in Appendix B, the descriptive statistics discussed in Chapter 6, and several of the inferential statistics presented in this chapter. However, we will focus on three research questions and three inferential statistics because they answer this research problem and fit our earlier recommendations for good choices. First, we will discuss two basic research questions, given the above specification of the variables and their measurement. Then, we will discuss a complex research question that could be asked instead of research questions 1 and 2.

1. Is there a difference between *male* and *female genders* on their average *math achievement scores*?

Type of research question. Using the text, Fig. 6.1 and Table 6.2, you should see that the first question is phrased as a **basic difference question** because there are only two variables and the focus is a group difference (the difference between the male group and the female group).

Selection of an appropriate statistic. If you examine Table 6.1, you will see that the first question should be answered with an **independent samples t test** because (a) the independent variable has only two values (male and female), (b) the design is between groups (males and females form two independent groups), and (c) the dependent variable (math achievement) is normal or scale data. We also would check other assumptions of the *t* test to be sure that they are not markedly violated.

Interpretation of the results for question 1. Let's assume that about 50 students participated in the study and that $t = 2.05$. SPSS will give you the exact **Sig**. In this case, $p < .05$ and, thus, t is statistically significant. However, if you had 25 participants this t would not have been significant (because the t value necessary for statistical significance is influenced strongly by sample size. Small samples require a larger t to be significant).

Deciding whether the statistic is significant only means the result is unlikely to be due to chance. You still have to state the direction of the result and the effect size and/or the confidence interval (see Fig. 6.3). To determine the direction, we need to know the mean (average) math achievement scores for males and females. Let's assume, as is true for the HSB data, that males have the higher mean. If so, you can be quite confident that males in the population are at least a little better at math achievement, on average, than females. So, you should state that males scored higher than females. If the difference was not statistically significant, it is best *not* to make any comment about which mean was higher because the difference could be due to chance. Likewise, if the difference was not significant, we recommend that you do not discuss or interpret the effect size. But you should provide the means and standard deviations so that effect sizes could be computed if a researcher wanted to use this study in a meta analysis

Because the t was statistically significant, we would calculate d and discuss the **effect size** as shown earlier. First, compute the pooled (weighted average) standard deviation for male and female math achievement scores. Let's say that the difference between the means was 2.0 and the pooled standard deviation was 6.0, then d would be .33, a small to medium size effect. This means that the difference is less than typical of the statistically significant findings in the behavioral sciences. A d of .33 may or may not be a large enough difference to use for recommending programmatic changes (i.e., be practically significant).

Confidence intervals might help you decide if the difference in math achievement scores was large enough to have practical significance. For example, say you found (from the lower bound of the confidence interval) that you could only be confident that there was a 1/2 point difference between males and females. Then you could decide whether that was a big enough difference to justify, for example, a programmatic change.

2. Is there an association between *math courses taken* and *math achievement?*

Type of research question. This second question is phrased as a **basic associational question** because there are only two variables and both have many ordered levels. Thus, use Table 6.2 for the second question.

Selection of an appropriate statistic. As you can see from Table 6.2, the second research question should be answered with a **Pearson correlation** because both math courses taken and math achievement are normally distributed data.

Interpretation of the results for research question 2. The interpretation of r is based on decisions similar to those made above for t. If $r = .30$ (with 50 subjects), it would be statistically significant at the $p < .05$ level. If the r is statistically significant, you still need to discuss the direction of the correlation and effect size. Because the correlation is positive, we would say that students with a relative *high* number of math courses taken tend to perform at the high end on math achievement and those with few math courses taken tend to perform poorly on math achievement. The **effect size** of $r = .30$, is medium or typical.

Note that if N were 25, the r of .30 would not be significant. On the other hand, if N were 500 and $r = .30$, p would be $< .0001$. With $N = 500$, even $r = .10$ would be statistically significant, indicating that you could be quite sure the association was not zero, but the effect size would be small, or less than typical.

Complex research question and statistics. As you will see in later chapters, there are advantages of considering the two independent variables (gender and math courses taken) together rather than separately as in questions 1 and 2. There are at least two statistics, that you will compute, that could be used to consider gender and math courses taken together. A research question, which subsumes both questions 1 and 2 above could be:

3. Is there a combination of *gender* and *math courses* that predicts *math achievement*?

Selection of an appropriate statistic. As just indicated, multiple regression could be used to answer this question. As you can see in Table 6.4, multiple regression is appropriate because we are trying to predict a normally distributed/scale variable (*math achievement*) from two independent variables. The independent or predictor variables are *math courses taken* (normal or scale) and *gender* (a dichotomous or dummy variable).

Based on our discussion of the general linear model (GLM), a **two-way factorial ANOVA** would be another statistic that could be used to consider both gender and test anxiety simultaneously. However, to use ANOVA, the many levels of math courses taken would have to be recoded into two or three (perhaps high, medium, and low). Because information is lost when you do such a recode, we would not recommend factorial ANOVA for this example. Another possible statistic to use for this example is **analysis of covariance** (ANCOVA) using gender as the independent variable and math courses taken as the covariate; ANOVA is discussed in Leech et al. (2003).

Interpretation of the results for research question 3. We will provide an introduction to multiple regression in Chapter 8 and to factorial ANOVA in Chapter 10, but extended treatment is beyond the scope of this book (see Leech et al., 2003). For now, let's just say that we would obtain more information about the relationships among these three variables by doing these complex statistics than by doing only the t test and correlation described above and in the next section.

Writing About Your Outputs

One of the goals of this book is to help you write a research report or thesis using the SPSS outputs. To help you, we have provided this section, which could be paragraphs from a research paper based on the expanded HSB data used in the assignments in this book.

Before demonstrating how you might write about the results of research questions 1 and 2 above, we would like to make several important points. There are several books listed in the bibliography that will help you write a research paper and make appropriate tables. Note especially the APA manual (2001), Nicol and Pexman (1999), and Morgan, Reichart, and

Harrison (2002). The example below and the samples provided in each output interpretation section give only one way to write about SPSS outputs. There are other good ways.

Based on your SPSS outputs, you should update the **Methods** chapter that you wrote as a proposal to include descriptive statistics about the demographics (e.g., gender, age, ethnicity) of the participants. You should add to any literature-based evidence about the reliability and validity of your measures/instruments your sample. You also should include in your report whether statistical assumptions of the inferential statistics were met or how adjustments were made.

The **Results** chapter includes a description (but not a discussion) of the findings in words and tables. Your Results section should include the following numbers about each statistically significant finding (in a table or the text):

1. The value of the statistic (e.g., $t = 2.05$ or $r = .30$)
2. The degrees of freedom (often in parenthesis) and for chi-square the N (e.g., $df = 2$, $N = 49$).
3. The p or Sig. Value (e.g., $p = .048$).
4. The direction of the finding (e.g., by showing which mean is larger or the sign of the correlation, if the statistic is significant).
5. An index of effect size from either the d family or the r family.

When not shown in a table, the above information should be provided in the text as shown below. *In addition* to the above numerical information, <u>describe your significant results in words, including the variables related, the direction of the finding, and an interpretive statement about the size/strength of the effect</u> based on Table 6.5 or, better still based on the effect sizes found in the literature on your topic. Realize that these effect size terms are only rough estimates of the magnitude of the "effect" based on what is typical in the behavioral sciences, but not necessarily applicable to your topic.

If your paper includes a table, it is usually not necessary or advisable to include all the details about the value of the statistic, degrees of freedom, and p in the text because they are in the table. <u>If you have a table, you must refer to it by number (e.g., Table 1) in the text</u> and <u>describe the main points, but don't</u> <u>repeat all of it</u> or the table is not necessary. You can mention relationships that are not significant, but do not discuss, in the text, the direction of the finding or interpret the effect size of nonsignificant findings because the results could well be due to chance. Do provide the information (e.g., ns, means, and standard deviation) necessary for other researchers to compute the effect size if your study is included in a meta-analysis.

The **Discussion** chapter puts the findings in context in regard to the research literature, theory, and the purposes of the study. You may also attempt to explain why the results turned out the way they did.

An Example of How to Write Results

Based on what we reported above about the results of research questions 1 and 2 we might make the following statements in our Results section:

Results

For research question 1, there was a statistically significant difference between male and female students on math achievement, $t(48)=2.05$. $p=.04, d=.33$. Males ($M=14.70$) scored higher than females ($M=12.70$), and the effect size was small to medium according to Cohen's (1988) guidelines. The confidence interval for the difference between the means was .50 to 6.50 indicating that the difference could be as little as half a point, which is probably not a practically important difference, but could be as large as six and half points.

For research question 2, there was a statistically significant positive correlation between math courses taken and math achievement $r(48)=.30, p=.03$. The positive correlation means that in general students who took more math courses tended to score high on the math achievement test and students who did not take many math courses scored low on math achievement. The effect size of $r=.30$ is considered medium or typical.

We will present examples of how to write about the results of each statistic that you compute in the appropriate chapter.

Conclusion

Now you should be ready to study each of the statistics in Tables 6.1 to 6.4 and learn more about their computation and interpretation. It may be tough going at times, but hopefully this overview has given you a good foundation. It would be wise for you to review this chapter, especially the tables and figures from time to time. If you do, you will have a good grasp of how the various statistics fit together, when to use them, and how to interpret the results. You will need this information to understand the chapters that follow.

Interpretation Questions

6.1. Compare and contrast a between groups design and a within groups design.

6.2. What information about variables, levels, and design should you keep in mind in order to choose an appropriate statistic?

6.3. Provide an example of a design which a researcher could appropriately choose two different statistics. Explain your answer.

6.4. When $p < .05$, what does this signify?

6.5. Interpret the following related to effect size:
   a) $d = .25$ c) $R = .53$ e) $d = 1.15$
   b) $r = .35$ d) $r = .13$ f) $\eta = .38$

6.6. What statistic would you use if you wanted to see if there was a difference between males and females on math achievement? Why?

6.7. What statistic would you use if you had two independent variables, income group (<$10,000, $10,000-$30,000, >$30,000) and ethnic group (Hispanic, Caucasian, African-American), and one normally distributed dependent variable (self-efficacy at work).

6.8.   What statistic would you use if you had one independent variable, geographic location (North, South, East, West), and one dependent variable (satisfaction with living environment, Yes or No)?

6.9   What statistic would you use if you had three normally distributed (scale) independent variables (weight of participants, age of participants, and height of participants) and one dichotomous independent variable (gender) and one dependent variable (positive self-image), which is normally distributed.

6.10. A teacher *ranked* the students in her Algebra I class from 1=highest to 25=lowest in terms of their grades on several tests. After the next semester, she checked the school records to see what the students received from their Algebra II teacher. The research question is 'Is there a relationship between rank in Algebra I and grades in Algebra II?' What statistic should she use?

CHAPTER 7

Cross-Tabulation, Chi-Square, and Non Parametric Measures of Association

In this chapter, you will learn how to make cross-tabulation tables from two variables, both of which have a few levels or values. You will learn how to decide if there is a statistically significant relationship between two nominal variables using **chi-square** and you will learn how to assess the strength of this relationship (i.e., the effect size) using **phi** (or **Cramer's V**). You will also compute and interpret **Kendall's tau-b** for ordinal, categorical variables and **eta** for one nominal and one normal/scale variable. We will see eta again in Chapter 10 as an effect size measure for ANOVA's. Finally, you will compute **Cohen's kappa,** which is used to assess interobserver reliability for two nominal variables.

- First logon and get **hsbdataB** (you saved it after computing new variables in Chapter 5).

Problem 7.1: Chi-Square and Phi (or Cramer's V)

The statistics discussed in this first problem are designed to analyze two nominal or dichotomous variables. Remember, nominal variables are variables that have distinct *unordered* levels; each subject is in only one level (you can only be male *or* female). Chi-square (χ^2) or phi/Cramer's V are good choices for statistics when analyzing two nominal variables. They are less appropriate if either variable has three or more *ordered* levels because these statistics do not take in account the order and, thus, sacrifice power if used with ordinal or scale variables.

Chi-square requires a relatively large sample size and/or a relatively even split of the subjects among the levels because the expected counts in 80% of the cells should be greater than 5. **Fisher's exact test** for 2x2 crosstabs should be reported instead of chi-square for small samples. Chi-square and the Fisher's exact test provide similar information about relationships among variables; however, they only tell us whether the relationship is statistically significant (i.e., not likely to be due to chance). They do not tell the effect size (i.e., the strength of the relationship). Another way to interpret chi-square is as a test of whether there are differences between the groups formed from one variable, (gender in this problem) on the incidence or counts of each category of the other variable (see the Table 6.1).

Phi and **Cramer's** V provide a test of statistical significance and also provide information about the *strength* of the association between two categorical variables and can be used as a measure of the effect size similar to r (see Table 6.5). If one has a 2x2 cross tabulation, phi is the appropriate statistic. For larger crosstabs, Cramer's V is used. The numbers in the crosstabs description refer to the number of levels in each of the variables. Thus, for *gender* and *religion* in the HSB data set, the crosstab would be 2x3 because *gender* has two levels and *religion* has three levels.

For phi and Cramer's V the strength of association measures are similar to the correlations you will compute in the next chapter. Like correlation, a strong phi or Cramer's V could be close to 1.00 while one close to zero would indicate no relationship. A problem with Phi and Cramer's V is that under some conditions, the maximum possible value of these statistics will be considerably less than 1.00. This makes them hard to interpret.

Assumptions and Conditions for the Use of Chi-square, Phi and Cramer's *V*
- The data for the variables must be independent. Each subject is assessed only once.
- Data are treated as nominal, even if ordered.
- For chi-square, if the expected frequencies, are less than 5, the test of significance is too liberal. At least 80% of the expected frequencies should be 5 or larger. All should be at least 5 if you have a 2x2 chi-square.

7.1.   Do males and females differ on whether they take geometry or not? If so, how strong is the relationship?

Let's see if *males* and *females* differ in terms of whether they *took geometry*. Remember, both variables are dichotomous; they have two values.

- Click on **Analyze => Descriptive Statistics => Crosstabs.**
- Put *geometry* in the **Rows** box using the arrow key and put *gender* in the **Columns** box (see Fig. 7.1).

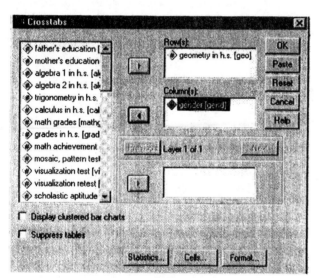

Fig. 7.1. Crosstabs.

- Next, click on **Statistics.**
- Check **Chi-square** and **Phi and Cramer's V**. The window should look like Figure 7.2.
- Click on **Continue.**

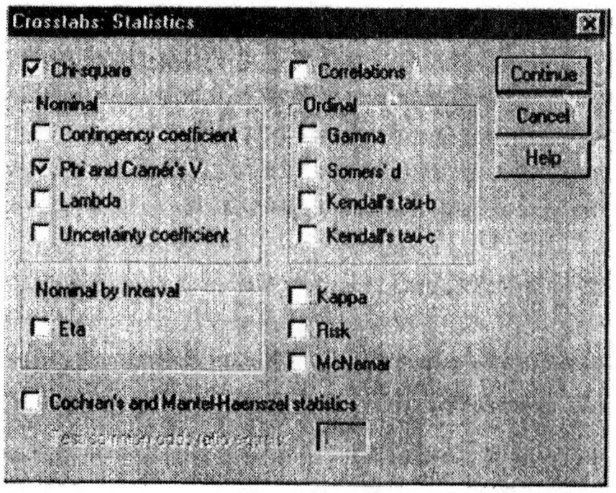

Fig. 7.2. Crosstabs statistics.

- Once you return to the **Crosstabs** menu, click on **Cells**.
- Now, click on **Expected** and **Total**; ensure that **Observed** is also checked (See Fig. 7.3).

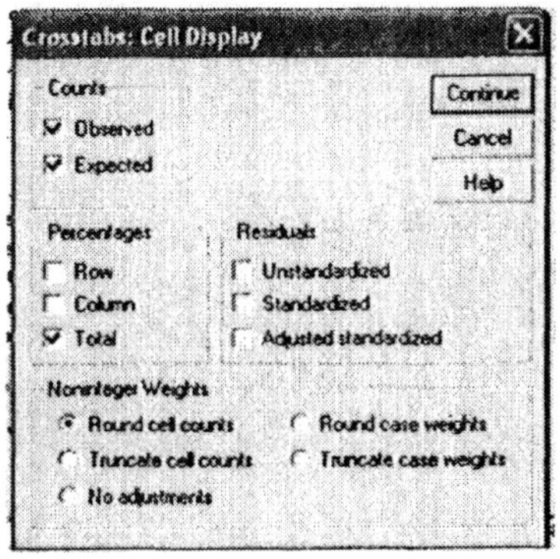

Fig. 7.3. Crosstabs: Cell display.

- Click on **Continue** then **OK**. Compare your output to Output 7.1.

Output 7.1: *Crosstabs With Chi-Square and Phi*

```
CROSSTABS
  /TABLES=geo  BY gender
  /FORMAT= AVALUE TABLES
  /STATISTIC=CHISQ PHI
  /CELLS= COUNT EXPECTED TOTAL
  /COUNT ROUND CELL .
```

Case Processing Summary

	Cases					
	Valid		Missing		Total	
	N	Percent	N	Percent	N	Percent
geometry in h.s. * gender	75	100.0%	0	.0%	75	100.0%

geometry in h.s. * gender Crosstabulation

			gender		Total
			male	female	
geometry in h.s.	not taken	Count	10	29	39
		Expected Count	17.7	21.3	39.0
		% of Total	13.3%	38.7%	52.0%
	taken	Count	24	12	36
		Expected Count	16.3	19.7	36.0
		% of Total	32.0%	16.0%	48.0%
Total		Count	34	41	75
		Expected Count	34.0	41.0	75.0
		% of Total	45.3%	54.7%	100.0%

Compare the expected and observed counts.

Chi-Square Tests

	Value	df	Asymp. Sig. (2-sided)	Exact Sig. (2-sided)	Exact Sig. (1-sided)
Pearson Chi-Square	12.714(b)	1	.000		
Continuity Correction(a)	11.112	1	.001		
Likelihood Ratio	13.086	1	.000		
Fisher's Exact Test				.000	.000
Linear-by-Linear Association	12.544	1	.000		
N of Valid Cases	75				

a Computed only for a 2x2 table
b 0 cells (.0%) have expected count less than 5. The minimum expected count is 16.32.

This is good.

Symmetric Measures

		Value	Approx. Sig.
Nominal by Nominal	Phi	-.412	.000
	Cramer's V	.412	.000
N of Valid Cases		75	

For 2x2 tables

a. Not assuming the null hypothesis.

b. Using the asymptotic standard error assuming the null hypothesis.

Interpretation of Output 7.1

The case processing summary table indicates that there are no participants with missing data. The **Crosstabulation** table includes the **Counts** and **Expected Counts,** and each cell also has a **% of Total.** For example, there are 10 *males* who had *not taken geometry*, this is 13.3% of the 75 students. The bottom row and the right hand column provide total percentages for the two levels of each variable. For example, 34 or 45% of the 75 students were *males*, and 36 or 48% of both genders *had taken geometry*.

Note, in the **Crosstabulation** table, that the **Expected Count** of the number of *male* students who *didn't take geometry* is 17.7 and the observed or actual **Count** is 10. Thus, there are 7.7 fewer *males* who *didn't take geometry* than would be expected by chance, given the **Total**s shown in the table. There are also the same discrepancies between observed and expected counts in the other three cells of the table. A question answered by the chi-square test is whether these discrepancies between observed and expected counts are bigger than one might expect by chance.

The **Chi-Square Tests** table is used to determine if there is a statistically significant relationship between two dichotomous or nominal variables. It tells you whether the relationship is statistically significant but <u>does not indicate the strength of the relationship</u>, like phi or a correlation does. In Output 7.1, we use the **Pearson Chi-Square** <u>or</u> (for small samples) the **Fisher's Exact Test** to interpret the results of the test. They are statistically significant ($p < .001$), which indicates that we can be quite certain that *males* and *females* are different on whether they *take geometry*. Note that footnote b states that no cells have expected counts less than 5. That is good because otherwise a condition for using of chi-square would be violated. (If so, we could then use the Fisher exact test.) A good guideline is that no more than 20% of the cells should have expected frequencies less than 5. For chi-square with 1 *df* (i.e., 2 x 2 cross-tabulation as in this case) *none* of the cells should have expected frequencies less than 5, some say 10.

The **Symmetric Measures** table provides measures of the strength of the relationships or effect size. If the association between variables is weak, the **Value** of the statistic will be close to zero. If the relationship or effect size is strong, the value should be +/- .50 or more. However, remember that the maximum value for phi and Cramer's V may be less than 1.00, the maximum for most measures of association. If both variables have two levels (i.e., 2 x 2 crosstabs) phi is the appropriate statistic.

In Output 7.1, **phi** is -.412, and like the chi-square it is statistically significant. Phi is also a measure of effect size for an associational statistic and, in this case, is a somewhat larger effect than typical in the behavioral sciences (see Table 6.5) or medium to large according to Cohen (1998).

Example of How to Write About the Results of Problem 7.1

Results

To investigate whether males and females differ on whether they take geometry or not, a chi-square statistic was used. Table 7.1 shows the Pearson chi-square results and indicates that males and females are significantly different on whether they are have taken or have not taken geometry ($\chi^2 = 12.71$, $df = 1$, $N = 75$, $p < .001$). Males are more likely than expected under the null hypothesis to take geometry than females. Phi, which indicates the strength of the association between the two variables, is -.412 and, thus, the effect size is considered to be medium to large according to Cohen (1988).

Table 7.1

Chi-square Analysis of Prevalence of Taking Geometry Among Males and Females

Variable	*n*	Geometry Taken	Not taken	χ^2	*p*
Gender				12.71	<.001
Males	*34*	*24*	*10*		
Females	41	12	29		
Totals	75	36	39		

Problem 7.2: Other Nonparametric Associational Statistics

In addition to phi and Cramer's *V*, there are several other nonparametric measures of association that we could have chosen in Fig. 7.2. They attempt, in different ways, to measure the strength of the association between two variables. If both variables are nominal and you have a 2x2 cross tabulation, like the one in Output 7.1, phi is the appropriate statistic to use from the symmetric measures table. For larger cross tabulations (like a 3 x 3) with nominal data, **Cramer's *V*** is the appropriate statistic. Note that with a 2 x 3 or a 3 x 2 cross tabulation Phi and Cramer's *V* are the same. If the variables are ordered (i.e., ordinal) you have several other choices. We will use **Kendall's tau-b** in this problem.

7.2. What is the relationship or association between *father's education* and *mother's education*?

- **Analyze => Descriptive Statistics => Crosstabs.**
- Put *mother's education revised* in the **Rows** box and *father's education revised* in the **Columns** box.
- Click on **Cells** and ask that the **Observed** and **Expected** cell counts and **Total** percentages be printed in the table. Click on **Continue** and then **Statistics.**
- Request the following **Statistics: Phi** and **Cramer's** *V* and **Kendall's tau-b** coefficient for ordinal data. Do not check chi-square.
- Click on **Continue** then **OK**. Compare your syntax and output to Output 7.2.

Output 7.2: Crosstabs and Nonparametric Associational Statistics

```
CROSSTABS
  /TABLES=maedRevis  BY faedRevis
  /FORMAT= AVALUE TABLES
  /STATISTIC=PHI BTAU
  /CELLS= COUNT EXPECTED TOTAL
  /COUNT ROUND CELL .
```

Crosstabs

Case Processing Summary

	Cases					
	Valid		Missing		Total	
	N	Percent	N	Percent	N	Percent
mother's educ revised * father's educ revised	73	97.3%	2	2.7%	75	100.0%

mother's education revised * father's education revised Crosstabulation

			father's education revised			Total
			HS grad or less	Some College	BS or More	
mother's education revised	HS grad or less	Count	33	9	4	46
		Expected Count	23.9	10.1	12.0	46.0
		% of Total	45.2%	12.3%	5.5%	63.0%
	Some College	Count	5	7	7	19
		Expected Count	9.9	4.2	4.9	19.0
		% of Total	6.8%	9.6%	9.6%	26.0%
	BS or More	Count	0	0	8	8
		Expected Count	4.2	1.8	2.1	8.0
		% of Total	.0%	.0%	11.0%	11.0%
Total		Count	38	16	19	73
		Expected Count	38.0	16.0	19.0	73.0
		% of Total	52.1%	21.9%	26.0%	100.0%

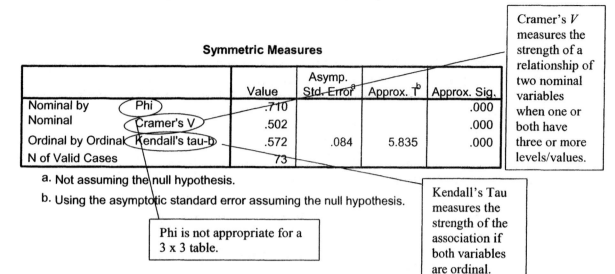

Symmetric Measures

		Value	Asymp. Std. Error[a]	Approx. T[b]	Approx. Sig.
Nominal by Nominal	Phi	.710			.000
	Cramer's V	.502			.000
Ordinal by Ordinal	Kendall's tau-b	.572	.084	5.835	.000
N of Valid Cases		73			

a. Not assuming the null hypothesis.

b. Using the asymptotic standard error assuming the null hypothesis.

> Cramer's *V* measures the strength of a relationship of two nominal variables when one or both have three or more levels/values.

> Kendall's Tau measures the strength of the association if both variables are ordinal.

> Phi is not appropriate for a 3 x 3 table.

Interpretation of Output 7.2

There are several nonparametric measures of association that we could have chosen from Fig. 7.2. All of them except chi-square attempt, in different ways, to measure the *strength* of the association between two variables roughly on the -1 to +1 scale used by the Pearson correlation (see Chapter 8). However, several of them, including phi and Cramer's *V* have maximum values considerably less than 1 under some conditions.

For tables <u>with nominal data</u> (like a 3 x 3 crosstabulation of *religion* and *ethnicity*), **Cramer's *V*** would be the appropriate statistic. In Problem 2, we also requested **Kendall's tau-b** because both *mother's education* and *father's education* are to be ordered variables and ordinal data. Cramer's *V* (and phi) treat the cross tabulated variables as if they were nominal, even if they are ordered so they would not be good choices for this problem. We requested them so you could compare them to Kendall's tau-b.

If the association between variables is weak, the value of the statistic will be close to zero and the significance level (**Sig.**) will be greater than .05, the usual cutoff to say that an association is statistically significant. However, if the association is statistically significant, the *p* will be small (<.05). In this case *p* is < .001 for Kendall's tau-b, which is clearly significant, and the effect size (tau-b = .572) is large (see Table 6.5).

Example of How to Write About Problem 7.2

Results

To investigate the relationship between father's education and mother's education, Kendall's tau-b was used. Kendall's tau-b analysis indicated a significant positive association between father's education and mother's education, tau (71) = .572, *p* < .001. This means that fathers with relatively high educations were married to mothers with relatively high educations and vice versa. This tau is considered to be a large effect (Cohen, 1988).

Problem 7.3: Cross-Tabulation and Eta

There is an important associational statistic, eta, that is used when one variable is nominal and the other is approximately normal or scale. We will use this statistic to describe the association between *gender* and *math courses taken* (an approximately normal variable with six values). **Eta squared** will be an important statistic in later chapters when we interpret the *effect size* of various ANOVAs.

7.3. What is the association between *gender* and number of *math courses taken*? How strong is it?

Follow these steps:
* Click on **Analyze => Descriptive Statistics => Crosstabs**.
* Put *math courses taken* in the **Rows** box using the arrow key and put *gender* in the **Columns** box (similar to Fig. 7.1).
* Next, click on **Statistics** and select **Eta**.
* Click on **Continue**.
* Now, click on **Cells** and select **Expected** and **Observed**.
* Click on **Continue**.
* Click on **OK**. Compare your syntax and output to Output 7.3.

Output for Problem 7.3: Eta for Gender and Math Courses Taken

```
CROSSTABS
  /TABLES=mathcrs  BY gender
  /FORMAT= AVALUE TABLES
  /STATISTIC=ETA
  /CELLS= COUNT EXPECTED
  /COUNT ROUND CELL .
```

Crosstabs

Case Processing Summary

	Cases					
	Valid		Missing		Total	
	N	Percent	N	Percent	N	Percent
Math courses taken * gender	75	100.0%	0	.0%	75	100.0%

Math courses taken * gender Crosstabulation

			gender		
			male	female	Total
Math courses taken	None taken	Count	4	12	16
		Expected Count	7.3	8.7	16.0
	1	Count	3	13	16
		Expected Count	7.3	8.7	16.0
	2	Count	9	6	15
		Expected Count	6.8	8.2	15.0
	3	Count	6	2	8
		Expected Count	3.6	4.4	8.0
	4	Count	7	5	12
		Expected Count	5.4	6.6	12.0
	All math courses	Count	5	3	8
		Expected Count	3.6	4.4	8.0
Total		Count	34	41	75
		Expected Count	34.0	41.0	75.0

Directional Measures

			Value	
Nominal by Interval	Eta	Math courses taken Dependent	.328	This is the appropriate eta for this problem.
		gender Dependent	.419	

Interpretation of Output 7.3
The second table shows the actual **Counts** and the **Expected Counts** of the number of persons in each cell. If there are positive discrepancies between the actual and expected counts in the upper left (male) columns and negative discrepancies in the lower left columns or vice versa, that would indicate that there is an association between the two variables. Like most measures of association, eta can vary from about -1.0 through zero to +1.0. High positive or negative values of eta indicate a strong association. In this case the appropriate eta is .328 because *math courses taken* is the dependent variable. It is a medium to large effect size (see Table 6.5). With 75 subjects, an eta of .33 probably would be statistically significant, but SPSS does not test it. Eta squared would be .11, indicating that the two variables share 11% common variance. We will see eta squared when interpreting the size of the "effect" in analysis of variance.

Example of How to Write About Problem 7.3
Results
Eta was used to investigate the strength of the association between gender and number of math courses taken (eta = .33). This is a medium to large effect size (Cohen, 1988). Males were more likely to take several or all the math courses than females.

Problem 7.4: Cohen's Kappa for Reliability With Nominal Data

When we have two nominal variables with the *same* values (usually two raters' observations or scores using the same codes), you can compute Cohen's kappa to check the reliability or agreement between the measures. Imagine that the ethnicity variables were based on school records. Then, a new variable was obtained by asking students to self-report the ethnicity. The question is, how reliable is the interobserver classification of ethnicity?

7.4. What is the reliability coefficient for the *ethnicity* codes (based on school records) and *ethnicity reported by the student*?

To compute the kappa:
- Click on **Analyze => Descriptive Statistics => Crosstabs**.
- Move *ethnic* to the **Rows** box and *ethnic 2* to the **Columns** box.
- Click on **Kappa** in the **Statistics** dialog box.
- Click on **Continue** to go back to the Crosstabs dialog window.
- Then click on **Cells** and request the **Observed** cell counts and **Total** under **percentages**.
- Click on **Continue** and then **OK**. Compare your syntax and output to Output 3.5.

Output 3.5: Cohen's Kappa with Nominal Data

```
CROSSTABS
  /TABLES=ethnic  BY ethnic2
  /FORMAT= AVALUE TABLES
  /STATISTIC=KAPPA
  /CELLS= COUNT TOTAL
  /COUNT ROUND CELL .
```

ethnicity * Ethnicity reported by student Crosstabulation

			Ethnicity reported by student				Total
			Euro =Amer	Afican =Amer	Latino =Amer	Asian =Amer	
ethnicity	Euro-Amer	Count	40	1	0	0	41
		% of Total	z56.3%	1.4%	.0%	.0%	57.7%
	African-Amer	Count	2	11	1	0	14
		% of Total	2.8%	15.5%	1.4%	.0%	19.7%
	Latino-Amer	Count	0	1	8	0	9
		% of Total	.0%	1.4%	11.3%	.0%	12.7%
	Asian-Amer	Count	0	1	0	6	7
		% of Total	.0%	1.4%	.0%	8.5%	9.9%
Total		Count	42	14	9	6	71
		% of Total	59.2%	19.7%	12.7%	8.5%	100.0%

One of six disagreements. They are in "squares" off the diagonal.

Agreements between school records and student's memory.

Case Processing Summary

	Cases					
	Valid		Missing		Total	
	N	Percent	N	Percent	N	Percent
ethnicity * Ethnicity reported by student	71	94.7%	4	5.3%	75	100.0%

Symmetric Measures

		Value	Asymp. Std. Error(a)	Approx. T(b)	Approx. Sig.
Measure of Agreement	Kappa	.858	.054	11.163	.000
N of Valid Cases		71			

a Not assuming the null hypothesis.
b Using the asymptotic standard error assuming the null hypothesis.

As a measure of reliability, kappa should be high (usually $\geq .70$) not just statistically significant.

Interpretation of Output 7.4

The **Crosstabulation** table of *ethnicity* and *ethnicity reported by student* shows the cases where the school records and the student self-reports are in agreement; they are on the diagonal and circled. There are 65 (40 + 11 + 8 + 6) students with such agreement or consistency. The **Case Processing Summary** table shows that 71 students have data on both variables. Thus, in 65 out of 71 cases with complete data, the student listed the same ethnicity as in the school records, but there were discrepancies for 6 students shown in boxes off the diagonal.

The **Symmetric Measures** table shows that **Kappa** is .86. This is good because for reliability measures; they should be high (>.70) and positive. Statistical significance is not relevant for reliability measures.

Interpretation Questions

7.1.   In Output 7.1: a) what do the terms "count" and "expected count" mean? b) What does the difference between them tell you?

7.2.   In Output 7.1: a) Is the (Pearson) chi-square statistically significant? Explain what it means. b) Are the expected values in at least 80% of the cells ≥ 5? How do you know?

7.3.   Because *father's* and *mother's education revised* are at least ordinal data, which of the statistics used in 7.2 is the most appropriate to measure the strength of the relationship: phi, Cramer's *V*, or Kendall's tau-b? Interpret the results. Why are tau-b and Cramer's *V* different?

7.4.   In Output 7.3: a) How do you know what is the appropriate valued eta? b) Do you think
        it is high or low? Why? c) How would you describe the results?

7.5.   Write a sentence or two describing the results of Output 7.4 that you might include in a
        research report.

Extra SPSS Problems

Using college student data from file, do the following problems. Print your outputs after typing
your interpretations on them. Please circle the key parts of the output that you discuss.

7.1.   Run crosstabs and interpret the results (as discussed in Chapter 6 and in the interpretation
        of Output 7.1) of chi-square, and phi (or Cramer's V) for: a) gender and marital status and
        b) age group and marital status.

7.2.   Select two other appropriate variables, run and interpret the output as we did in Output
        7.1.

7.3.   Is there an association between having children or not and watching TV sitcoms?

7.4.   Is there a difference between students who have children and those who do not in regard
        to their age group?

7.5.   Compute an appropriate statistic and effect size measure for the relationship between
        gender and evaluation of social life.

CHAPTER 8

Correlation and Regression

In this chapter, you will learn how to compute several associational statistics. First, you will learn how to make **scatterplots** and how to interpret them. An assumption of the **Pearson product moment correlation** is that the variables are related in a linear (straight line) way so we will examine the scatterplots to see if that assumption is reasonable. Second, the **Pearson correlation**, and the **Spearman rho** will be computed. The Pearson correlation is used when you have two variables that are normal/scale, and the Spearman is used when the two variables are ordinal. Second, you will compute a **correlation matrix** indicating the associations among all the pairs of three or more variables. Fourth, we will show you how to compute Cronbach's alpha, the most common measure of **reliability,** which is based on a correlation matrix. Fifth, you will compute simple or **bivariate regression**, which is used when one wants to predict scores on a normal/scale dependent variable from one normal or scale dependent variable. Last, we will provide an introduction to a complex associational statistic, **multiple regression**, which is used to predict a scale/normal dependent variable from two or more independent variables.

The correlations in this chapter can vary from –1.0 (a perfect negative relationship or association) through 0.0 (no correlation) to +1.0 (a perfect positive correlation). Note that +1 and –1 are equally high or strong, but they lead to different interpretations. A high *positive correlation* between anxiety and grades would mean that students with higher anxiety tended to have higher grades, those with lower anxiety had lower grades, and those in between had grades that were neither especially high or especially low. A high *negative correlation* would mean that students with high anxiety tended to have low grades; also, high grades would be associated with low anxiety. With a *zero correlation* there are no consistent associations. A student with high anxiety might have low, medium, or high grades.

Assumptions and Conditions for the Pearson Correlation (r)
1. The two variables have a linear relationship. We will show how to check this assumption with a scatterplot in Problem 8.1. (Pearson *r* will not detect a curvilinear relationship unless you transform the variables, which is beyond the scope of this book.)
2. Scores on one variable are normally distributed for each value of the other variable and vice versa. (If degrees of freedom are greater than 25, failure to meet this assumption has little consequence.)
3. Outliers can have a big effect on the correlation.

Assumptions and Conditions for Spearman Rho (r_s)
1. Data on both variables are at least ordinal.
2. Scores on one variable are monotonically related to the other variable. This means that as the values of one variable increase, the other should also increase but not necessarily in a linear (straight line) fashion. The curve can flatten but cannot go both up and down as in a **U** or **J**
3. Rho is computed by ranking the data for each variable and then computing a Pearson product moment correlation. (SPSS will do this for you automatically when you request a Spearman correlation.)

- Retrieve **hsbdataB.sav**.

Problem 8.1: Scatterplots to Check Assumptions

A **scatterplot** is a plot or graph of two variables that shows how the score for an individual on one variable associates with his or her score on the other variable. If the correlation is *high positive,* the plotted points will be close to a straight line (the **linear regression line**) from the lower left corner of the plot to the upper right. The linear regression line will slope downward from the upper left to the lower right if the correlation is *high negative.* For correlations *near zero* the regression line will be flat with many points far from the line.

Doing a scatterplot with SPSS is somewhat cumbersome, as you will see, but it provides a visual picture of the correlation. The plot also allows you to see if there are extreme outliers (far from the regression line), and it may show that a better fitting line would be a curve rather than a straight line. In this case the assumption of a linear relationship is violated and a Pearson correlation would not be the best choice.

8.1. What are the Scatterplots, and linear regression line, a) for *grades* and *math achievement* and for b) *mosaic* and *math achievement?*

To develop a scatterplot of *math achievement* with *grades,* follow these commands:

- **Graphs => Scatter**. This will give you Fig. 8.1.
- Click on **Simple.**

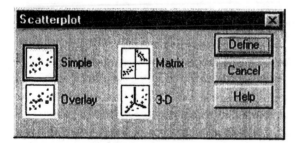

Fig. 8.1. Scatterplot.

- Click on **Define** which will bring you to Fig. 8.2.
- Now, move *math achievement* to the **Y Axis** and *grades* to the **X Axis**. <u>Note: the presumed outcome or dependent variable goes on the Y axis.</u> However, in the correlation itself there is no distinction between independent and dependent variable.

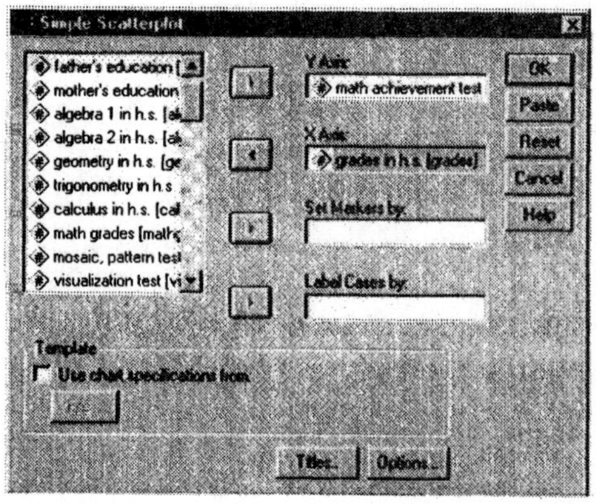

Fig. 8.2. Simple scatterplot.

- Next, click on **Titles** (in Fig. 8.2). Type **Correlation of math achievement with high school grades** (see Fig. 8.3). Note, we put the title on two lines so it will all fit.
- Click on **Continue** then on **OK.** You will get Output 8.1a, the scatterplot. You will not print this now because we want to add the regression line first.

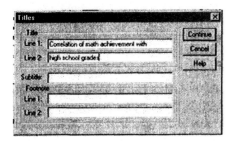

Fig. 8.3. Titles.

Output 8.1a. Scatterplot without Regression Line

```
GRAPH
    /SCATTERPLOT(BIVAR)=grades WITH mathach
    /MISSING=LISTWISE
    /TITLE= 'Correlation of math achievement with' 'high school grades'.
```

Graph

Correlation of math achievement with

high school grades

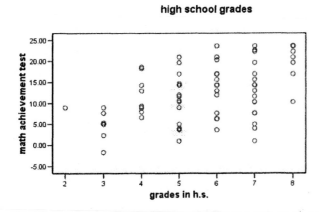

Now let's put the regression lines on the scatterplot so we can get a better sense of the correlation and how much scatter or deviation from the line there is.

- Double click on the scatterplot in Output 8.1a. The Chart Editor window will appear (see Fig. 8.4).

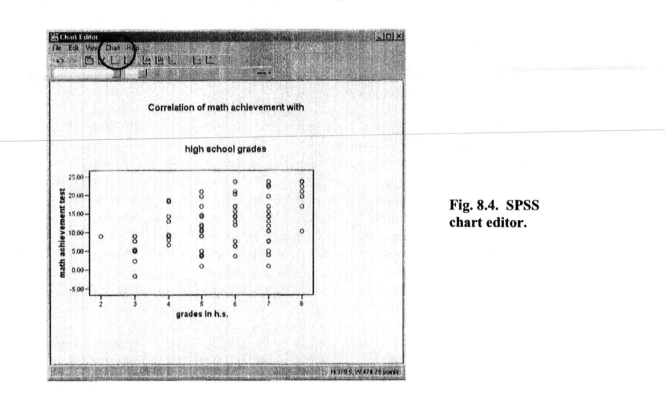

Fig. 8.4. SPSS
chart editor.

- Click on the one of the circles in the scatterplot in the **Chart Editor**. The circles (points) will turn blue.
- Click on **Chart => Add Chart Element => Fit Line at Total**. The **Properties** window (see Fig. 8.5) will appear as well as a blue fit line in the Chart Editor.
- Be sure that **Linear** is checked (see Fig. 8.5).
- Close the Chart Editor window to return to the Output window (Output 8.1b).

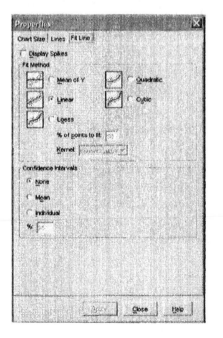

Fig. 8.5. Properties.

Now <u>add a new scatterplot</u> to Output 8.1b by doing the same steps as Problem 1 <u>for a new pair of variables</u>: *math achievement* (**Y-Axis**) with *mosaic* (**X-Axis**). Don't forget to click on **Titles** and change the second line before you run the scatterplot so that the title reads: correlation of *math achievement* with(1st line) *mosaic pattern* score (2nd line). Then, add the regression line as you did above. <u>Now, once more</u> do the scatterplot for *math achievement* and *mosaic*, <u>but this time click on</u> **Quadratic** instead of **Linear** in the **Properties** window (Fig. 8.5). You will see that a curved line was added to the second scatterplot in Output 8.1b below.

Do the these scatterplots look like the ones in Output 8.1b?

Output 8.1b: Three Scatterplots

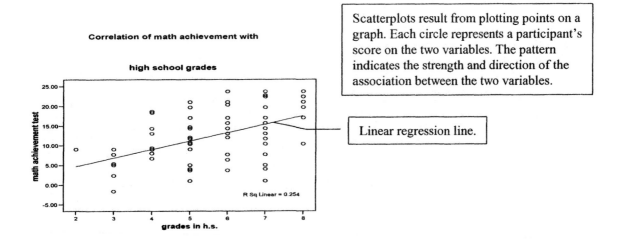

Scatterplots result from plotting points on a graph. Each circle represents a participant's score on the two variables. The pattern indicates the strength and direction of the association between the two variables.

Linear regression line.

Graph

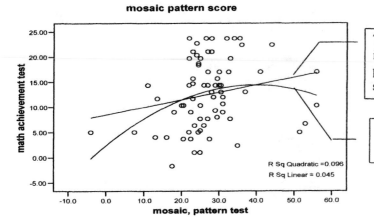

The linear regression line. Note that in contrast to the above plot, more points are not near the line. This plot shows a poor fit and low correlation.

The quadratic regression line seems to be a somewhat better fit to the points.

Interpretation of Output 8.1b

Both scatterplots shown in Output 8.1b show the best fit for a straight **linear regression line** (i.e., it minimizes the squared differences between the points and the line). Note that for the first scatterplot (*grades in h.s.*) the points fit the line pretty well; $r^2 = .25$ and, thus, r is .50. The second scatterplot shows that *mosaic* and *math achievement* are not well correlated; the points do not fit the line very well, $r^2 = .05$, and r is .21, which is not statistically significant. Note that in the second scatterplot we asked SPSS to fit a quadratic (one bend) curve as well as a linear line. It seems to fit the points better; $r^2 = .10$. If so, the linear assumption would be violated and a Pearson correlation may not be the most appropriate statistic.

Problem 8.2: Bivariate Pearson and Spearman Correlations

The **Pearson product moment correlation** is a bivariate parametric statistic used when both variables are approximately normally distributed (i.e., scale data). When you have ordinal data or when assumptions are markedly violated, one should use a nonparametric equivalent of the Pearson correlation coefficient. One such nonparametric, ordinal statistic is the **Spearman rho** (another is Kendall's tau, which we computed in the last chapter). Here you will compute both parametric and nonparametric correlations and then compare them. The variables of interest for Problem 8.2 are *mother's education* and *math achievement*. We found in Chapter 4 that *mother's education* was somewhat skewed, but that *math achievement* was normally distributed.

8.2. What is the association between *mother's education* and *math achievement*?

To compute Pearson and Spearman correlations follow these commands:

- **Analyze => Correlate => Bivariate**.
- Move *math achievement* and *mother's education* to the **Variables** box.
- Next, ensure that the **Spearman** and **Pearson** boxes are checked.
- Make sure that the **Two-tailed** (under **Test of Significance**) and **Flag significant correlations** are checked (see Fig. 8.6). Unless one has a clear directional hypothesis, two-tailed tests are used. Flagging the significant correlations (with an asterisk) is optional but helps you quickly identify the statistically significant correlations.

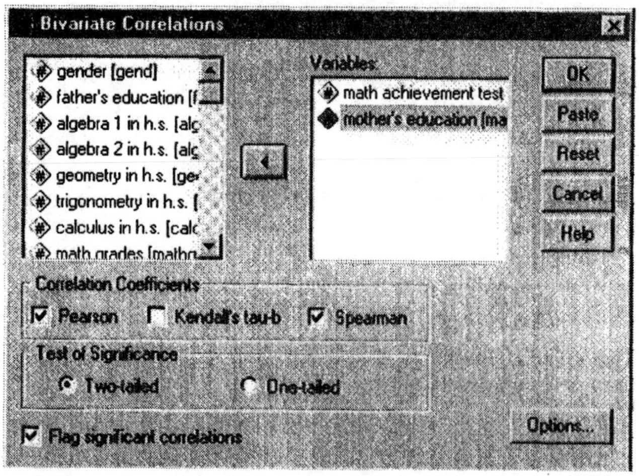

Fig. 8.6. Bivariate correlations.

- Now click on **Options** to get Fig. 8.7.
- Click on **Means and standard deviations** and click on **Exclude cases listwise.** When requesting only one correlation listwise and pairwise exclusion are the same, but, as described below, which one you select may make a difference in a correlation matrix.

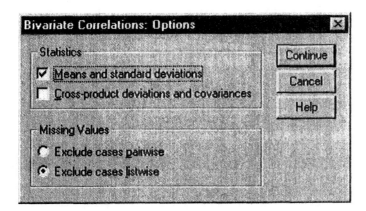

Fig. 8.7. Bivariate correlations: Options.

- Click on **Continue** then on **OK**. Compare Output 8.2 to your output and syntax.

Output 8.2: Pearson and Spearman Correlations

```
CORRELATIONS
  /VARIABLES=mathach maed
  /PRINT=TWOTAIL NOSIG
  /STATISTICS DESCRIPTIVES
  /MISSING=LISTWISE .
```

Correlations

Descriptive Statistics

	Mean	Std. Deviation	N
math achievement test	12.5645	6.67031	75
mother's education	4.11	2.240	75

There are 75 persons with data on both of these variables.

117

Correlations[a]

		math achievement test	mother's education
math achievement test	Pearson Correlation	1	.338*
	Sig. (2-tailed)	.	.003
mother's education	Pearson Correlation	.338**	1
	Sig. (2-tailed)	.003	.

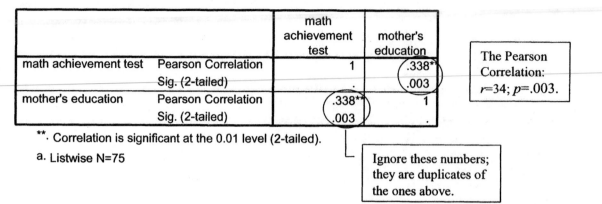

The Pearson Correlation: $r=34$; $p=.003$.

Ignore these numbers; they are duplicates of the ones above.

. Correlation is significant at the 0.01 level (2-tailed).

a. Listwise N=75

Nonparametric Correlations

```
NONPAR CORR
  /VARIABLES=mathach maed
  /PRINT=SPEARMAN TWOTAIL NOSIG
  /MISSING=LISTWISE .
```

Correlations[a]

			math achievement test	mother's education
Spearman's rho	math achievement test	Correlation Coefficient	1.000	.315**
		Sig. (2-tailed)	.	.006
	mother's education	Correlation Coefficient	.315**	1.000
		Sig. (2-tailed)	.006	.

. Correlation is significant at the .01 level (2-tailed).

a. Listwise N = 75

Again these are duplicates.

Interpretation of Output 8.2
The first table provides **descriptive statistics** (mean, standard deviation, and *N*) for the variables to be correlated, in this case *math achievement* and *mother's education*. The two tables labeled **Correlations** are our primary focus. The information is displayed in matrix form, which unfortunately means that every number is presented twice. We have provided a call out box to help you.

The **Pearson Correlation** coefficient is .34; the significance level **(sig.)** or *p* is .003 and the number of participants with both variables (*math achievement* and *mother's education*) is 75. In a report, this would usually be written as: *r* (73) =.34, *p* = .003. Note that the degrees of freedom (*N*-2 for correlations) is put in parentheses after the statistic (*r* for **Pearson** correlation), which is usually rounded to two decimal places. The significance, or *p* value, follows and is stated as .003.

The correlation value for **Spearman's rho** (.32) is somewhat different from *r*, but usually, as in this case, it has a similar significance level (*p*=.006). The nonparametric Spearman correlation is based on ranking the scores (1st, 2nd, etc.) rather than using the actual raw scores. It should be used when the scores are ordinal data or when assumptions of the Pearson correlation (such as normality of the scores) are markedly violated. Note, you should *not* report both the Pearson and Spearman correlations; they provide similar information. Pick the one whose assumptions best fit the data. In this case, because *mother's education* was somewhat skewed, Spearman would be the more appropriate choice, although either would yield significant results. Problem 1 showed you a way to check the Pearson assumption that there is a linear relationship between the variables (i.e., that it is reasonable to use a straight line to describe the relationship).

It is usually best to choose two-tailed tests as we did in Fig. 8.6. We also chose to flag (put asterisks beside) the correlation coefficients that are statistically significant so that they can be identified quickly. The output also prints the exact significance level (*p*), which is redundant with the asterisk. It is best in a thesis or paper table to report the exact *p*, but if space is tight you can use asterisks with a footnote, as SPSS did in Output 8.2.

As indicated earlier, the correlation between *mother's education* and *math achievement* is statistically significant because the "sig" is less than .05. Thus we can reject the null hypothesis of no association and state that there is an association between *mother's education* and *math achievement*. In nontechnical language, students who have mothers with high (a lot of) education generally have high *math achievement* scores and vice versa. Because the correlation is positive this means that high *mother's education* is generally associated with high achievement, medium education with medium achievement, and low with low. If the correlation were significant and *negative* (e.g., -.50), high *mother's education* would be associated with low achievement and vice versa. If the correlation were not significant, there would be *no* systematic association between a *mother's education* and her child's achievement. In that case you could not predict anything about *math achievement* from knowing someone's *mother's education*. In addition to statistical significance and the sign of the Pearson correlation, you should note and comment on the effect size for a full interpretation of the correlation. In this case, the correlation is .34, so, using Cohen's (1988) guideline, the effect size is medium (see Table 6.5).

> **Example of How to Write About Problem 8.2**
> Results
> To investigate if there was a statistically significant association between mother's education and math achievement, a correlation was computed. Mother's education was skewed (skewness = 1.13) which violated the assumption of normality. Thus, the Spearman rho statistic was calculated, r_s (73) = .32, p = .006. The direction of the correlation was positive, which means that students who have highly educated mothers tend to have higher math achievement test scores and vice versa. Using Cohen's (1988) guidelines, the effect size is medium or typical for studies in this area. The r squared indicates that approximately 10% of the variance in math achievement test scores can be predicted from mother's education.

Problem 8.3: Correlation Matrix for Several Variables

If you have more than two ordinal or normally distributed variables that you want to correlate, SPSS will produce a matrix showing the correlation of each selected variable with each of the others. With SPSS you can print a matrix scatterplot to check the linear relationship for each pair of variables (see Fig. 8.3).

8.3. What are the associations among the four variables: *visualization, mosaic pattern test, grades in h.s.,* and *math achievement?*

Now, compute **Pearson** correlations among all pairs of the following scale/normal variables: *visualization, mosaic, grades in h.s.,* and *math achievement.* Move all four into the **Variable** box. Follow procedures outlined previously except:

- Do not check Spearman (under **Correlation Coefficients**) but do use **Pearson**.
- For **Options,** click **Means and standard deviations,** and **Exclude cases listwise.** The latter will only use participants who have no missing data on any of these four variables.

This will produce Output 8.3. To see if you are doing the work right, compare your syntax and output to Output 8.3.

Output 8.3: Pearson Correlation Matrix

```
CORRELATIONS
   /VARIABLES=visual mosaic grades mathach
   /PRINT=TWOTAIL NOSIG
   /STATISTICS DESCRIPTIVES
```

Correlations

Descriptive Statistics

	Mean	Std. Deviation	N
visualization test	5.2433	3.91203	75
mosaic, pattern test	27.416	9.5738	75
grades in h.s.	5.68	1.570	75
math achievement test	12.5645	6.67031	75

Chapter 8 – Correlation and Regression

Correlations of other variables with *math achievement*

Correlations[a]

		visualization test	mosaic, pattern test	grades in h.s.	math achievement test
visualization test	Pearson Correlation	1	.030	.127	.423**
	Sig. (2-tailed)	.	.798	.279	.000
mosaic, pattern test	Pearson Correlation	.030	1	-.012	.213
	Sig. (2-tailed)	.798	.	.920	.067
grades in h.s.	Pearson Correlation	.127	-.012	1	.504**
	Sig. (2-tailed)	.279	.920	.	.000
math achievement test	Pearson Correlation	.423**	.213	.504**	1
	Sig. (2-tailed)	.000	.067	.000	.

**. Correlation is significant at the 0.01 level (2-tailed).

a. Listwise N=75

Interpretation of Output 8.3

Notice that after the descriptive statistics table, there is a larger **Correlations** table that shows the **Pearson Correlation** coefficients, and two-tailed significance **(Sig.)** levels. These numbers are, as in Output 8.2, each given twice so you have to be careful in reading matrix. It is a good idea to look only at the numbers above or below the diagonal (the 1s). There are 6 different correlations in the table. In the last column, we have circled the correlation of each of the other variables with *math achievement*. In the second to last column, each of the other three variables is correlated with *grades in h.s.*, but note that the .504 below the diagonal for *grades in h.s.* and *math achievement* is the same as the correlation of *math achievement* and *grades in h.s.* in the last column, so ignore it the second time.

The Pearson correlations on this table are interpreted similarly to the one in Output 8.2. However, because there are 6 correlations, the odds are increased that one could be statistically significant by chance. Thus, it would be prudent to require a smaller value of *p*. The Bonferroni correction is a conservative approach designed to keep the significance level at .05 for the whole study. Using Bonferroni, you would divide the usual significance level (.05) by the number of tests. In this case a $p < .008$ (.05/6) would be required for statistical significance. Another approach is simply to set alpha (the *p* value required for statistical significance) at a more conservative .01 instead of .05.

Note that if we had checked **Excluded cases pairwise** in Fig. 8.6, the correlations would be the same because there were no missing data ($N = 75$) on any of the four variables. However, if some variables had missing data, the correlations would be at least somewhat different. Each correlation would be based on the cases that have no missing data <u>on those two variables</u>. One might use pairwise exclusion to include as many cases as possible in each correlation; however, the problem with this approach is that different correlations will include data from somewhat different pairs of individuals. Multivariate statistics, such as multiple regression, use listwise data and correlations.

If you checked **One-Tailed Test of Significance** in Fig. 8.6, the **Pearson Correlation** values would be the same as in Output 8.3, but the **Sig.** values would be half what they are here. For example the Sig. for the correlation between *math achievement* and *mosaic* would be .0335 instead of .067. One-tailed tests are only used if you have a clear directional hypothesis (e.g., there is a *positive* correlation between the variables), and if the output has an apparently significant correlation in the direction opposite from that predicted, it must be ignored.

Example of How to Write About Problem 8.3
Results
Table 8.1 shows that two of the six pairs of variables were significantly correlated. The strongest positive correlation, which would be considered a large effect size, was between grades in high school and math achievement test scores, $r(73) = -.504$, $p < .001$. This means that students who had relatively high grades in high school were likely to have high math achievement test scores. Math achievement was also positively correlated with visualization test scores ($r = .42$); this is a medium to large size according to Cohen (1988).

Table 8.1

Intercorrelations, Means, and Standard Deviations for Four Variables (N = 75)

Variable	1	2	3	4	M	SD
1. Visualization	--	.03	.13	.42*	5.24	3.91
2. Mosaic	--	--	-.01	.21	27.41	9.57
3. Grades	--	--	--	.50*	5.68	1.57
4. Math ach.	--	--	--	--	12.56	6.67

*p < .001

Problem 8.4. Internal Consistency Reliability with Cronbach's Alpha

A very common measure of reliability in the research literature is **Cronbach's alpha.** It is used to assess the **internal consistency reliability** of several items or scores that the researcher wants to add together to get a summary or **summated scale** score. Alpha is based on a correlation matrix and is interpreted similarly to other measures of reliability; alpha should be positive and usually greater than .70 in order to provide good support for internal consistency reliability. Remember that in Chapter 7 we computed Cohen's Kappa to assess interobserver reliability for nominal data. In Chapter 9, we will compute test-retest or parallel forms reliability.

8.4. What is the internal consistency reliability for the four items in the *pleasure* with math *scale*?

To compute Cronbach's alpha:
- Select **Analyze => Scale => Reliability Analysis.**
- Move item02, item06 reversed, item 10 reversed, and item 14 to the right into the **Items** box. Be sure you use the reversed versions of items 2 and 10.
- Check to be sure that the **Model** is **Alpha.**
- Click in statistics to get the **Reliability Analysis: Statistics** window.
- Under **Inter Item** check **Correlation.**
- Click on **Continue** and **OK.**

Compare your output to Output 8.4.

Output 8.4 Cronbach's Alpha for the Pleasure Scale

Reliability

Warnings

The covariance matrix is calculated and used in the analysis.

Case Processing Summary

		N	%
Cases	Valid	75	100.0
	Excluded (a)	0	.0
	Total	75	100.0

a Listwise deletion based on all variables in the procedure.

Reliability Statistics

Cronbach's Alpha	Cronbach's Alpha Based on Standardized Items	N of Items
.688	.704	4

Inter-Item Correlation Matrix

	item02 pleasure	item06 reversed	item10 reversed	item14 pleasure
item02 pleasure	1.000	.285	.347	.504
item06 reversed	.285	1.000	.203	.461
item10 reversed	.347	.203	1.000	.436
item14 pleasure	.504	.461	.436	1.000

The covariance matrix is calculated and used in the analysis.

> *Interpretation of Output 8.4*
> The **Inter-Item Correlation Matrix** is read similarly to the correlation matrix in Output 8.3. Remember that each correlation (*r*) is given twice, both above and below the diagonal (1.000). Use only one. Note that the six correlations are all positive and range from .20 to .50.
>
> The **Reliability Statistics** table provide the **Cronbach's Alpha** (.69) and an alpha based on standardizing the items (.70). Unless the items have very different means and *SDs*, you would use the unstandardized alpha (.69). This alpha is marginal in terms of acceptability as a measure of reliability because it is (slightly) less than .70. However, alpha is highly dependent on the number of items in the proposed summated scale so .69 is probably acceptable to most researchers for a four item scale.

Problem 8.5: Bivariate or Simple Linear Regression

As stated above in relation to the Pearson, correlation is the best choice for a statistic when you are interested in associating two variables that have normal or scale level measurement for the two variables. Correlations do not indicate prediction of one variable from another; however, there are times when researchers wish to make such predictions. To do this one needs to use bivariate regression (which is also called simple regression or simple linear regression). For simple regression, the variables should be approximately normally distributed.

8.5. Can we predict *math achievement* from *grades in high school*?

To answer this question, a bivariate regression is the best choice. Follow these commands:

- **Analyze** => **Regression** => **Linear...**
- Highlight *math achievement*. Click the arrow to move it into the **Dependent** box.
- Highlight *grades in high school* and click on the arrow to move it into the **Independent(s)** box. The window should look like Figure 8.8.
- Click on **OK.**

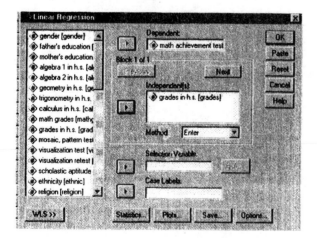

Fig. 8.8. Linear regression.

- Compare your output with Output 8.5

Output 8.5 Bivariate regression

```
REGRESSION
  /MISSING LISTWISE
  /STATISTICS COEFF OUTS R ANOVA
  /CRITERIA=PIN(.05) POUT(.10)
  /NOORIGIN
  /DEPENDENT mathach
  /METHOD=ENTER grades   .
```

Regression

Variables Entered/Removed[b]

Model	Variables Entered	Variables Removed	Method
1	grades in h.s.[a]	.	Enter

a. All requested variables entered.

b. Dependent Variable: math achievement test

> Notice that with bivariate regression the R is the same as the r in Output 8.3.

Model Summary

Model	R	R Square	Adjusted R Square	Std. Error of the Estimate
1	.504[a]	.254	.244	5.80018

a. Predictors: (Constant), grades in h.s.

ANOVA[b]

Model		Sum of Squares	df	Mean Square	F	Sig.
1	Regression	836.606	1	836.606	24.868	.000[a]
	Residual	2455.875	73	33.642		
	Total	3292.481	74			

a. Predictors: (Constant), grades in h.s.

b. Dependent Variable: math achievement test

> This is the regression coefficient, which is the slope of the best-fit line or regression line. Note that it is not equal to the correlation coefficient. The standardized regression coefficient (.504) for simple regression is the correlation.

Coefficients[a]

Model		Unstandardized Coefficients		Standardized Coefficients	t	Sig.
		B	Std. Error	Beta		
1	(Constant)	.397	2.530		.157	.876
	grades in h.s.	2.142	.430	.504	4.987	.000

a. Dependent Variable: math achievement test

> ### *Interpretation of Output 8.5*
> In the fourth table, labeled Coefficients, the **Unstandardized** regression **Coefficient** in bivariate regression is simply the slope of the "best fit" regression line for the scatterplot showing the association between two variables. The **Standardized** regression **Coefficient** is equal to the correlation between those same two variables. (In problem 8.6, multiple regression, we will see that when there is more than one predictor, the relation between correlation and regression becomes more complex, and there is more than one standardized regression coefficient.) The primary distinction between bivariate regression and bivariate correlation (e.g., Pearson) is that in regression, one wants to predict one variable from another variable; whereas, in correlation, you simply want to know how those variables are related.
>
> The **Unstandardized Coefficients** give you a formula that one can use to predict the y scores (dependent variable) from the x scores (independent variable). Thus, if one did not have access to the real y score, this formula would tell one the best way of estimating an individual's y score based on that individual's x score. For example, if we want to predict *math achievement* for a similar group knowing only *grades in h.s.*, we could use the regression equation to estimate an individual's achievement scores: predicated *math achievement* = .397 + 2.14x (the person's *grades* score). Thus, if a student has mostly Bs (6) for their grades, their predicted math achievement would be 13.24: math achievement = .40 + 2.14*6.
>
> One should be cautious in doing this, however; we know that *grades in h.s.* only explains 25% of the variance in *math achievement*, so this would not yield a very accurate prediction. A better use of simple regression is to test a directional hypothesis: *grades in h.s* predicts *math achievement*. If one really thinks that this is the direction of the relationship (and not that *math achievement* predicts *grades in h.s.*), then regression is more appropriate than correlation.

> ### *An Example of How to Write About Output 8.5*
> #### Results
> Simple regression was conducted to investigate how well grades in high school predict math achievement scores. The results were statistically significant $F(1,73) = 24.87, p < .001$. The identified equation to understand this relationship was math achievement = .40 + 2.14*(grades in high school). The adjusted R squared value was .244. This indicates that 24% of the variance in math achievement was explained by the grades in high school. According to Cohen (1988) this is a large effect.

Problem 8.6: Multiple Regression

The purpose of multiple regression is similar to bivariate regression, but with more predictor variables. Multiple regression attempts to predict a normal (or scale) dependent variable from a combination of several scale and/or dichotomous independent/predictor variables. In this problem, we will see if *math achievement* can be predicted better from a combination of several of our other variables, *gender, grades in high school*, and *mother's* and *father's education*. There are many different methods provided in SPSS to analyze data with multiple regression. We will use one where we assume that all four of the predictor variables are important and that we want to see what is the highest possible multiple correlation of these variables with the dependent variable. For this purpose, we will use the method that SPSS calls **Enter** (often called **simultaneous regression**), which tells the computer to consider all the variables at the same time. Our *SPSS for Intermediate Statistics* book (Leech et al., 2004) provides more examples and discussion of multiple regression assumptions, methods, and interpretation.

Assumptions and Conditions of Multiple Regression

There are many assumptions to consider, but we will only focus on the major ones that are easily tested with SPSS. These include the following: the relationship between each of the predictor variables and the dependent variable is linear, the errors are normally distributed, and the variance of the residuals (difference between actual and predicted scores) is constant. A condition that can be problematic is **multicollinearity**; it occurs when there are high intercorrelations among some set of the predictor variables. In other words, multicollinearity happens when two or more predictors contain the same information.

8.6.   How well can you predict math achievement from a combination of four variables: *grades in high school, father's and mother's education*, and *gender*?

In this problem, the computer will enter/consider all the variables at the same time. We will ask which of these four predictors contribute significantly to the multiple correlation/regression.

Let's compute the regression for these variables. To do this, follow these steps:

- Click on the following: **Analyze => Regression => Linear**. The Linear Regression window (Fig. 8.9) should appear.
- Select *mathach* and click it over to the **Dependent** box (Dependent variable).
- Next select the variables *grades in h.s., father's education, mother's education,* and *gender* and click them over to the **Independent(s)** box (Independent variables).
- Under **Method**, be sure that **Enter** is selected.
- Click on **Statistics**, at the bottom of Fig 8.9 to get Fig. 8.10.
- Click on **Estimates** (under **Regression coefficients**), click on **Model fit,** and **Descriptives**. (See Fig. 8.10.)

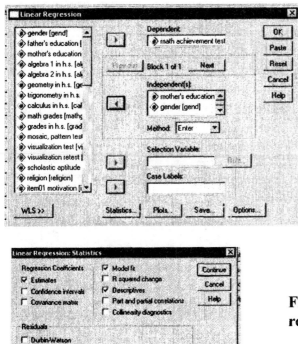

Fig. 8.9. Linear regression.

Fig. 8.10. Linear regression: Statistics.

- Click on **Continue**.
- Click on **OK**.

Compare your output and syntax to Output 8.6.

Output 8.6: Multiple Regression

```
REGRESSION
  /DESCRIPTIVES MEAN STDDEV CORR SIG N
  /MISSING LISTWISE
  /STATISTICS COEFF OUTS R ANOVA
  /CRITERIA=PIN(.05) POUT(.10)
  /NOORIGIN
  /DEPENDENT mathach
  /METHOD=ENTER grades faed maed gender   .
```

Regression

Descriptive Statistics

	Mean	Std. Deviation	N
math achievement test	12.6621	6.49659	73
grades in h.s.	5.70	1.552	73
father's education	4.73	2.830	73
mother's education	4.14	2.263	73
gender	.55	.501	73

N is 73 because 2 participants have some missing data.

Regression

This is a high correlation among these independent variables. It indicates there might be a problem with multicollinearity

Correlations with *math achievement*, the dependent variable.

Correlations

		math achievement test	grades in h.s.	father's education	mother's education	gender
Pearson Correlation	math achievement test	1.000	.472	.381	.345	-.274
	grades in h.s.	.472	1.000	.269	.190	.144
	father's education	.381	.269	1.000	.681	-.265
	mother's education	.345	.190	.681	1.000	-.202
	gender	-.274	.144	-.265	-.202	1.000
Sig. (1-tailed)	math achievement test	.	.000	.000	.001	.010
	grades in h.s.	.000	.	.011	.054	.112
	father's education	.000	.011	.	.000	.012
	mother's education	.001	.054	.000	.	.043
	gender	.010	.112	.012	.043	.
N	math achievement test	73	73	73	73	73
	grades in h.s.	73	73	73	73	73
	father's education	73	73	73	73	73
	mother's education	73	73	73	73	73
	gender	73	73	73	73	73

Significance level of correlations with *math achievement*.

Variables Entered/Removed[b]

Model	Variables Entered	Variables Removed	Method
1	gender, grades in h.s., mother's education, father's education[a]	.	Enter

> This indicates that we used the Enter method in the calculation. If we chose a different method, this box and the outputs would be different.

a. All requested variables entered.

b. Dependent Variable: math achievement test

> Multiple correlation coefficient.

> This indicates that 34% of the variance can be predicted from the independent variables.

Model Summary

Model	R	R Square	Adjusted R Square	Std. Error of the Estimate
1	.616[a]	.379	.343	5.26585

a. Predictors: (Constant), gender, grades in h.s., mother's education, father's education

> This indicates that the combination of these variables significantly predicts the dependent variable.

ANOVA[b]

Model		Sum of Squares	df	Mean Square	F	Sig.
1	Regression	1153.222	4	288.305	10.397	.000[a]
	Residual	1885.583	68	27.729		
	Total	3038.804	72			

a. Predictors: (Constant), gender, grades in h.s., mother's education, father's education

b. Dependent Variable: math achievement test

Coefficients[a]

Model		Unstandardized Coefficients		Standardized Coefficients	t	Sig.
		B	Std. Error	Beta		
1	(Constant)	1.047	2.526		.415	.680
	grades in h.s.	1.946	.427	.465	4.560	.000
	father's education	.191	.313	.083	.610	.544
	mother's education	.406	.375	.141	1.084	.282
	gender	-3.759	1.321	-.290	-2.846	.006

a. Dependent Variable: math achievement test

> Only grades and gender are significantly contributing to the equation. However, all of the variables need to be included to obtain this result, since the overall *F* value was computed with all the variables in the equation.

Interpretation of Output 8.6

This output begins with the usual **Descriptive Statistics** for all five variables in the first table. Note that the *N* is 73 because two participants are missing a score on one or more variables. Multiple regression uses only the participants who have complete data (listwise exclusion) for all the variables. The next table is a **Correlation** matrix. The first column shows the correlations of the other variables with *math achievement*. Note that all of the independent/predictor variables are significantly correlated with *math achievement*. Also notice that two of the predictor/ independent variables are highly correlated with each other; i.e., *mother's* and *father's education* (.681).

The **Model Summary** table shows that the multiple correlation coefficient (*R*), using all the predictors simultaneously, is .62 and the **Adjusted R^2** is .34, meaning that 34% of the variance in math achievement can be predicted from the combination of *father's education, mother's education, grades in h.s.,* and *gender*. Note that the adjusted R^2 is lower than the unadjusted R^2 (.38). This is, in part, related to the number of variables in the equation. As you will see from the coefficients table, only *grades in h.s.* and *gender* are significant, but the other variables will always add a little to the prediction of *math achievement*. Because several independent variables were used, a reduction of the number of variables might help us find an equation that explains more of the variance in the dependent variable, once the correction is made. It is helpful to use the concept of parsimony with multiple regression, and use the smallest number of predictors needed. The **ANOVA** table shows that *F* = **10.40** and is statistically significant. This indicates that the combination of the predictors significantly combine together to predict *math achievement*.

One of the most important tables is the **Coefficients** table. It shows the **standardized beta coefficients**, which are interpreted much like correlation coefficients. The **t** value and the **Sig** opposite each independent variable indicates whether that variable is significantly contributing to the equation for predicting *math achievement*. Thus, *grades* and *gender*, in this example, are the only variables that are significantly adding anything to the prediction <u>when the other three variables are already considered</u>. It is important to note that all the variables are being considered together when these values are computed. Therefore, if you delete one of the predictors, even if it is not significant, it can affect the levels of significance for other predictors. For example, if we deleted *father's education*, it is quite possible that *mother's education* would be a significant predictor.

How to Write About Output 8.6

Results

Simultaneous multiple regression was conducted to investigate the best predictors of math achievement test scores. The means, standard deviations, and intercorrelations can be found in Table 8.2a. When the combination of variables to predict math achievement test included grades in h.s., father's education, mother's education, and gender, $F(4, 68) = 10.40$, $p < .001$.

The beta coefficients are presented in Table 8.2b. Note that high grades and male gender significantly predict math achievement when all four variables are included. The adjusted R squared value was .343. This indicates that 34% of the variance in math achievement was explained by the model. According to Cohen (1988) this is a large effect.

Table 8.2a

Means, Standard Deviations, and Intercorrelations for Math Achievement and Predictors Variables (N=73)

Variable	M	SD	Grades in h.s.	Father's education	Mother's education	Gender
Math Achievement	12.66	6.50	.47**	.38**	.35*	-.27*
Predictor variable						
1. Grades in h.s.	5.70	1.55	- -	.27*	.19	.14
2. Father's education	4.73	2.83		- -	.68**	-.27*
3. Mother's education	4.14	2.26			- -	-.20*
4. Gender	.55	.50				- -

*$p < .05$; **$p < .01$.

Table 8.2b

Simultaneous Multiple Regression Analysis Summary for Grades in High School, Father's and Mother's Education, and Gender Predicting Math Achievement (N = 73)

Variable	B	SEB	β
Grades in h.s.	1.95	.43	.47**
Father's education	.19	.31	.08
Mother's education	.41	.38	.14
Gender	-.38	1.32	-.29*
Constant	1.05	2.53	

Note. $R^2 = .38$; $F(4,68) = 10.40$, $p < .001$.
*$p < .01$; **$p < .001$.

Interpretation Questions

8.1. Why would we graph scatterplots and regression lines?

8.2. In Output 8.2: a) What do the correlation coefficients tell us? b) What is r^2 for the Pearson correlation? What does it mean? c) Compare the Pearson and Spearman correlations on both correlation size and significance level. d) When should you use which type in this case?

8.3. In Output 8.3, how many of the Pearson correlation coefficients are significant? Write an interpretation of a) one of the significant and b) one of the nonsignificant correlations in Output 8.3. Include whether or not the correlation is significant, your decision about the null hypothesis, *and* a sentence or two describing the correlations in nontechnical terms. Include comments related to the sign and to the effect size.

8.4. Interpret the Cronbach alpha in Output 8.4? What is the internal consistency reliability?

8.5. Using Output 8.5, find the regression (B) coefficient or weight and the standardized regression (Beta) coefficient. a) How do these compare to the correlation between the same variables in Output 8.3?) What does the regression (B) weight tell you? c) Give an example of a research problem in which the Pearson correlation would be more appropriate than bivariate regression, and one in which bivariate regression would be more appropriate than Pearson correlation.

8.6. In Output 8.6, what do the Beta weights (standardized regression weights or coefficients) tell you about the ability of the predictors to predict the dependent variable?

Extra SPSS Problems

Using your College Student data do the following problems. Print your outputs after typing your interpretations on them. Please circle the key parts of the output that you discuss.

8.1.   What is the correlation between students' height and parent's height? Also produce a scatterplot. Interpret the results, including statistical significance, direction, and effect size.

8.2.   Write a question that can be answered via correlational analysis with two approximately normal or *scale* variables. Run the appropriate statistics to answer the question. Interpret the results.

8.3.   Make a correlation matrix using at least four appropriate variables. Identify, using the variable names, the two strongest and two weakest correlations. What were the *r* and *p* values for each correlation?

8.4.   Is there a combination of gender and same sex parent's height that predicts student's height better than either one of these variables alone?

8.5.   Is there a combination of hours of TV watching, hours of studying, and hours of work that predicts current GPA?

CHAPTER 9

Comparing Groups with *t* Tests
and Similar Nonparametric Tests

In this chapter, we will use a number of statistics to compare groups. In Problem 1, we will use a **one-sample *t* test** to compare one group or sample to a hypothesized population mean. Then we will examine two parametric and two nonparametric/ordinal statistics that compare two groups of participants. Problem 2 compares two independent groups (between groups design), males and females, using the **independent samples *t* test**. Problem 3 uses the **Mann-Whitney** nonparametric test, which is similar to the independent *t* test. Problem 4 is a within subjects design that uses a **paired samples *t*** to compare the average levels of education of students' mothers and fathers. Problem 5 will also use the **paired *t*** but, in this case, to check the **reliability** of a repeated measure, namely the *visualization test* and *visualization retest*. Problem 6 shows how to use the nonparametric **Wilcoxon** test for a within subjects design.

The top right side of Table 9.1 distinguishes between **between groups** and **within subjects designs.** This helps determine the specific statistic to use. The other determinant of which statistic to use has do with statistical assumptions. If the assumptions are not markedly violated, you can use a parametric test. If the assumptions are markedly violated, one can use a nonparametric test, as indicated by the left side of Table 9.1. Another alternative is to transform the variable so that it meets the assumptions, but this is beyond the scope of this book. Note that chi-square has been demonstrated in Chapter 7 so we will not use it here. The McNemar test, which is rarely used, will not be demonstrated.

Table 9.1. *Selection of an Appropriate Inferential Statistic for Basic, Two Variable Difference Questions or Hypotheses*

	Level of Measurement of Dependent Variable	Compare	One Factor or Independent Variable With 2 Categories or Levels/Groups/Samples	
			Independent Samples or Groups (Between)	Repeated Measures or Related Samples (Within)
Parametric Statistics	Dependent Variable Approximates **Normal (Scale) Data** and Assumptions Not Markedly Violated	Means	INDEPENDENT SAMPLES *t* TEST (or ONE - WAY ANOVA)	PAIRED SAMPLES *t* TEST
Nonparametric Statistics	Dependent Variable Clearly **Ordinal Data** or the ANOVA Assumptions Are Markedly Violated	Mean Ranks	MANN-WHITNEY	WILCOXON
	Dependent Variable is **Nominal** or (dichotomous) Data	Counts	CHI-SQUARE	MC NEMAR

You might ask, why would you compute a t test when one-way ANOVA (F) can be used to compare *two* groups as well as three or more groups? Because $F = t^2$, both statistics provide the same information. Thus, the choice is mostly a matter of personal preference. However, t tests can be either one tailed or two-tailed, while ANOVAs are always two tailed. Thus, if you have a clear directional hypothesis that predicts which group will have the higher mean, you may want to use a t test rather than one-way ANOVA when comparing two groups. In addition, the t test output provides an adjustment to deal with the problem of unequal variances; whereas, the remedy for such problems in ANOVA may be less satisfactory. Finally, it is just more customary to use t test if one is comparing only two groups. You *must* use ANOVA if you want to compare three or more groups.

- Retrieve **hsbdataB** from your data file.

Problem 9.1. One-Sample t Test

Sometimes you want to compare the mean of a sample with a hypothesized population mean to see if your sample is significantly different. For example, the scholastic aptitude test was originally standardized so that the mean was 500 and the standard deviation was 100. In our modified HSB data set, we made up mock *SAT-Math* data for each student. You may remember from chapter 3 that the mean *SAT-Math* score for our sample was 490.53.

Assumptions of the One-Sample t Test:
  1. The dependent variable is normally distributed within the population.
  2. The data are independent (scores of one participant are not dependent on scores of the others).

9.1. Is the mean *SAT-Math* score in the modified HSB data set significantly different from the presumed population mean of 500?

To compute the one-sample t test, use the following commands:
- **Analyze => Compare Means => One-Sample T test**
- Move *scholastic aptitude test-math* to the **Test Variables** box.
- Type 500 in the **Test Value** box (the test value is the hypothesized population mean).
- Click **OK.**

```
T-TEST
  /TESTVAL = 500
  /MISSING = ANALYSIS
  /VARIABLES = satm
  /CRITERIA = CI(.95) .
```

One-Sample Statistics

	N	Mean	Std. Deviation	Std. Error Mean
scholastic aptitude test - math	75	490.53	94.553	10.918

One-Sample Test

This *t* test compares the sample mean of 490.53 with the test value.

	Test Value = 500				95% Confidence Interval of the Difference	
	t	df	Sig. (2-tailed)	Mean Difference	Lower	Upper
scholastic aptitude test - math	-.867	74	.389	-9.47	-31.22	12.29

Interpretation of Output 9.1
The **One-Sample Statistics** table provides basic descriptive statistics for the variable under consideration. The **Mean** *SAT-Math* for the students in the sample will be compared to the hypothesized population mean, displayed as the **Test Value** in the **One-Sample Test** table. On the bottom line of this table, are the *t* value, *df*, and the two tailed sig. (*p*) value, which is circled. Note the $p = .389$ so we can say that the sample mean (491) is not significantly different from the population mean. The table also provides the difference (-9.47) between the sample and population means and the 95% **Confidence Interval.** The difference between the sample and the population mean is likely to be between 12.29 and -31.72 points. Notice that this range includes the value of zero, so it is possible that there is no difference. Thus, the difference is not statistically significant.

Problem 9.2: Independent Samples *t* Test

When investigating the difference between two unrelated or independent groups (in this case males and females) on an approximately normal dependent variable it is appropriate to choose an independent samples *t* test if the following assumptions are not markedly violated.

Assumptions of the Independent Samples t Test:
1. The variances of the dependent variable in the two populations are equal.
2. The dependent variable is normally distributed within each population.
3. The data are independent (scores of one participant are not related systematically to scores of the others).

SPSS will automatically test assumption 1 with the **Levene test** for equal variances. Assumption 2 could be tested, as we did in Chapter 4, Problem 4.3, with the **Explore** command, to see that the dependent variables are at least appropriately normally distributed for each gender. Because the *t* test is quite robust to violations of this assumption, we won't test it here. Assumption 3 probably is met because the genders are not matched or related pairs and there is no reason to believe that one person's score might have influenced another person's. This assumption is best addressed during design and data collection. In addition to ensuring that the data meet these assumptions, the researcher should try to ensure that groups or samples are of similar size, as the assumption of homogeneity of variance is most important and more likely to be violated if samples differ markedly in size.

9.2. Do male and female students differ significantly in regard to their average *math achievement* scores, *grades in high school,* and *visualization test* scores?

One feature of SPSS is that it can do several *t* tests in a single output, if they have the same independent or grouping variable (e.g., gender). In this problem, we have asked SPSS to compute three separate *t* tests, one each for *math achievement, grades in high school,* and *visualization test* scores.

With more than one dependent variable, one could have chosen to use MANOVA (see Fig. 6.1), especially if these variables were conceptually related and correlated with each other. MANOVA would enable us to see how a linear *combination* of these three variables was different for boys than for girls. We will not demonstrate MANOVA in this book, but see Leech et al. (2004) *SPSS for Intermediate Statistics* for how to compute and interpret MANOVA.

For the *t* tests, follow these commands:

- Click on **Analyze => Compare means => Independent Samples T Test.**
- Move *math achievement, grades in high school,* and *visualization* to the **Test** (dependent) **Variable(s)** box and move *gender* to the **Grouping** (independent) **Variable(s)** box (see Fig. 9.1).

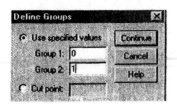

Fig. 9.1. Independent-samples *t* test.

- Next click on **Define Groups** in Fig. 9.1 to get Fig. 9.2.
- Type **0** (for males) in the **Group 1** box and **1** (for females) in the **Group 2** box (see Fig. 9.2). This will enable us to compare males and females on each of the three dependent variables.

Fig. 9.2. Define groups.

- Click on **Continue** then on **OK**. Compare your output to Output 9.2.

Output 9.2: Independent Samples t Test

```
T-TEST
  GROUPS=gender(0 1)
  /MISSING=ANALYSIS
  /VARIABLES=mathach grades visual
  /CRITERIA=CIN(.95) .
```

SPSS for Introductory Statistics

Group Statistics

Each circle contains the means to be compared.

	gender	N	Mean	Std. Deviation	Std. Error Mean
math achievement test	male	34	14.7550	6.03154	1.03440
	female	41	10.7479	6.69612	1.04576
grades in h.s.	male	34	5.50	1.638	.281
	female	41	5.83	1.515	.237
visualization test	male	34	6.4265	4.47067	.76671
	female	41	4.2622	3.10592	.48506

Independent Samples Test

		Levene's Test for Equality of Variances		t-test for Equality of Means					95% Confidence Interval of the Difference	
		F	Sig.	t	df	Sig. (2-tailed)	Mean Difference	Std. Error Difference	Lower	Upper
math achievement test	Equal variances assumed	.537	.466	2.697	73	.009	4.0070	1.48548	1.04648	6.96760
	Equal variances not assumed			2.724	72.472	.008	4.0070	1.47092	1.07515	6.93894
grades in h.s.	Equal variances assumed	.574	.451	-.903	73	.369	-.33	.365	-1.056	.397
	Equal variances not assumed			-.897	68.145	.373	-.33	.367	-1.062	.403
visualization test	Equal variances assumed	6.510	.013	2.466	73	.016	2.1643	.87778	.41486	3.91369
	Equal variances not assumed			2.385	57.150	.020	2.1643	.90727	.34761	3.98094

This is *not* the *t* test. It is a test of the assumption equal variances.

Circled numbers are discussed in the Interpretation box.

Interpretation of Output 9.2

The first table, **(Group Statistics)** shows descriptive statistics for the two groups (males and females) separately. Note that the means within each of the three pairs look somewhat different. This might be due to chance, so we will check the *t* tests in the next table.

The second table, **Independent Samples Test**, provides two statistical tests. In the left two columns of numbers, is the **Levene test** for the assumption that the variances of the two groups are equal. <u>This is *not* the *t* test; it only assesses an assumption!</u> If this *F* test is not significant (as in the case of *math achievement* and *grades in high school*), the assumption is not violated, and one uses the **Equal variances assumed** line for the *t* test and related statistics. However, if Levene's *F* is statistically significant (sig ≤ .05), as is true for *visualization*, then variances are significantly different and the assumption of equal variances is violated. In that case, the **Equal variances *not* assumed** line is used; and SPSS adjusts the *t, df* and **Sig**. The appropriate lines are circled.

Thus, for *visualization*, the appropriate $t = 2.39$, degrees of freedom (df) = 57.15, and $p = .020$. This *t* is statistically significant so, based on the means, we can say that boys have higher *visualization scores* than girls. We used *visualization* to provide an example where the assumption of equal variances was violated (Levene's test was significant). Note that for *grades in high school* the *t* is not statistically significant ($p = .369$) so we conclude that there is no difference between boy and girls on grades. On the other hand, *math achievement* is statistically significant because $p < .05$.

The **95% Confidence Interval of the Difference** is shown in the two right hand columns of the Output. The confidence interval tells us that if we repeated the study 100 times, 95 of the times the true (population) difference would fall within the confidence interval, which for *math achievement* is between 1.05 points and 6.97 points. Note that if the **Upper** and **Lower** bounds have the same sign (either + and + or - and -), we know that the difference is statistically significant because this means that the null finding of zero difference lies *outside* of the confidence interval. On the other hand, if zero lies between the upper and lower limits, there could be no difference, as is the case for *grades in h.s.*. The lower limit of the confidence interval on *math achievement* tells us that the difference between males and females could be as small as 1.05 points out of 25.

Effect size measures for *t* tests are not provided in the printout but can be estimated relatively easily. See Chapter 6 for the formula and interpretation of *d*. For math achievement, the difference between the means (4.01) would be divided by about 6.4, an estimate of the pooled (weighted average) standard deviation. Thus, *d* would be approximately .60, which is, according to Cohen (1988), a medium to large sized "effect." Because you need means and standard deviations to compute the effect size, you should include a table with means and standard deviations in your results section for a full interpretation of *t* tests.

How to Write About Output 9.2.

Results

Table 9.1 shows that males were significantly different from females on *math achievement*, (*p*=.009). Inspection of the two group means indicates that the average math achievement score for female students (10.75) is significantly lower than the score (14.76) for males. The difference between the means is 4.01 points on a 25-point test. The effect size *d* is approximately .6, which is typical in this discipline. Males did not differ significantly from females on grades in high school (*p*=.369), but males did score higher on the visualization test (*p*=.020). The effect size, *d*, is again approximately .6.

Table 9.1

Comparison of Male and Female High School Students on a Math Achievement Test, Grades, and a Visualization Test (n = 34 males and 41 females)

Variable	*M*	*SD*	*t*	*df*	*p*
Math achievement			2.70	73	.009
Males	14.76	6.03			
Females	10.75	6.70			
Grades			-.90	73	.369
Males	5.50	1.64			
Females	5.83	1.52			
Visualization			2.39[a]	57.2[a]	.020
Males	6.43	4.47			
Females	4.26	3.11			

[a]The *t* and *df* were adjusted because variances were not equal.

Problem 9.3: The Nonparametric Mann-Whitney *U* Test

What should you do if the *t* test assumptions are markedly violated (e.g., what if the dependent variable data are grossly nonnormally distributed or are ordinal)? One answer is to run the appropriate nonparametric statistic, which in this case is called the Mann-Whitney (M-W) U test. The M-W is used with a between groups design with two levels of the independent variable.

Assumptions of the Mann-Whitney test:
1. The dependent variable is assumed to be continuous before it is ranked. It is assumed there is an underlying continuity in the dependent variable even if the actual data are discrete numbers such as 1, 2, 3, 4, 5, on a Likert rating.
2. The data are independent (scores of one participant are not dependent on scores of the others).

9.3. Do boys and girls differ significantly on *visualization, math achievement*, and *grades*? Assume that the scores for the three dependent variables are ordinal level data or violate other assumptions of the *t* tests.

- Click on **Analyze => Nonparametric Tests => 2 Independent Samples**.
- Move *visualization, math achievement, grades in h.s.* to the **Test** (dependent) **Variable List**.
- Next, click on *gender* and move it over to the **Grouping** (independent) **Variable** box.
- Click on **Define Groups** and enter 0 and 1 for groups because males are 0 and females are 1.
- Ensure that **Mann-Whitney U** is checked. Your window should look like Fig. 9.3.
- Click on **OK**.

Compare your syntax and output to Output 9.3 to check your work.

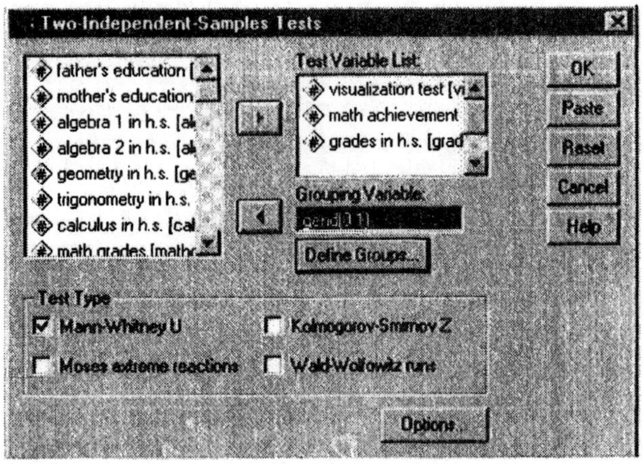

Fig. 9.3. Nonparametric tests for two independent samples.

Output 9.3   Non Parametric Test : Mann-Whitney U

```
NPAR TESTS
 /M-W= visual mathach grades   BY gender(0 1)
 /MISSING ANALYSIS.
```

Ranks

	gender	N	Mean Rank	Sum of Ranks
visualization test	male	34	43.65	1484.00
	female	41	33.32	1366.00
	Total	75		
math achievement test	male	34	45.10	1533.50
	female	41	32.11	1316.50
	Total	75		
grades in h.s.	male	34	35.78	1216.50
	female	41	39.84	1633.50
	Total	75		

> Mean ranks to be compared. The group with the higher rank had the higher grades and test scores.

Test Statistics[a]

	visualization test	math achievement test	grades in h.s.
Mann-Whitney U	505.000	455.500	621.500
Wilcoxon W	1366.000	1316.500	1216.500
Z	-2.052	-2.575	-.818
Asymp. Sig. (2-tailed)	.040	.010	.413

a. Grouping Variable: gender

Interpretation of Output 9.3

The **Ranks** table shows the mean or average ranks for males and females on each of the three dependent variables. SPSS ranks the 75 students from 75 (highest) to 1 (lowest) so that, in contrast to the typical ranking procedure, a high mean rank indicates the group scored higher.

The second table provides the **Mann-Whitney U**, **z score**, and the **Sig.** (significance) level or *p*, which are circled. Note that the mean ranks of the genders differ significantly on *visualization* and *math achievement* but not on *grades in high school*, as was the case for the similar *t* tests in Problem 2. The Mann-Whitney test is only slightly less powerful than the *t* test, so it is a good alternative if the assumptions of the *t* test are violated, as was the case with *visualization*.

Problem 9.4: Paired Samples *t* Test

In this problem, you will compare the average scores of each HSB student's father's and mother's scores on the same measure, namely their educational level. Since *father's* and *mother's education* are not independent of each other, the paired *t* test is the appropriate test to perform. The paired samples *t* test is also used when the two scores are repeated measures, such as the *visualization test* score and the *visualization retest* score (see Problem 9.5). Another example would be in a single group quasi-experimental study in which the same assessment is used as the pretest, before the intervention, and as the posttest, after the intervention.

Assumptions and Conditions for Use of the Paired Samples t test:
1. The independent variable is dichotomous and its levels (or groups) are paired, or matched, in some way (e.g., husband-wife, pre-post, etc.).
2. The dependent variable is normally distributed in the two conditions.

9.4.   Do students' fathers or mothers have more education?

We will determine if the fathers of these students have more education than their mothers. Remember that the fathers and mothers are paired; that is, each child has a pair of parents. (Note that SPSS allows you to do more than one paired *t* test at a time, so we could have compared the *visualization test* and *retest* scores in the same run as we compared *father's* and *mother's* *education,* but we decided to do them separately.)

- Select on **Analyze => Compare Means => Paired Samples T Test**.
- Click on <u>both</u> of the variables, *father's education* and *mother's education,* and move them simultaneously to the **Paired Variable(s)** box (see Fig. 9.4).
- Click on **OK**.

Compare your syntax and output to Output 9.4.

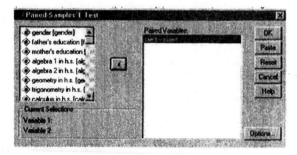

Fig. 9.4. Paired-samples *t* test.

Output 9.4: Paired Samples t Tests

```
T-TEST
  PAIRS= faed WITH maed (PAIRED)
  /CRITERIA=CIN(.95)
  /MISSING=ANALYSIS.
```

T-Test

Paired Samples Statistics

> The circled means are to be compared.

		Mean	N	Std. Deviation	Std. Error Mean
Pair 1	father's education	4.73	73	2.830	.331
	mother's education	4.14	73	2.263	.265

Paired Samples Correlations

> This is information about the <u>correlations</u> of mother's education with father's education. <u>Not</u> the result of the paired *t*.

		N	Correlation	Sig.
Pair 1	father's education & mother's education	73	.681	.000

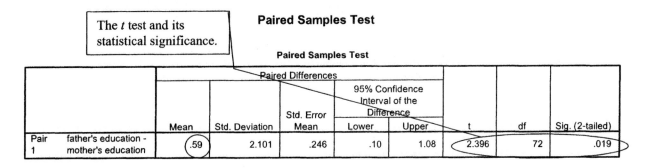

The *t* test and its statistical significance.

Paired Samples Test

Paired Samples Test

		Paired Differences					t	df	Sig. (2-tailed)
					95% Confidence Interval of the Difference				
		Mean	Std. Deviation	Std. Error Mean	Lower	Upper			
Pair 1	father's education - mother's education	.59	2.101	.246	.10	1.08	2.396	72	.019

Interpretation of Output 9.4

The first table shows the descriptive statistics used to compare *mother's* and *father's education* levels. The second table **Paired Samples Correlations,** provides correlations between the two paired scores. The correlation ($r = .68$) between *mother's* and *father's education* indicates that highly educated men tend to marry highly educated women and vice versa. It doesn't tell you whether men or women have more education. That is what *t* in the third table tells you.

The last table shows the **Paired Samples *t* Test**. The **Sig.** for the comparison of the average education level of the students' mothers and fathers was, $p = .019$. Thus, the difference in educational level is statistically significant, and we can tell from the means in the first table that fathers have more education; however, the effect size is small ($d= .59/2.1 = .28$). We can tell from the confidence interval that the difference in the means could be as small as .10 of a point or as large as 1.08 points on the 2 to 10 scale.

It is important that you understand that the correlations in the second table provide you with different information than the paired *t*. If not, read this interpretation again.

How to Write About Output 9.4

Results

A paired or correlated samples *t* test indicated that the students' fathers had on average significantly more education than their mothers, $t(72)=2.40$, $p=.019$, $d=.28$. The difference, although statistically significant, is small using Cohen's (1988) guidelines.

Problem 9.5: Using the Paired *t* Test to Check Reliability

In addition to comparing the means for two paired or matched samples, the paired *t* can be used to check reliability, especially **test-retest** or **parallel** (equivalent) **forms reliability.** These reliability measures are often done using a correlation coefficient so we could have demonstrated test-retest reliability for the *visualization* scores in the last chapter. However, the paired *t* test may be a better way to go because it produces not only the correlation but also comparison of the test and retest means. Thus we can see not only whether the test scores were strongly associated (relatively high test scores have high retests and vice versa) but also whether, on the average, scores on the retest were the same (versus higher or lower) as the test scores.

9.5.   What is the test-retest reliability of the *visualization* test scores?

To compute reliability with the paired *t* test program:
• Select **Analyze => Compare Means => Paired Samples T Test.**

- Click on both *visualization test* and *visualization retest* and move them simultaneously to the **Paired Variables** box (see Fig 9.4 if you need help).
- Click on **OK.**

Compare your output to Output 9.5.

Output 9.5: Test-Retest Reliability for Visualization Scores

```
T-TEST
  PAIRS = visual  WITH visual2 (PAIRED)
  /CRITERIA = CI(.95)
  /MISSING = ANALYSIS.
```

Note the means seem different.

Paired Samples Statistics

		Mean	N	Std. Deviation	Std. Error Mean
Pair 1	visualization test	5.2433	75	3.91203	.45172
	visualization retest	4.5467	75	3.01816	.34851

Paired Samples Correlations

Focus on the size of the correlation, not the Sig. when checking reliability.

		N	Correlation	Sig.
Pair 1	visualization test & visualization retest	75	.885	.000

Paired Samples Test

		Paired Differences					t	df	Sig. (2-tailed)
					95% Confidence Interval of the Difference				
		Mean	Std. Deviation	Std. Error Mean	Lower	Upper			
Pair 1	visualization test - visualization retest	.6967	1.87637	.21666	.2650	1.1284	3.215	74	.002

Interpretation of Output 9.5
The first table, **Paired Samples Statistic**, shows the **Mean** for the *visualization test* (5.24) and the *visualization retest* (4.55). These means will be compared in the third table. In addition, the *n*s, *SD*s, and standard errors are shown.

The second table shows the **Paired Samples Correlations**, which will be used to assess the test-retest reliability of the *visualization* scores. Note that the *r* = .89, which is a high positive correlation and seems to provide good support for test-retest reliability. This correlation indicates that students who scored highly on the test were very likely to score high on the retest, and students who scored low were very likely to score poorly on the retest.

The **Paired Samples Test** table shows that the means of the test and the retest are significantly different (*p*=.002). Although the correlation is very high, a significant *t* test is usually not desirable for a reliability measure. It indicates that, although the same students tended to score high (or low) on the test and the retest, the group average was lower on the retest. For some reason the retest seemed to be harder. Perhaps the retest was actually an alternate form or version of the test that was supposed to be equivalent but turned out to be more difficult.

Problem 9.6: Nonparametric Wilcoxon Test for Two Related Samples

Let's assume that education levels and visualization scores are not normally distributed and/or other assumptions of the paired *t* are violated. In fact, *mother's education* was quite skewed (see Chapter 4). Let's run the **Wilcoxon signed-ranks test** nonparametric test to see if fathers have significantly higher educational levels than mothers and to see if the *visualization test* is significantly different from *visualization retest*. The assumptions of the Wilcoxon tests are similar to those for the Mann-Whitney test.

9.6.   a) Are *mother's* and *father's education* levels significant different? b) Are the *visualization* and *visualization retest* scores different?

- To do this, select **Analyze => Nonparametric => 2 Related Samples.**
- Highlight both *father's education* and *mother's education* and move them together into the **Test Pair(s) List** box. Then, highlight *visualization* and *visualization retest* and move them into the box.
- Ensure that **Wilcoxon** is checked in the **Test Type** dialog box.
- Compare your syntax and output to Output 9.6.

Output 9.6

```
NPAR TEST
  /WILCOXON=faed visual  WITH maed visual2 (PAIRED)
  /MISSING ANALYSIS.
```

Wilcoxon Signed Ranks Test

Ranks

		N	Mean Rank	Sum of Ranks
mother's education - father's education	Negative Ranks	27[a]	29.20	788.50
	Positive Ranks	21[b]	18.45	387.50
	Ties	25[c]		
	Total	73		
visualization retest - visualization test	Negative Ranks	55[d]	34.02	1871.00
	Positive Ranks	14[e]	38.86	544.00
	Ties	6[f]		
	Total	75		

a. mother's education < father's education

b. mother's education > father's education

c. father's education = mother's education

d. visualization retest < visualization test

e. visualization retest > visualization test

f. visualization test = visualization retest

Test Statistics [b]

	mother's education - father's education	visualization retest - visualization test
Z	-2.085[a]	-3.975[a]
Asymp. Sig. (2-tailed)	.037	.000

a. Based on positive ranks.

b. Wilcoxon Signed Ranks Test

Interpretation of Output 9.6
Output 9.6 shows the nonparametric (Wilcoxon) analyses that are similar to the paired *t* tests. Note that the first table shows not only the mean ranks, but also the number of students who, for example, had mothers with less education than the fathers (27). Note that there were lots of ties (25) and almost as many women (21) that have more education than their spouse. The second table shows the significance level for the two tests. Note that the *p* or sig. values are quite similar to those for the paired *t*s.

Interpretation Questions

9.1.   a) Under what conditions would you use a one-sample *t* test? b) Provide another possible example of its use from the HSB data.

9.2.   In Output 9.2: a) Are the *variances* equal or significantly different for the three dependent variables? b) List the appropriate *t*, *df*, and *p* (significance level) for each *t* test as you would in an article. c) Which *t* tests are statistically significant? d) Write sentences interpreting the gender difference between the means of *grades in high school* and also *visualization*. e) Interpret the 95% confidence interval for these two variables. f) Comment on the effect sizes.

9.3.   a) Compare the results of Output 9.2 and 9.3. b) When would you use the Mann-Whitney U test?

9.4.   In Output 9.4: a) What does the paired samples correlation for mother's and father's education mean? b) Interpret/explain the results for the *t* test. c) Explain how the correlation and the *t* test differ in what information they provide. d) Describe the results if the *r* was .90 and the *t* was zero. e) What if *r* was zero and *t* was 5.0?

9.5.   Interpret the reliability for the *visualization test* and *retest* scores using Output 9.5.

9.6.   a) Compare the results of Outputs 9.4 and 9.5 with Output 9.6. b) When would you use the Wilcoxon test?

Extra SPSS Problems

Using the College Student data file, do the following problems. Print your outputs after typing your interpretations on them. Please circle the key parts of the output that you use for your interpretation.

9.1.   Is there a significant difference between the genders on average student height? Explain. Provide a full interpretation of the results.

9.2.   Is there a difference between the number of hours students study and the hours they work? Also, is there an association between the two?

9.3.   Write another question that can be answered from the data using a paired sample *t* test. Run the *t* test and provide a full interpretation.

9.4.   Are there differences between males and females in regard to the average number of hours they a) study, b) work, and c) watch TV? Hours of study is quite skewed so compute an appropriate nonparametric statistic.

CHAPTER 10

Analysis of Variance (ANOVA)

In this chapter, you will learn how to compute two types of analysis of variance (ANOVA) and an appropriate nonparametric statistic. In Problem 1, we will use the **one-way** or **single factor ANOVA** to compare three levels of *father's education* on several dependent variables (e.g., *math achievement*). If the ANOVA is statistically significant, you will know that there is a difference somewhere, but you will not know which pairs of means were significantly different. In Problem 2, we show you when and how to do appropriate **post hoc** tests to see which pairs of means were different. In Problem 3, you will compute the **Kruskal-Wallis (K-W)** test, a nonparametric test similar to one-way ANOVA. In Problem 4, we will introduce you to two-way or **factorial ANOVA.** This complex statistic is discussed in more detail in our companion book, Leech et al. (2004), *SPSS for Intermediate Statistics.*

- Retrieve your **hsbdataB.sav** file.

Problem 10.1: One-Way (or Single Factor) ANOVA

In this problem, you will examine a statistical technique for comparing two or *more* independent groups on the dependent variable. The appropriate statistic, called **One-Way ANOVA** in SPSS, compares the *means* of the samples or groups in order to make inferences about the population means. One-way ANOVA is also called single factor analysis of variance because there is only one independent variable or factor. The independent variable has nominal levels or a few ordered levels.

Remember that, in Chapter 9, we used the independent samples *t* to compare two groups (males and females). The one-way ANOVA *may* be used to compare two groups, but ANOVA is necessary if you want to compare three or more groups (e.g., three levels of *father's education*). Review Fig. 6.1 and Table 6.1 to see how these statistics fit into the overall selection of an appropriate statistic.

Assumptions of ANOVA
1. Observations are independent (the value of one observation is not related to any other observation. In other words, one person's score should not provide any clue as to how any of the other people should score).
2. Variances on the dependent variable are equal across groups.
3. The dependent variable is normally distributed for each group.

Because ANOVA is robust, it can be used when variances are only approximately equal if the number of subjects in each group is equal. ANOVA also is robust if the dependent variable data are even approximately normally distributed. Thus, if assumption #2, or, even more so, #3 is not fully met, you may still be able to use ANOVA. There are also several choices of post hoc tests to use depending on whether the assumption of equal variances has been violated. **Dunnett's C** and **Games Howell** are appropriate post hoc tests if the assumption of equal variances is violated.

10.1. Are there differences among the three *father's education revised* groups on *grades in high school, visualization test* scores, and *math achievement*?

We will use the **One-Way ANOVA** procedure because we have one independent variable with three ordered levels. SPSS allows us to do several one-way ANOVAs at a time so we will do three ANOVAs in this problem, one for each of the three dependent variables. Note that you could do MANOVA (see Fig. 6.1) instead of three ANOVAs, especially if the dependent variables are correlated and conceptually related, but that is beyond the scope of this book. See our companion book (Leech et al., 2004).

To do the three one-way ANOVAs, use the following commands:

- **Analyze** => **Compare Means** => **One-Way ANOVA**.
- Move *grades in h.s., visualization test,* and *math achievement* into the **Dependent List** box in Fig. 10.1.
- Click on *father's educ revised* and move it to the **Factor** (independent variable)box.
- Finally, click on **Options** and choose **Descriptives** and **Homogeneity of variance**. See Fig. 10.2.

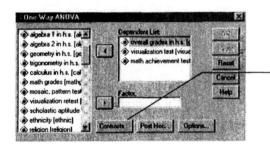

Fig. 10.1. One-way ANOVA.

Note: Instead of doing post hoc (after the fact) tests, you could do planned contrasts if you have a prediction about expected differences or trends.

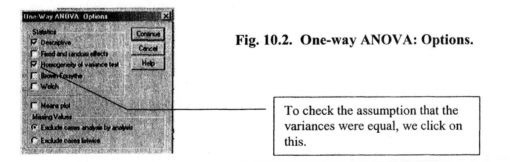

Fig. 10.2. One-way ANOVA: Options.

To check the assumption that the variances were equal, we click on this.

- Click on **Continue** then **OK**. Compare your output to Output 10.1.

Output 10.1. One-Way ANOVA

```
ONEWAY
  grades visual mathach BY faedRevis
  /STATISTICS DESCRIPTIVES HOMOGENEITY
  /MISSING ANALYSIS .
```

SPSS for Introductory Statistics

Means to be compared.

Descriptives

		N	Mean	Std. Deviation	Std. Error	95% Confidence Interval for Mean Lower Bound	Upper Bound	Minimum	Maximum
grades in h.s.	HS grad or less	38	5.34	1.475	.239	4.86	5.83	3	8
	Some College	16	5.56	1.788	.447	4.61	6.52	2	8
	BS or More	19	6.53	1.219	.280	5.94	7.11	4	8
	Total	73	5.70	1.552	.182	5.34	6.06	2	8
visualization test	HS grad or less	38	4.6711	3.96058	.64249	3.3692	5.9729	-.25	14.8
	Some College	16	6.0156	4.56022	1.14005	3.5857	8.4456	-.25	14.8
	BS or More	19	5.4605	2.79044	.64017	4.1156	6.8055	-.25	9.75
	Total	73	5.1712	3.82787	.44802	4.2781	6.0643	-.25	14.8
math achievement test	HS grad or less	38	10.0877	5.61297	.91054	8.2428	11.9326	1.00	22.7
	Some College	16	14.3958	4.66544	1.16636	11.9098	16.8819	5.00	23.7
	BS or More	19	16.3509	7.40918	1.69978	12.7798	19.9221	1.00	23.7
	Total	73	12.6621	6.49659	.76037	11.1463	14.1779	1.00	23.7

The Levene Test is significant for *math achievement* so the variances are significantly different. Note: This tests an assumption of ANOVA; not the central hypotheses.

Test of Homogeneity of Variances

	Levene Statistic	df1	df2	Sig.
grades in h.s.	1.546	2	70	.220
visualization test	1.926	2	70	.153
math achievement test	3.157	2	70	.049

a Groups with only one case are ignored in computing the test of homogeneity of variance for grades in h.s.
b Groups with only one case are ignored in computing the test of homogeneity of variance for visualization test.
c Groups with only one case are ignored in computing the test of homogeneity of variance for math achievement test.

ANOVA

		Sum of Squares	df	Mean Square	F	Sig.
grades in h.s.	Between Groups	18.143	2	9.071	4.091	.021
	Within Groups	155.227	70	2.218		
	Total	173.370	72			
visualization test	Between Groups	22.505	2	11.252	.763	.470
	Within Groups	1032.480	70	14.750		
	Total	1054.985	72			
math achievement test	Between Groups	558.481	2	279.240	7.881	.001
	Within Groups	2480.324	70	35.433		
	Total	3038.804	72			

These are the degrees of freedom: 2, 70.

The between group differences for *grades in high school* and *math achievement* are significant (p<.05) while those for *visualization* are not.

150

Interpretation of Output 10.1

The first table, **Descriptives,** provides familiar descriptive statistics for the three father's education groups on each of the three dependent variables that we requested (*grades, visualization test,* and *math achievement,*) for this analysis. Remember that although these three dependent variables appear together in each of the tables, <u>we have really computed three separate one-way ANOVAs.</u>

The second table (**Test of Homogeneity of Variances**) provides the <u>Levene test to check the assumption</u> that the variances of the three *father's education* groups are equal; i.e., not significantly different. Notice that for *grades* (*p*=.220) and *visualization* (*p*=.153) the Levene tests are *not* significant. Thus, the assumption is *not* violated. However, for *math achievement, p*=.049; therefore, the Levene test is significant and, thus, the assumption of equal variances is violated. In this latter case, we could use the similar nonparametric test (Kruskal-Wallis). Or, if the overall *F* is significant (as you can see it was in the ANOVA table), you could use a post hoc test designed for situations in which the variances are unequal. We will do the latter in Problem 2 and the former in Problem 3 for *math achievement.*

The **ANOVA** table in Output 10.1 is the key table because it shows whether the overall *F*s for these three ANOVAs were significant. Note that the three *father's education* groups differ significantly on *grades and math achievement* but not *visualization.* When reporting these findings one should write, for example, $F(2, 70)=4.09, p=.021$, for *grades.* The 2, 70 (circled for *grades* in the ANOVA table) are the degrees of freedom (*df*) for the between groups "effect" and within-groups "error," respectively. *F tables* also usually include the mean squares, which indicates the amount of variance (sums of squares) for that "effect" divided by the degrees of freedom for that "effect." You also should report the means (and SDs) so that one can see which groups were high and low. Remember, however, that if you have three or more groups you will not know which specific pairs of means are significantly different, unless you do a post hoc or a priori comparison test, as shown in Problem 10.2. We provide an example of appropriate APA-format tables and how to write about these ANOVAs after Problem 10.2.

Problem 10.2: Post Hoc Multiple Comparison Tests

Now, we will introduce the concept of **post hoc multiple comparisons**, sometimes called **follow-up tests**. When you <u>compare three or more group means</u>, you will know that there will be a statistically significant <u>difference somewhere</u> if the **ANOVA** *F* (sometimes called the **overall** *F* or **omnibus** *F*) is significant.

However, we would usually like to know which specific means are different from which other ones. In order to know this, you can use *one* of several post hoc tests that are built into the SPSS one-way ANOVA program. The **LSD** post hoc test is quite liberal and the **Scheffe** test is quite conservative so many statisticians recommend a more middle of the road test such as the **Tukey HSD** (honestly significant differences) test, if the Levene test was not significant, or the **Games-Howell** test, if the Levene test was significant. Ordinarily, you <u>do post hoc tests only if the overall *F* is significant</u>. For this reason, we have separated Problems 1 and 2, which could have been done in one step. Fig. 10.3 shows the steps one should use in deciding whether to use post hoc multiple comparison tests.

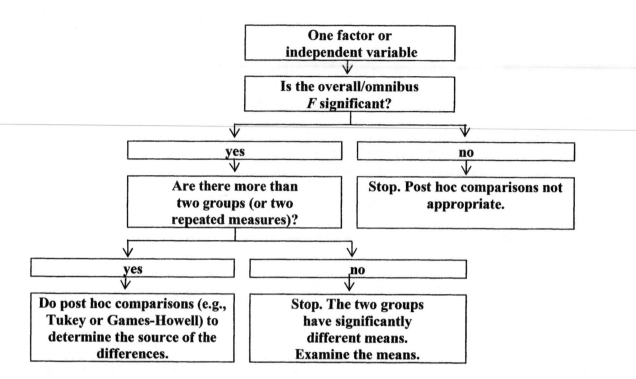

Fig. 10.3. Schematic representation of when to use post hoc multiple comparisons with a one-way ANOVA.

10.2.   If the overall F is significant, which pairs of means are significantly different?

After you have examined Output 10.1 to see if the overall F (ANOVA) for each variable was significant, you will do appropriate post hoc multiple comparisons for the statistically significant variables. We will use the **Tukey HSD** if variances can be assumed to be equal (i.e., the Levene's Test is *not* significant) and the **Games-Howell** if the assumption of equal variances can not be justified (i.e., the Levene's Test is significant).

First we will do the Tukey HSD for *grades*. Get the **One-Way ANOVA** dialog box *again* by doing the following:
- Select **Analyze => Compare Means => One-Way ANOVA** to see Fig. 10.1 again.
- Move *visualization* out of the **Dependent List** by highlighting it and clicking on the arrow pointing left because the overall F for *visualization* was not significant. (See interpretation for Output 10.1.)
- Also move *math achievement* to the left because the Levene test for it <u>was</u> significant. (We will use it below.)
- Keep *grades* in the **Dependent List** because it had a significant ANOVA, and the Levene test was not significant.
- Insure that *father's educ revised* is in the **Factor** box.
- Next, click on **Options** and remove the check for **Descriptive** and **Homogeneity of Variances** (in Fig. 10.2) because we do not need to do them again; they would be the same.
- Then click on **Continue**.
- In the main dialogue box (Fig. 10.1), click on **Post Hoc** to get Fig. 10.4.
- Check **Tukey** because, for *grades,* the Levene test was not significant so we assume that the variances are approximately equal.

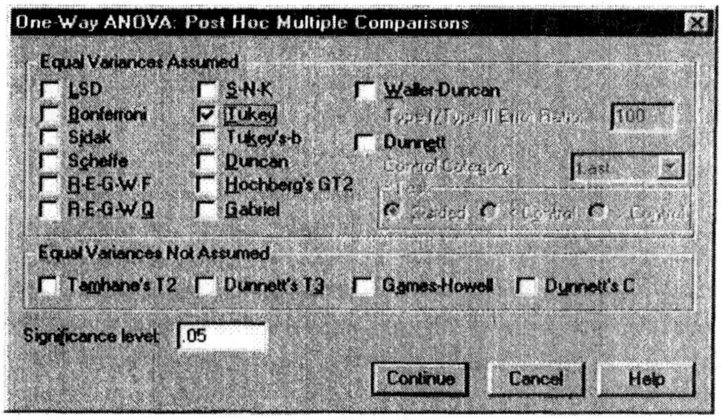

Fig. 10.4. One-way ANOVA: Post hoc multiple comparisons.

- Click on **Continue** and then **OK** to run this post hoc test.

Compare your output to Output 10.2a

Output 10.2a

```
ONEWAY
  grades BY faedRevis
  /MISSING ANALYSIS
  /POSTHOC = TUKEY ALPHA(.05).
```

ANOVA

grades in h.s.

	Sum of Squares	df	Mean Square	F	Sig.
Between Groups	18.143	2	9.071	4.091	.021
Within Groups	155.227	70	2.218		
Total	173.370	72			

Post Hoc Tests

The Tukey HSD is a common post hoc test to use when variances are equal. This table is most appropriate when the group *n*s are similar. Here they are quite different.

Multiple Comparisons

Dependent Variable: grades in h.s.
Tukey HSD

(I) father's education revised	(J) father's education revised	Mean Difference (I-J)	Std. Error	Sig.	95% Confidence Interval	
					Lower Bound	Upper Bound
HS grad or less	Some College	-.22	.444	.873	-1.28	.84
	BS or More	-1.18*	.418	.017	-2.19	-.18
Some College	HS grad or less	.22	.444	.873	-.84	1.28
	BS or More	-.96	.505	.144	-2.17	.25
BS or More	HS grad or less	1.18*	.418	.017	.18	2.19
	Some College	.96	.505	.144	-.25	2.17

*. The mean difference is significant at the .05 level.

These are the differences between the means and the significance levels you would use if the group sizes were similar. Ignore duplicates.

Homogeneous Subsets

grades in h.s.

Tukey HSD[a,b]

father's education revised	N	Subset for alpha = .05	
		1	2
HS grad or less	38	5.34	
Some College	16	5.56	5.56
BS or More	19		6.53
Sig.		.880	.096

Means for groups in homogeneous subsets are displayed.

a. Uses Harmonic Mean Sample Size = 21.209.

b. The group sizes are unequal. The harmonic mean of the group sizes is used. Type I error levels are not guaranteed.

> This way of computing and displaying the post hoc tests is more appropriate when group sizes are quite different. Groups listed in the same subset are not significantly different. Thus, the grades of students whose father's were *HS grads or less* are not different from those whose father's had *some college*. Likewise, those with *some college* are not different from those with a *BS or more*, but *HS grads or less* are different from those with a *BS or more*.

After you do the Tukey test, let's go back and do **Games-Howell**. Follow these steps:

- Select **Analyze => Compare Means => One-Way ANOVA**.
- Move *grades* out of the **Dependent List** by highlighting it and clicking on the arrow pointing left.
- Move *math achievement* into the **Dependent List box**.
- Insure that *father's educ revised* is still in the **Factor** box.
- In the main dialogue box (Fig. 10.1), press **Post Hoc** to get Fig. 10.4.
- Check **Games-Howell** because equal variances cannot be assumed for *math achievement*.
- Remove the check mark from Tukey.
- Click on **Continue** and then **OK** to run this post hoc test.
- Compare your syntax and output to Output 10.2b.

Output 10.2b

```
ONEWAY
  mathach BY faedRevis
  /MISSING ANALYSIS
  /POSTHOC = GH ALPHA(.05).
```

ANOVA

math achievement test

	Sum of Squares	df	Mean Square	F	Sig.
Between Groups	558.481	2	279.240	7.881	.001
Within Groups	2480.324	70	35.433		
Total	3038.804	72			

Post Hoc Tests

Use Games-Howell when the Levene test indicates that the variances are unequal.

Multiple Comparisons

Dependent Variable: math achievement test

Games-Howell

(I) father's education revised	(J) father's education revised	Mean Difference (I-J)	Std. Error	Sig.	95% Confidence Interval	
					Lower Bound	Upper Bound
HS grad or less	Some College	-4.3081*	1.47969	.017	-7.9351	-.6811
	BS or More	-6.2632*	1.92830	.008	-11.0284	-1.4980
Some College	HS grad or less	4.3081*	1.47969	.017	.6811	7.9351
	BS or More	-1.9551	2.06147	.614	-7.0308	3.1205
BS or More	HS grad or less	6.2632*	1.92830	.008	1.4980	11.0284
	Some College	1.9551	2.06147	.614	-3.1205	7.0308

*. The mean difference is significant at the .05 level.

Interpretation of Output 10.2

The first table in both 10.2a and 10.2b repeats appropriate parts of the **ANOVA** table from Output 10.1. The second table in 10.2a shows the **Tukey HSD** test for *grades* that you would use if the three group sizes (*n*=38, 16, 19 from the first table in Output 10.1) had been similar. For *grades*, this Tukey table indicates that there is only a small mean difference (.22) between the mean grades of students whose fathers were *high school grads or less* (*M* = 5.34 from Output 10.1) and those fathers who had *some college* (*M*=5.56). The **Homogenous Subsets** table shows an adjusted Tukey that is appropriate when group sizes are not similar, as in this case. Note that there is not a statistically significant difference (*p*=.880) between the grades of students whose fathers were *high school grads or less* (low education) and those with *some college* (medium education) because their means are both shown in **Subset 1**. In **Subset 2,** the medium and high education group means are shown, indicating that they are not significantly different (*p*=.096). By examining the two subset boxes, we can see that the low education group (*M*=5.34) is different from the high education group (*M*=6.53) because these two means do not appear in the same subset.

Output 10.2b shows, for *math achievement,* the **Games-Howell** test, which we use for variables that have unequal variances. Note that each comparison is presented twice. The **Mean Difference** between students whose fathers were *high school grads or less* and those with fathers who had *some college* was -4.31. The **Sig**. (*p* =.017) indicates that this is a significant difference. We can also tell that this difference is significant because the confidence interval's lower and upper bounds both have minus signs. Similarly, students whose fathers had a *B.S. degree* were significantly different on *math achievement* from those whose fathers had a *high school degree or less* (*p*=.008).

An Example of how to Write About Output 10.1 and 10.2.

Results

A statistically significant difference was found among the three levels of father's education on grades in high school, *F* (2, 70) = 4.09, *p* = .021, and on math achievement, *F* (2, 70) = 7.88, *p* = .001. Table 10.2a shows that the mean grades in high school is 5.34 for students whose father's had low education, 5.56 for students whose father's attended some college (medium), and 6.53 for students whose father's received a BS or more (high). Post hoc Tukey HSD Tests indicate that the low education group and high education group differed significantly in their grades (*p*<.05, *d*=.85). Likewise, there were also significant mean differences on math achievement between the low education and both the medium education group (*p*<.017, *d*=.80) and the high education group (*p*=.008, *d*=1.0) using the Games-Howell post hoc test.

Table 10.2a

Means and Standard Deviations Comparing Three Father's Education Groups

		Grades in H.S.		Math Achievement		Visualization	
Father's Education	*n*	*M*	*SD*	*M*	*SD*	*M*	*SD*
HS grad or less (low)	38	5.34	1.48	10.09	5.61	4.67	3.96
Some college (medium)	16	5.56	1.79	14.40	4.67	6.02	4.56
BS or more (high)	19	6.53	1.22	16.35	7.41	5.46	2.79
Total	73	5.70	1.55	12.66	6.50	5.17	3.83

Table 10.2b

One-Way Analysis of Variance Summary Table Comparing Father's Education Groups on Grades in High School, Math Achievement, and Visualization Test

Source	*df*	SS	*MS*	*F*	*p*
Grades in High School					
Between groups	2	18.14	9.07	4.09	.021
Within groups	70	155.23	2.22		
Total	72	173.37			
Math Achievement					
Between groups	2	558.48	279.24	7.88	.001
Within groups	70	2480.32	35.43		
Total	72	3038.80			
Visualization Test					
Between groups	2	22.51	11.25	.76	.470
Within groups	70	1032.48	14.75		
Total	72	1054.99			

Problem 10.3: Nonparametric Kruskal-Wallis Test

What else can you do if the homogeneity of variance assumption is violated (or if your data are ordinal)? The answer is a nonparametric statistic. Let's make comparisons similar to Problem 1, assuming that the data are ordinal or the assumption of equality of group variances is violated.

Remember that the variances for the three fathers' education groups were significantly different on *math achievement*, and the *competence* scale was not normally distributed (see Chapter 4).

10.3. Are there statistically significant differences among the three father's education groups on *math achievement* and the *competence scale?*

Follow these commands:

- **Analyze => Nonparametric Test => K Independent Samples**.
- Move the dependent variables of *math achievement* and *competence* to the **Test Variable List** (see Fig. 10.5).
- Move the independent variable *father's educ revised* to the **Grouping Variable** box.
- Click on **Define Range** and insert **1** and **3** into the **minimum** and **maximum** boxes (Fig. 10.6) because *faedRevis* has values of 1, 2, and 3.
- Click on **Continue**.
- Ensure that **Kruskal-Wallis H** (under **Test Type**) in the main dialogue box is checked.
- Then, click on **OK**. Do your results look like Output 10.3?

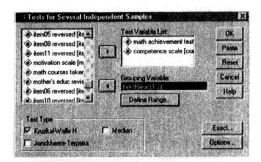

Fig. 10.5. Tests for several independent samples.

Fig. 10.6. Define.

Output 10.3: Kruskal-Wallis Nonparametric Tests

```
NPAR TESTS
  /K-W=mathach competence   BY faedRevis(1 3)
  /MISSING ANALYSIS.
```

High mean ranks indicate high *math achievement* and *competence* scores.

Ranks

	father's education revised	N	Mean Rank
math achievement test	HS grad or less	38	28.43
	Some College	16	43.78
	BS or More	19	48.42
	Total	73	
Competence scale	HS grad or less	37	36.04
	Some College	16	35.78
	BS or More	18	36.11
	Total	71	

157

Kruskal-Wallis Test

Test Statistics [a,b]

	math achievement test	Competence scale
Chi-Square	13.384	.003
df	2	2
Asymp. Sig.	.001	.999

a. Kruskal Wallis Test

b. Grouping Variable: father's education revised

Interpretation of Output 10.3

As in the case of the Mann-Whitney test (Chapter 9), the **Ranks** table provides **Mean Ranks** for the two dependent variables, *math achievement* and *competence*. In this case, the **Kruskal-Wallis** test will compare the mean ranks for the three *father's education* groups.

The **Test Statistics** table shows whether there is an overall difference among the three groups. Notice that the p (sig.) value for *math achievement* is .001, which is the same as it was in Output 10.1 using the One-Way ANOVA. This is because K-W and ANOVA have similar power to detect a difference. Note also that there is not a significant difference among the father's education groups on the *competence scale* (p=.999).

Unfortunately, there are not post hoc tests built into the K-W test, as there are for the one-way ANOVA. Thus, you cannot tell which of the pairs of father's education means are different on *math achievement*. One method to check this would be to run three Mann-Whitney (M-W) tests comparing each pair of *father's education* mean ranks. Note, you would only do the post hoc M-W tests if the K-W test was statistically significant; thus, so you would not do the M-W for *competence*. It also would be prudent to adjust the significance level by dividing .05 by 3 (the Bonferonni correction) so that you would require that the M-W Sig.<.017 to be statistically significant.

Problem 10.4: Two-Way (or Factorial) ANOVA

In the previous problems, we compared two or more groups based on the levels of only one independent variable or factor using t tests and one-way ANOVA. These were called single factor designs. In this problem, we will compare groups based on *two* independent variables. The appropriate statistic for this is called a two-way or factorial ANOVA. This statistic is used when there are two different independent variables with a between groups design.

10.4. Do *math grades* (not grades in h.s.) and *gender* each seem to have an effect on *math achievement*, and do *math grades* and *gender* interact?

Follow these commands:

*   **Analyze => General Linear Model => Univariate**.
*   Move *math achievement* to the **Dependent** (variable) box.
*   Move the first independent variable, *math grades*, to the **Fixed Factor(s)** box.
*   Then, also move the second independent variable, *gender*, to the **Fixed Factor(s)** box (see Fig. 10.7).

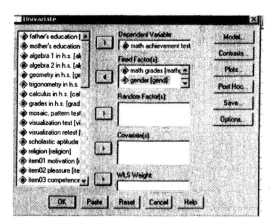

Fig. 10.7. GLM -Univariate.

Now that we know the variables we will be dealing with, let's determine our options.
- Click on **Plots** and move *mathgr* to the **horizontal axis** and *gender* to **Separate Lines** box.
- Then press **Add**. Your window should now look like Fig. 10.8.
- Click on **Continue** to get back to Fig. 10.7.

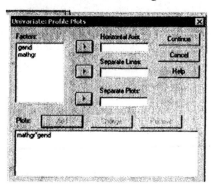

Fig. 10.8. Univariate: Profile plots.

- Select **Options** and click **Descriptive statistics** and **Estimates of effect size**. See Fig. 10.9.
- Click on **Continue**.
- Click on **OK**. Compare your syntax and output to Output 10.4.

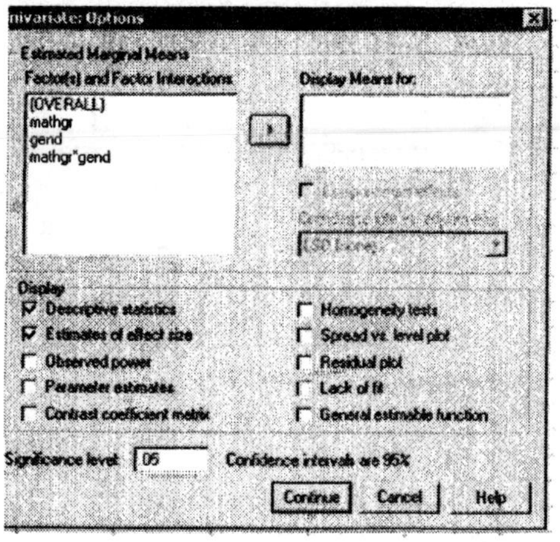

Fig. 10.9. General factorial:
Options.

Output 10.4: Two-Way ANOVA

```
UNIANOVA
  mathach  BY mathgr gender
  /METHOD = SSTYPE(3)
  /INTERCEPT = INCLUDE
  /PLOT = PROFILE( mathgr*gender )
  /PRINT = DESCRIPTIVE ETASQ
  /CRITERIA = ALPHA(.05)
  /DESIGN = mathgr gender mathgr*gender.
```

Between-Subjects Factors

		Value Label	N
math grades	0	less A-B	44
	1	most A-B	31
gender	0	male	34
	1	female	41

Descriptive Statistics

Dependent Variable: math achievement test

math grades	gender	Mean	Std. Deviation	N
less A-B	male	12.8751	5.73136	24
	female	8.3333	5.32563	20
	Total	10.8106	5.94438	44
most A-B	male	19.2667	4.17182	10
	female	13.0476	7.16577	21
	Total	15.0538	6.94168	31
Total	male	14.7550	6.03154	34
	female	10.7479	6.69612	41
	Total	12.5645	6.67031	75

> The cell means are important for interpreting factorial ANOVAs and describing the results.

Tests of Between-Subjects Effects

Dependent Variable: math achievement test

Source	Type III Sum of Squares	df	Mean Square	F	Sig.	Partial Eta Squared
Corrected Model	814.481[a]	3	271.494	7.779	.000	.247
Intercept	11971.773	1	11971.773	343.017	.000	.829
MATHGR	515.463	1	515.463	14.769	.000	.172
GEND	483.929	1	483.929	13.866	.000	.163
MATHGR * GEND	11.756	1	11.756	.337	.563	.005
Error	2478.000	71	34.901			
Total	15132.393	75				
Corrected Total	3292.481	74				

a. R Squared = .247 (Adjusted R Squared = .216)

> These *F*s and significance levels tell you important information about differences between means and the interaction.

> Percent of variance in *math achievement* predictable from both independent variables.

> Eta squared is an index of the effect size. Thus, about 17% of the variance in *math achievement* can be predicted from *math grades*.

Estimated Marginal Means of math achievement test

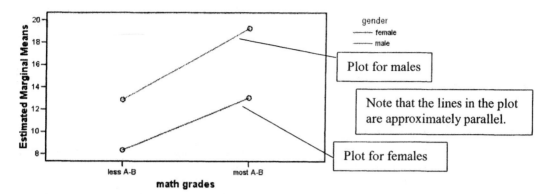

Interpretation of Output 10.4

The GLM Univariate program allows you to print the means for each sub group (cell). It also provides measures of effect size (eta^2), and plots the interaction, which is helpful in interpreting it. The first table in Output 10.4 shows that 75 participants (44 with less than A-B math grades and 31 mostly A-B math grades) are included in the analysis because they had data on all of the variables. The **Descriptive Statistics** table shows the cell and marginal (total) means; both are very important for interpreting the ANOVA table and explaining the results of the test for the interaction.

The ANOVA table, called **Tests of Between Subjects Effects**, is the key table. Note that the word "effect" in the title of the table can be misleading because this study was not a randomized experiment. Thus, you cannot say in your report that the differences in the dependent variable were *caused* by or the effect of the independent variable. Usually you will ignore the corrected model and intercept lines and skip down to the **interaction** *F* (*mathgr * gend*) that, in this case, is not statistically significant, $F(1,71)=.337$, $p=.563$. If the interaction was significant, we would need to be cautious about the interpretation of the main effects because they could be misleading.

Next we examine the main effects of *math grades* and of *gender*. Note that both are statistically significant. The significant *F* for *math grades* means that students with less than an A-B math average scored lower ($M = 10.81$ vs. 15.05) on *math achievement* than those with high math grades; and this difference is statistically significant ($p<.001$). *Gender* is also significant ($p < .001$). Because the interaction (*mathgr*gend*) is not significant, the "effect" of *math grades* on *math achievement* is about the same for both genders. If the interaction were significant, we would say that the "effect" of math grades depended on which gender you were considering. For example, it might be large for boys and small for girls. If you find a significant interaction you should examine the **profile plots** of cell means to visualize the differential effects. When the lines on the profile plot are parallel there is not a significant interaction. If the interaction is significant, you should also analyze the differences between cell means (the simple effects).

Note also the callout boxes about the adjusted *R* squared and eta squared. Eta, the correlation ratio, is used when the independent variable is *nominal* and the dependent variable (*math achievement* in this problem) is normal. Eta is an indicator of the proportion of variance that is due to between groups differences. Adjusted R^2 refers to the multiple correlation coefficient squared. Like r^2, these statistics indicate how much variance or variability in the dependent variable can be predicted if you know the independent variable scores. In this problem, the eta^2 percentages for these key *F*s vary from .5% to 17.2%. Because eta and *R*, like *r*, are indexes of association, they can be used to interpret the effect size. However, the rules for small, medium, and large are somewhat different (for eta, small= .10, medium=.24, and large=.37; for R, small=.14, medium= .36, and large=.51).

In this example, eta (not squared) for *math grades* is about .42 and, thus, a large effect. Eta for *gender* is about .40, a large effect. The overall adjusted R is about .46, almost a large effect. Notice that the adjusted R^2 is lower than the unadjusted (.22 versus .25). The reason for this is that the adjusted R^2 takes into account (and adjusts for) the fact that not just one but three factors (*math grades, gender*, and the interaction) were used to predict *math achievement*.

An important point to remember is that statistical significance depends heavily on the sample size so that with 1000 subjects a much lower F or r will be significant than if the sample is 10 or even 100. Statistical significance just tells you that you can be quite sure that there is at least a little relationship between the independent and dependent variables. Effect size measures, which are more independent of sample size, tell you how strong the relationship is and, thus, give you some indication of its importance.

An Example of How to Write About Output 10.4
Results

Table 10.4a shows the means and standard deviations for math achievement separately for the two genders and math grades groups. Table 10.4b shows that there was not a significant interaction between gender and math grades on math achievement ($p = .563$). There was, however, a significant main effect of gender on math achievement, $F(1,71) = 13.87$, $p < .001$. Eta for gender was about .42, which, according to Cohen (1988), is a large effect. Furthermore, there was a significant main effect of math grades on math achievement, $F(1,71) = 14.77$, $p < .001$. Eta for math grades was about .40, a large effect.

Table 10.4a

Means, Standard Deviations, and n for Math Achievement as a Function of Gender and Math Grades

Math Grade	Males			Females			Total	
	n	*M*	*SD*	*n*	*M*	*SD*	*M*	*SD*
Less A-B	24	12.88	5.73	20	8.33	5.33	10.81	5.94
Most A-B	10	19.27	4.17	21	13.05	7.17	15.05	6.94
Total	34	14.76	6.03	41	10.75	6.70	12.56	6.67

Table 10.4b

Analysis of Variance for Math Achievement as a Function of Gender and Math Grades

Variable and source	df	MS	F	η^2
Math Achievement				
Math Grades	1	515.46	14.77**	.172
Gender	1	483.93	13.87**	.163
Math Grades*Gender	1	11.76	.34	.005
Error	71	34.90		

** $p < .001$

Interpretation Questions

10.1. In Output 10.1: a) Describe the *F*, *df*, and *p* values for each dependent variable as you would in an article. b) Describe the results in nontechnical terms for visualization and grades. Use the group means in your description.

10.2. In Outputs 10.2 a and b what pairs of means were significantly different?

10.3. In Output 10.3, interpret the meaning of the sig. values for math achievement and competence. What would you conclude, based on this information, about differences between groups on each of these variables?

10.4. Compare Outputs 10.1 and 10.3 in regards to math achievement. What are the most important differences and similarities?

10.5. In Output 10.4: a) Is the interaction significant? b) Examine the profile plot of the cell means that illustrates the interaction. Describe it in words. c) Is the main effect of gender significant? Interpret the eta squared. d) How about the "effect" of math grades? e) Why did we put the word effect in quotes? f) Under what conditions would focusing on the main effects be misleading?

Extra SPSS Problems

Using your College Student data file, do the following problems. Print your outputs after typing your interpretations on them. Please circle the key parts of the output that you use for your interpretation.

10.1. Identify an example of a variable measured at the scale/normally distributed level for which there is a statistically significant overall difference (*F*) between the three marital status groups. Complete the analysis and interpret the results. Do appropriate post hoc tests.

10.2. Use the Kruskal-Wallis test, with Mann-Whitney post hoc follow-up tests if needed, to run the same problem as 10.1. Compare the results.

10.3. Do gender and marital status seem to have an effect on student's height and do gender and marital status interact? Run the appropriate SPSS analysis and interpret the results.

10.4. Do gender and having children interact and do either seem to affect current GPA?

10.5. Are there differences between the age groups in regard to the average number of hours they a) study, b) work, and c) watch TV?

APPENDIX A

Quick Reference Guide

Joan Naden Clay and Laura Jensen

Introduction

The Quick Reference Guide is intended as a supplemental resource to use while the SPSS program is open. It provides a brief overview of many of the most basic and commonly utilized procedures in SPSS. This guide presents one basic method for accomplishing each command, however, there are often multiple ways to accomplish any given task in SPSS. The intent of this guide is to provide a brief description of each subject area in addition to giving step-by-step directions for performing specific actions for each subject.

Throughout the Quick Reference Guide, each subject area (e.g., variable, cell, file) is organized alphabetically and written in *ALL CAPITAL, BOLD ITALICS*. Common actions (e.g., cut, paste, insert) are itemized for each subject and are indicated with an arrow. Stepwise directions for functions are designated with a round bullet. Items within the stepwise directions that are bolded indicate either that the user should select the item with the click of the mouse or represent window items that require you to make a selection. Each step of a function is sequentially represented with arrows. For example, the instructions to *Open a File* would be: **File** (select the word "file" in the header) => **Open** (select the word "open" in the drop down window) => **Data** (select the word data in the subsequent drop down menu) =>using the **Files of Type** pull down menu (click the arrow on the "Files of Type" window to get the drop down men), choose the type of data file to bring into SPSS=>locate the file=>double click on the file name.

SPSS Commands

BAR CHARTS Bar charts are useful for displaying frequency information for categorical data and SPSS allows several options for creating them. Types of bar charts available include: **simple** (presents a single bar for each category, case or variable); **clustered** (presents a group of bars on the category axis and bars within a cluster can represent groups of cases, separate variables or individual cases); and **stacked** (there is one bar stack for each category, case, or variable on the category axis and segments of each stack can represent groups of cases, separate variables, or individual cases).

- **Graphs** => **Bar** => select type of chart (simple, clustered, or stacked) => choose if the **Data in Chart Are** either summaries for groups of cases, summaries of separate variables, or values of individual cases => **Define** => at this point, the dialog box varies based on the type of chart and type of data to be displayed. Highlight variables and move them to the appropriate boxes (**bars represent, category axis, define clusters by, define stacks by**, etc.) by clicking the arrows. For summaries of groups of cases, choose if each **Bar Represents** the number of cases, cumulative cases, percent of cases, cumulative percent of cases, or other summary function => **Titles** => type in title, subtitles, and footnotes => **Continue** => **OK.**

BOX PLOTS This type of graphic provides a visual display of the distribution of data by presenting the median, quartiles, and extreme values for the category or variable. Box plots can be **simple** (with a single box plot for each category or variable) or **clustered** (has a cluster of plots for each category or variable on the category axis and the plots within each cluster are defined by a separate definition variable). Box plots are automatically generated by the **Explore** command or can be custom generated with the **Graphs** command.

- **Graphs** => **Boxplot** => select type of plot (simple or clustered) => choose if the **Data in Chart Are** either summaries for groups of cases or summaries of separate variables => **Define** => at this point, the dialog box varies based on the type of chart and type of data to be presented. Highlight variables and move them to the appropriate boxes (variable, category axis, define clusters by, label cases by, or boxes represent) => **OK**.

CASES are the individual records for each subject and are organized by rows for each record/case. SPSS numbers each case down the left side of the Data View window.

➤ *Insert Cases* This command allows data to be added for new subjects or cases anywhere in the dataset.

- Click on the case number below where the case is to be inserted => **Data** => **Insert Cases** => enter data for the new case.

➤ *List Cases (Case Summaries)* This command allows the user to list either an entire dataset or a subset of the data. Case summaries are especially helpful for ensuring that data are computed or entered correctly. Various options allow the user to select one or all variables, create an order for listing the cases using a grouping variable, limit the number of cases shown, and conduct basic descriptive statistics on the cases selected.

- **Analyze** => **Reports** => **Case Summaries** => select variables to be summarized with a left click => click the top arrow in the middle of the dialog box to move the selected variable to the **Variables** box => if desired, select categorical variables with a left click => click the bottom arrow in the middle of the dialog box to move the selected variable to the **Grouping Variables** box => utilize check boxes in lower left corner to display individual cases, limit number of cases show, show valid cases or show case numbers => **Statistics** => highlight desired statistic with a left click => click the arrow in the middle of the dialog to move the selected statistic to the **Cell Statistics** box => **Continue** => **OK**.

➤ *Select Cases* The select cases command permits the analysis of a specific subset of the data. Once a subset is selected the user can either revert back to the entire dataset or delete the unselected cases to create a subset data file. Users can **Select** data in a variety of ways including: **If condition is satisfied** (a conditional expression is used to select cases); **Random sample of cases** (cases are selected randomly based on a percent or number of cases); **Based on time or case range** (case selection is based on a range of case numbers or a range of dates/time); or, **Use filter variable** (a numeric variable can be used as the filter – any cases with a value other than 0 or missing are selected). **Unselected cases** may be **Filtered** (remain in data file, but excluded in the analysis) or **Deleted** (removed from the working data file and cannot be recovered if the data file is saved after the deletion).

- **Data** => **Select Cases** => **Select** (choose method: all cases, if condition is satisfied, random sample of cases, range, filter variable) => **Unselected cases are** (choose either filtered or deleted) => **OK**. (Save your work before deleting cases, just in case you change your mind!)

➢ **Sort Cases** This procedure allows the user to rearrange the order in which data are displayed using one or more variables of interest. Data can be sorted in **ascending** (small to large numbers or alphabetical) or **descending** (large to small numbers or reverse alphabetical) order.

- **Data** => **Sort Cases** => select a variable with a left click => click the arrow in the middle of the dialog box to move the variable to the **Sort By list** => choose either the **Ascending or Descending** display => **OK.**

CELLS A cell is a single data point where a row and column intersect within the dataset. Cells can be manipulated individually or in blocks. Data can be edited using **Copy** (puts a duplicate of the cell value(s) on the clipboard, but leaves original cells in place), **Cut** (puts the cell value(s) on the clipboard and deletes the original cell values), or **Paste** (inserts cell value(s) from the clipboard into cell(s) at a new location).

➢ **Copy and Paste Cells** This command makes a copy of data in a cell while leaving the original cell in place. The copy can be inserted in another location.

- Highlight the data (cell, row, column, etc.) to copy => **Edit** => **Copy** => click on the individual cell or the upper left cell of the group of cells to paste to (Note: <u>if data are pasted over already existing cells, the data in those cells will be erased! It may be necessary to create space by inserting variables or cases. Pay close attention to cell alignment.</u>) => **Edit** => **Paste.** (Save your work or experiment on a copy of your data, just in case the unexpected happens!).

➢ **Cut and Paste Cells** This command removes the data from a cell so you can insert it in a different location.

- Highlight data (cell, row, column, etc.) that you want to cut => **Edit** => **Cut** => click on the individual cell or the upper left cell of the group of cells you want to paste to (<u>If you paste data over already existing cells, the data in those cells will be erased! You may need to create space by inserting variables or cases. Pay close attention to your alignment.</u>) => **Edit** => **Paste.**

CHART EDITOR Existing charts may be edited using the SPSS chart editor. Common actions include adding titles, changing labels, altering color and fill patterns, and adjusting axis intervals.

- Double click on a chart in the output (chart appears in the **Chart Editor** window) => double click on the element of the chart to edit (**Palettes** window opens) => select appropriate tab of the palettes window => utilize various dialog boxes, check boxes, etc. to edit the element of interest => **Apply** (repeat process on all the various elements of the chart to edit).

CODEBOOK This feature allows information for all of the variables in the dataset to be printed including: variable names, measurement level, column width, number of decimal places, values and value labels.

- **Utilities** => **File Info** (the codebook is printed into the output).

DATA The values entered into the cells that are created by the intersection of the rows (cases) and columns (variables).

➤ *Copy Data* (see Cells – copy and paste or cut and paste).

➤ *Enter (Edit) Data* Values can be entered into blank cells or existing values may be changed.

- Left click the cell of interest => type (or edit) value => **Enter.**

➤ *Export Data* Datasets can be saved in other file formats for use in other applications (e.g., other versions of SPSS, Excel, dBASE, SAS).

- **File** => **Save As** => click the drop down arrow in the **Save as type** dialog box => select the file type => type the file name in the **File name** dialog box => click the drop down arrow in the **Save in** dialog box => select a drive or folder for the file => **Save.**

➤ *Import Data* This command copies data from a word document and pastes it into SPSS.

- In the word document, highlight the data to be pasted into SPSS => in the Data View of SPSS, set the mouse on the first cell to receive the incoming data => **Edit** => **Paste.**
- Alternatively, in the word document, highlight the data to be pasted into SPSS => in the Data View of SPSS, set the mouse on the first cell to receive the incoming data => right click to **Paste.**

➤ *Open Data* See Files (Open Data File).

➤ *Print Data* This command allows some or all of the data to be printed.

- *Print All Data* With the database open go to Data View => **File** => **Print** => in the **Print Range** dialog box use the radio button to select **All** => **OK.**
- *Print Selected Data* With the database open go to Data View => highlight the cells to print => **File** => **Print** => in the **Print Range** dialog box use the radio button to select **Selection** => **OK.**

➤ *Save Data* This command should be used often to avoid losing work!

- *Initially saving a new dataset* **File** => **Save** => (**Save Data As** dialog box appears) select the appropriate drive and folder using the **Save in** drop down menu => type the file name in the **File Name** dialog box => select SPSS (*.sav) in the **Save as type** dialog box => **Save.**
- *Resaving an existing dataset under the same filename* **File** => **Save.** (SPSS automatically resaves the data using the existing filename).
- *Saving existing dataset under a different filename* **File** => **Save As** => select the appropriate drive and folder using the **Save in** drop down menu => type the file name in the **File Name** dialog box => select SPSS (*.sav) in the **Save as type** dialog box => **Save.**

EXPLORE DATA This command produces summary statistics and graphical displays for entire datasets or selected subsets. This command is useful for screening data, generating descriptive information, checking assumptions and looking for differences among groups of cases.

- **Analyze** => **Descriptive Statistics** => **Explore** => highlight one or more dependent variables to explore and move them to the **Dependent List** box by clicking the arrow => if desired, move one or more categorical variables to the **Factor List** box in order to obtain separate analyses for groups of cases based upon the factor => **Statistics** => check desired statistics => **Continue** => **Plots** => select types of plots desired using (box plots, stem-and-leaf, histogram, normality plots) => **Continue** => **OK.**

FILES There are three different common file types in SPSS (data, output, and syntax) that are differentiated with unique file extensions (data = .sav; output = .spo; syntax = .sps). Script is a fourth type of SPSS file and is designated with a .sbs extension, however, discussion of script files is beyond the scope of this chapter. Each of the different file types will open in its own type of window. Data files are presented in the **SPSS Data Editor** window, output files are displayed in the **SPSS Viewer**, and syntax is viewed in the **SPSS Syntax Editor**. (Only one data file can be open in any one session.)

➤ *Create a New File* This command will open a blank file. Remember to save files frequently as you generate data, output and syntax!

  - *New Data File (.sav)* **File** => **New** => **Data** => see chapter 2 for information about entering data (Remember to save your work frequently!).
  - *New Output File (.spo)* **File** => **New** => **Output** => this provides a blank SPSS Viewer (SPSS will automatically open the SPSS Viewer when the first analysis is run, however, more than one SPSS viewer/output file can be open at any given time).
  - *New Syntax File (.sps)* **File** => **New** => **Syntax** => this provides a blank syntax editor – syntax can be typed directly into the editor or pasted in from a word processing program (e.g., Word). Information about writing syntax can be found in the SPSS Syntax Reference Guide in the Help Menu – **Help** => **Syntax Guide** => **Base** => this opens an Adobe portable document format (PDF) file that can be printed or viewed online (Adobe Reader software is required to open this file and is available free online at www.adobe.com).

➤ *Open File* This command helps locate and open existing files (data, output, syntax). The dialog box provides a pull down menu that allows for the selection of the type of data file to import/open.

  - *Open Data File* **File** => **Open** => **Data** => use the **Look In** drop down menu to select the appropriate directory/folder => using the **Files of Type** pull down menu, choose the type of data file to bring into SPSS. Common file types and file name extensions include SPSS (.sav), Excel (.xls), and dBase Files (.dbf). In searching for the data file to open, only those files of the specified type will be shown in the dialog box => locate the desired file, select the file name with a left click => **Open.** *(Only one data file can be open in any given session.)*
  - *Open Output File* **File** => **Open** => **Output** => use the **Look In** drop down menu to select the appropriate directory/folder => using the **Files of Type** pull down menu, choose **.spo** => when you locate the file you want, select the file name with a left click => **Open.**
  - *Open Syntax File* **File** => **Open** => **Syntax** => use the **Look In** drop down menu to select the appropriate directory/folder => using the **Files of Type** pull down menu, choose **.sps** => locate the desired file, select the file name with a left click => **Open.**

➤ **Save File** This command should be performed frequently to prevent unwanted loss of work! The first time a file is saved, the **Save As** dialog box will appear to allow the selection of a directory/folder and allow the user to name the file. If a file is saved that is already named, the program copies over the existing file. The directions presented below represent saving a file for the first time.

- **Save Data File** In the **SPSS Data Editor** => **File** => **Save** => use the **Save in** drop down menu to select the appropriate directory/folder => using the **Save as type** drop down menu, choose **SPSS (*.sav)** (unless another file format is desired, then simply choose the appropriate file type) => type in a name in the **File name** dialog box => **Save.**
- **Save Output File** In the **Output - SPSS Viewer** => **File** => **Save** => use the **Save in** drop down menu to select the appropriate directory/folder => using the **Save as type** drop down menu, choose **Viewer Files (*.spo)** => type in a name in the **File name** dialog box => **Save.**
- **Save Syntax File** In the **Syntax – SPSS Syntax Editor** => **File** => **Save** => use the **Save in** drop down menu to select the appropriate directory/folder => using the **Save as type** drop down menu, choose **SPSS Syntax Files (*.sps)** => type in a name in the **File name** dialog box => **Save.**

HELP SPSS provides online help in a variety of ways including the help menu, dialog box help, and tutorials. Every window has a Help menu on the menu bar.

➤ **Help Menu** This command is accessed from the menu bar in any window.

- **Help => Topics** => click the **Index** tab => type in a keyword or simply scroll down through the topic list => double click on the topic of interest => information and links to related topics will be displayed.
- **Help** => **Topics** => click the **Search** tab => type in a word or phrase to search for => click **List Topics** => browse results using the scroll bar => double click on the topic of interest => information and links to related topics will be displayed.

➤ **Dialog Box Help Button** Dialog boxes offer a context sensitive help button that brings up a standard help window that contains information on the current dialog box.

➤ **Dialog Box Quick Help** Right click on any control in a dialog box and a brief description of the item will appear.

MISSING VALUES SPSS defines missing values as "system-missing" versus "user-missing". System missing values are omissions in the dataset and are designated with a period in the cell. A user-missing value is an actual value that the user defines to indicate that a value is known to be missing. Up to three different discrete values or a range of values can be coded to define reasons for missing data.

➤ **Define User-Missing Values** This procedure allows the user to specify data values that indicate why information is missing.

- Select the **Data Editor** as the active window => click the Variable View tab => click on the cell in the **Missing** column that corresponds to the variable of interest => click on the

shaded box that appears in the right of the cell to get the **Missing Values** dialog box =>
select either **discrete missing values** or **range plus one optional discrete missing value**
=> type in the values to be assigned in the appropriate boxes => **OK**.

➢ **Replace Missing Values** Missing values may make datasets difficult to work with and may
hinder certain types of analyses. For these reasons, it may be appropriate to replace missing
values using techniques such as interpolation, inserting a mean or median of nearby values,
etc.

- **Transform** => **Replace Missing Values** => highlight the variable(s) of interest and
  move them to the **New Variable(s)** box by clicking the arrow in the center of the dialog
  box => highlight one of the variables in the **New Variable(s)** box => the variable name
  will appear in the **Name** box => click on the down arrow for the **Method** box to display
  the techniques for replacing the missing value => if either **mean of nearby points** or
  median of nearby points are chosen, the span of points to be used must be designated
  => **OK**.

OUTPUT This term refers to the display of commands and analyses. Output is generated into
its own window and can be saved as a separate file that has a .spo filename extension.

➢ **Copy and Paste Output** This allows the user to move output to another place while leaving
the original where it is.

- Left click on the output item of interest (or highlight the item in the outline view) to
  select the item => right click to get the drop down menu => **Copy** => left click to place
  the cursor over the area to copy to => right click => **Paste.**

➢ **Delete Output**

- Left click on the output to select => right click to **Delete.**

➢ **Display Syntax (Command Log) in the Output** This procedure will write the syntax for
everything a user does in SPSS and will post the syntax in the output window. The user can
then paste that syntax into a new syntax file enabling the user to repeat procedures without
having to use a point-and-click approach. This can help to ensure consistency across analyses
and eliminate errors. It is also useful because it shows which file is used for each analysis so
that results in the output can be easily identified.

- **Edit** => **Options** => **Viewer** => check the box to **Display Commands in the Log** =>
  Apply => **OK.**

➢ **Edit Output** Charts, tables, and text can all be edited in a variety of ways. Double clicking
on any item will activate chart editors, pivot tables, and text boxes to allow editing.

➢ **Export Output to Word**

- Left click to highlight table or graphic to copy => right click to **Copy** (NOT copy object)
  => proceed to the word document => **Edit** => **Paste** => **OK.**

➢ *Format Output* SPSS users may adjust the size, shape, color, or other features of any displayed output.

- Double click on the portion of the output to format => double click on the specific output cell to format => right click and select the appropriate formatting option. To edit the text of an output cell, instead of right clicking just double click again to begin typing.

➢ *Hide Results Within an Output File* Results in the output can be hidden if the user does not want them displayed or printed but still wants them in the file. Conversely, results previously hidden can be shown again.

- In the SPSS Viewer, go to the outline view on the left side of the screen => scroll down to the output item to hide => click on the minus sign (-) to the left of the output name to hide the item (a plus sign will appear to indicate the item has been collapsed and is hidden) => click on the plus sign (+) to unhide the output.

➢ *Insert Text/Title to Output* This command allows the user to insert descriptive titles or detailed notes directly into the output.

- In the output or in the output outline, click where the text will be inserted => **Insert** => **NewText (or NewTitle)** => type desired text => right click.

➢ *Open Output* See FILES (Open Output File).

➢ *Print Output*

- **File** => **Print** => choose to print **All Visible Output** or just a **Selection** (when printing a selection, one or more output items in the outline must be highlighted before accessing the print command).

➢ *Resize/Rescale Output* This allows larger tables to be fit onto a single printed page.

- Double click on the table to be resized to enter editing mode => right click **=> Table Properties** => select the **Printing** tab=> check to **Rescale Wide Table to Fit Page** and/or **Rescale Long Table to Fit Page** => **OK**.

➢ *Save Output* See FILES (Save Output File).

PIVOT TABLES When using the SPSS viewer, this feature can be used to quickly rearrange rows, columns, and layers in output tables in order to present results more clearly.

- Double click on the table to be formatted to enter editing mode=> right click => **Pivoting Trays** => left click on the icon of the row, column, or layer to be moved => drag the icon to the desired row, column, or layer and release.

PRINT PREVIEW This feature allows the user to see what will print on each page of output. Items that may not be visible in the viewer, but can be seen in print preview include: page breaks, hidden layers of pivot tables, breaks in wide tables, headers, and footers.

- Highlight all or some of the output in the output outline => **File** => **Print Preview** => use buttons at the top of the print preview window to navigate the document, print, close, etc.

RESULTS COACH Explains how to interpret specific output.

- Double click on the output table or graphic => right click and select **Results Coach** => use arrows at the bottom right of the screen to page through the explanation of the output.

STATISTICS COACH This feature prompts the novice user with questions and examples to help in the selection of basic statistical and charting features that are most appropriate for the data. The Statistics Coach only covers the basic, most commonly used statistical procedures.

- **Help** => **Statistics Coach** => complete the wizard to step through the coaching process.

SYNTAX SPSS provides a command language that can be used instead of the point-and-click (windows) method to run SPSS. A syntax file is simply a text file that contains commands that can be used to repeat an analysis at a later time. Use of syntax files can help to ensure consistency across analyses and eliminate errors.

➤ *Create syntax* See FILES (Create a New File – New Syntax File).

➤ *Run syntax* The user can choose to run some or all of the commands in the syntax file.

  - *All Syntax* With the appropriate syntax file as the active window => **Run** => **All**
  - *Selected Syntax* With the appropriate syntax file as the active window => highlight the portion of syntax to be run => **Run** => **Selection**.

➤ *Print Syntax* With the appropriate syntax file as the active window => **File** => **Print** => select printing options => **OK**.

➤ *Save Syntax* See FILES (Save File – Save Syntax File).

TABLES SPSS allows the user to build a variety of tables using the custom, basic, and general tables command. Only the basic tables command will be presented.

- **Analyze** => **Tables** => **Basic Tables** => select one or more variables to be summarized within the cells and move to the **Summaries** dialog box using the arrow => select categorical variables to create row subgroups and move to the **Subgroups – Down** dialog box using the arrow => select categorical variables to create column subgroups and move to the **Subgroups -- Across** dialog box using the arrow => select categorical variables whose values create separate tables and move to the **Subgroups – Separate Tables** dialog box using the arrow => **Statistics** => choose options for presentation of statistics => **Continue** => **Layout** => select layout options => **Totals** => select totals options => **Continue** => **Titles** => type in titles as desired => **Continue** => **OK**.

VARIABLES These are characteristics of the cases (e.g., participants) in the study that are able to vary or have different values.

➢ *Compute Variable* This procedure allows the user to create new variables from existing variables by either using numeric expressions to mathematically generate the new values or by using an "If" statement to conditionally select values to compute into a new variable.

- *Numeric Expression Procedure:* **Transform** => **Compute** => type name of the new variable in the **Target Variable** box => click on **Type & Label** => type in label to describe the new variable in the **Label** box => choose whether the variable is numeric or string in the **Type** section => **Continue** => create a numeric expression by highlighting variables and moving them to the **Numeric Expression** box with the arrow in conjunction with the calculator pad to create mathematical expressions (or alternatively highlight a preset mathematical function from the **Functions** box and move it up to the **Numeric Expression** box with the arrow) => **OK.**

- *"IF" Procedure:* **Transform** => **Compute** => type name of the new variable in the **Target Variable** box => click on **Type & Label** => type in label to describe the new variable in the **Label** box => choose whether the variable is numeric or string in the **Type** section => **Continue** => click **If...** => select whether the condition should "**include all cases**" vs. "**include if case satisfies condition:**" => create a numeric expression by highlighting variables and moving them to the computation box with the arrow in conjunction with the calculator pad to create mathematical expressions (or alternatively highlight a preset mathematical function from the **Functions** box and move it up to the **Numeric Expression** box with the arrow) => **Continue** => enter a value or computation in the **Numeric Expression** box that creates the value of the new variable when the conditional statement is met => **OK.**

➢ *Copy/Paste Variable*

- To avoid pasting over an already defined variable, a new variable must be created to hold the spot. This is accomplished by in Variable View, set the mouse where the new variable will be => **Data** => **Insert Variable**. Then, highlight with a left click the variable to copy => right click to **Copy Variable** => highlight with a left click to paste the variable => right click to **Paste Variable**.

➢ *Cut/Paste Variable*

- Highlight with a left click the variable to cut => right click to **Cut Variable** => highlight with a left click to paste the variable => right click to **Paste Variable**. To avoid pasting over an already defined variable, a new variable must be created to hold the spot (see Insert Variable).

➢ *Information on Variables* This function presents a dialog box that displays a variety of information about the selected variable including: data format, variable label, user-missing values, and value labels.

- **Utilities** => **Variables** => highlight the variable of interest in the **Variables** dialog box => Variable Information is listed on the right side of the dialog box.

➢ *Insert Variable* A new variable can be added to the dataset either in Data View or Variable View.

- Select any cell in the variable to the right of (Data View) or below (Variable View) the position where the new variable will be inserted => **Data** => **Insert Variable**.

➢ *Move Variable* This process allows you to relocate a variable.

- Click the variable name in Data View once and release (this highlights the variable column) => click and drag the variable or case to a new location => drop the variable in the new location (to place the variable between two existing variables, drop the variable on the variable column to the right of where the variable will be placed).

➢ *Recode Into Different Variable* This process reassigns the values of an existing variable into a new set of values for a new variable.

- **Transform** => **Recode** => **Into Different Variables** => select the variable to recode and move it to the **Numeric Variable – Output Variable** dialog box using the arrow => type in the new variable name and label in the **Output Variable** dialog box => **Change** => **Old and New Values** => select and define the **Old Value** to change => define the **New Value** it will become => **Add** => **Continue** => **OK**.

➢ *Recode Into Same Variables* This process assigns new values in place of the old values of an existing variable (be very cautious when using this procedure to collapse data because the original data will be lost unless an original copy of the dataset is saved).

- **Transform** => **Recode** => **Into Same Variables** => select the variable to recode and move it to the **Variables** dialog box using the arrow => **Old and New Values** => select and define the **Old Value** to change => define the **New Value** it will become => **Add** => **Continue** => **OK**.

Z SCORES This procedure standardizes data to a standard score that has a mean of zero and a standard deviation of one.

- **Analyze** => **Descriptive Statistics** => **Descriptives** => select a variable with a left click => click the arrow in the middle of the dialog box to move the variable to the **Variables** box => check the box to **Save Standardized Values as Variables** => **OK**.

APPENDIX B

WRITING RESEARCH PROBLEMS AND QUESTIONS

Frameworks for Stating Research Problems

Although a common definition of a research problem is that it is a statement that asks what relationship exists between two or more variables, most research problems are more complex than this definition implies. The research problem should be a broad statement that covers the several more specific research questions to be investigated, perhaps by using summary terms that stand for several variables. Several ways to state the research problem are provided below. Underlines indicate that you fill in the appropriate name for the variable or group of variables.

Format

One way that you could phrase the problem as follows: The research problem is to investigate whether (put independent variable 1 or group of variables here) (and independent variable 2, if any, here) (and independent variable 3, if any) are related to (dependent variable 1, here) (and dependent variable 2, if any) in (population here).

Except in a totally descriptive study, there always must be at least two variables (one is usually called the independent variable and one the dependent variable). However, there can be two or more of each, and there often are. In the statement of the problem, in contrast to the research questions/hypotheses, it is desirable to use broad descriptors for groups of similar variables. For example, demographics might cover four variables: gender, mother's and father's education, and ethnicity. Spatial performance might include a mosaic pattern test score and a visualization score. Likewise, grades and mathematics attitudes could refer to more than one variable. Concepts such as self-esteem or teaching style have several aspects that usually result in more than one variable. The first example below is in the above format. The second and third are suggested variations when the approach is quasi-experimental, comparative, or associational.

Examples
If your study uses the randomized experimental approach, you could phrase the problem as:

1. The research problem is to investigate the effect of a new curriculum on grades, math attitudes, and quantitative/spatial achievement in high school students.

For other studies that compare groups or associate/relate variables, you could phrase the problem as follows:

2. The problem is to investigate whether gender and grades are related to mathematics attitudes and achievement in high school students.

If you have several *independent variables* and want to predict some outcome, you could say:

3. The problem is to investigate the variables that predict or *seem* to influence mathematics achievement.

This latter format is especially useful when the approach is a complex (several independent variables) associational one that will use multiple regression.

Framework for Stating Research Questions/Hypotheses

Although it is okay to phrase a randomized experimental research problem (in the format of the first example above) as a "study of the effect of...," we think it is best to phrase your research questions or hypotheses so that they do not appear to imply cause and effect (i.e., as *difference* or *associational* questions/hypotheses and/or as *descriptive* questions). The former are answered with inferential statistics, and descriptive questions are answered with descriptive statistics. There are several reasonable ways to state research questions. Below, we show one way to state each type of question, which we have found useful and, hopefully, clear for our students.

Descriptive Questions

Basic descriptive questions. These questions are about some aspect of one variable. Descriptive questions ask about the central tendency, frequency distribution, percentage in each category, variability, or shape of the distribution. Some descriptive questions are intended to test assumptions. Some questions simply describe the sample demographics; others describe a dependent variable. A few *examples* are as follows:

1. Is mathematics achievement distributed approximately normally?
2. What percentage of participants is of each gender?
3. What are the mean, mode, and median of the mathematics achievement scores?

Complex descriptive questions. These questions deal with two or more variables at a time, but do not involve inferential statistics. Cross-tabulations of two categorical variables, factor analysis, and measures of reliability (e.g., Cronbach's alpha) are examples.

An *example* is:
1. What is the internal consistency reliability of the pleasure scale items?

Difference Questions/Hypotheses

Basic difference questions. The *format* is as follows:

Are there differences between the (insert number) levels of (put the independent variable name here) (you could name the levels here in parentheses) in regard to the average (put the dependent variable name here) scores?

An *example* is as follows:
1. Are there differences between the three levels (high, medium, and low) of father's education in regard to the average mathematics achievement scores of the students?

Appropriate analyses: One-way ANOVA (see Chapter 10). A *t* test could be used if there were only two levels of the independent variable (see Chapter 9).

Complex difference and interaction questions. When you have two categorical independent variables considered together, you will have *three* research questions or hypotheses. There are advantages of considering two or three independent variables at a time. See Chapter 10 for an introduction about how to interpret the *interaction* question. Sample *formats* for a set of three questions answered by *one* 2-way ANOVA are as follows:

1. Is there a difference between (<u>insert the levels of independent variable 1</u>) in regard to the average (<u>put dependent variable 1 here</u>) scores?
2. Is there a difference between (<u>insert the levels of independent variable 2</u>) in regard to the average (<u>dependent variable 1</u>) scores?
3. Is there an interaction of (<u>independent **variable 1**</u>) and (<u>independent **variable 2**</u>) in regard to the (<u>**dependent** variable 1</u>)?

(Repeat these three questions, for the second dependent variable, if there is more than one.) An *example* is as follows:

1. Is there a difference between students who have high versus low math grades in regard to their average mathematics achievement scores?
2. Is there a difference between male and female students in regard to their average math achievement scores?
3. Is there an interaction between mathematics grades and gender in regard to math achievement?

Note that the first question states the *levels* or categories of the first independent variable; that is; it states the groups that are to be compared (high vs. low math grade students). The second question does the same for the second independent variable; that is, states the *levels (*male and female) to be compared. However, the third (interaction) question, asks whether the first *variable* itself (mathematics grades) interacts with the second variable (gender). No mention is made, at this point, of the values/levels/groups.

An appropriate analysis: Factorial ANOVA (see Chapter 10).

Associational/Relationship Questions/Hypotheses

Basic associational questions. When both variables are ordered and essentially continuous (i.e., have five or more ordered categories) we consider the approach and research question to be associational. There are two main types of basic associational statistics: corrlelation and regression.

The *format* for a correlation is as follows:

Is there an association between (<u>variable 1</u>) and (<u>variable 2</u>)?

In this case it is arbitrary which variable is independent or antecedent and which is dependent or outcome. An *example* for a single association or relationship is as follows:

1. Is there an association between grades in high school and mathematics achievement?

If there are more than two variables, which is common, and each pair of variables is associated separately, you can have a series of questions asking whether there is an association between *each* variable and every other variable. This would produce a *correlation matrix*.

An *example* that would produce a correlation matrix is as follows:
2. Are there associations among the three mathematics attitude scale scores?

Note that what is said to be associated in these questions is the variable itself; no mention is made of the levels or values here.

If one variable is clearly the independent or predictor, you would phrase the question as follows and use *bivariate regression* analyses:

3. Can we predict math achievement test scores (the dependent variable) from grades in high school (the independent variable)?

Appropriate analyses: Bivariate regression, if there is a clear independent or antecedent variable and you want to make a prediction; correlation if no clear independent variable (see Chapter 8).

Complex associational questions. In the associational approach, when two or more *independent* variables are considered together, rather than separately, as in the basic format above, you get a new kind of question. The *format* can be phrased something like:

How well does the combination of (list the several specific independent variables here) predict (put dependent variable here)?

An *example* is as follows:
1. How well does the combination of number of mathematics courses taken, gender, and father's education predict mathematics achievement?

An appropriate analysis: Multiple regression (see Chapter 8).

This complex question can also be expanded into a set of questions. This set first asks about the association of each of the predictors (or independent) variables and the dependent (or outcome) variable and then states the complex or combination question as above.

For *example*:
1. Is there an association between the number of mathematics courses taken and mathematics achievement test scores?
2. Is there an association between gender and mathematics achievement?
3. Is there an association between father's education and mathematics achievement?
4. How well does the combination of the number of mathematics courses taken, gender, and father's education predict mathematics achievement test scores?

Appropriate analysis: The multiple regression output will provide you with the three bivariate, Pearson correlations in a matrix as well as the multiple regression statistics (see, for example, Output 8.6).

APPENDIX C

Getting Started With SPSS and Printing the Syntax

This section includes step-by-step instructions for three procedures related to getting started with SPSS: a) making a working file from the CD in the back of the book, b) opening and starting SPSS and getting familiar with the **SPSS data editor**, and c) setting your computer so that SPSS will print the **syntax** or **log** along with each output.

Copy the Data Files From the Compact Disk

It is wise to make a working **copy** of the files from the compact disk (CD) provided with this book. The files are:

> **hsbdata.sav (11KB)**
> **college student data.sav (4KB)**
> **alternative hsbdataB.sav (13 KB)** (Use if you skip Chapter 5 or messed it up.)

Note: you may not see the file extension (.sav) depending on your computer setup.

There are several ways to copy the files. Also our letters for the computer drives may not be the same on your computer. The method described below assumes that your CD drive is E: (some systems use D: or F:) and that you will be copying to the A: drive. Insert the compact disk found with this book in your CD drive.

- Point at the **Start** button in the lower left corner of your screen and click the **right** button (not the left) on your mouse.
- Click **Explore** with the **left** button.
- On the left side of the Window click the **CD icon, SPSS Data (E:).**
- The display should look something like Fig C.1.

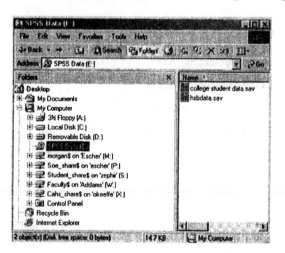

Fig. C.1. Copying the SPSS files using the exploring window.

- Click and drag each of the **two files** in the right column of Fig.C.1 to the **(A:) icon** on the left or to wherever you want to have you working file (hard drive, SD, diskette, etc.).
- Close the **Explore** window.

Open and Start the SPSS Application

- Begin at the **Start** button (bottom left of the Windows Desktop). Click **Start** => **Programs** => **SPSS for Windows** (see Fig. C.2). *Alternatively*, if an **SPSS icon** is available on the desktop, double click on it (see Fig. C.2). If **SPSS for Windows** is not listed in the **Programs** menu, it will need to be installed on your computer. It is not part of the Microsoft Windows package or the CD that accompanies this book and must be loaded separately.

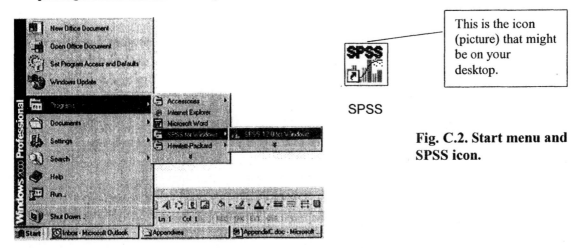

This is the icon (picture) that might be on your desktop.

SPSS

Fig. C.2. Start menu and SPSS icon.

After you start SPSS, you will see the **SPSS Startup screen** shown in Fig. C.3. Notice that in the Startup screen there is a list of all SPSS files available on your computer or diskette.

- Click on the SPSS file you wish to use *or* click the **Cancel** button shown in Figs. C.3, which will bring up a new SPSS desktop screen, called the **SPSS Data Editor** as shown in Fig C.5 and C.6. If no files are listed, click OK to bring up the **Open File** dialogue box to search for the file you want to open. In any one session, only one data file can be open at time.

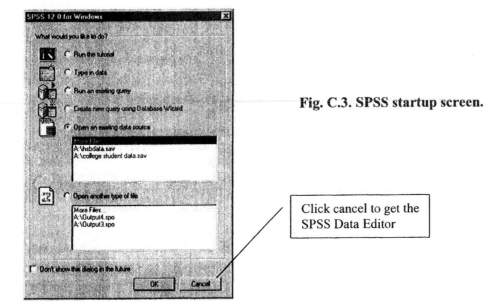

Fig. C.3. SPSS startup screen.

Click cancel to get the SPSS Data Editor

Existing files as well as new data files are opened in the **SPSS Data Editor** screen. In this screen, there are two tabs at the bottom left side of the screen; the **Data View** tab and the **Variable View** tab (see Fig. C.4).

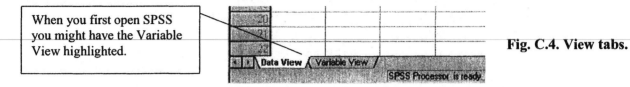

| When you first open SPSS you might have the Variable View highlighted. |

Fig. C.4. View tabs.

If you have SPSS 9.0 or a lower version, you will not have the Variable View screen option and will have to define and label variables differently. Please refer to your SPSS Help menu for further information on how to do this in earlier versions.

Although the toolbar at the top of the data editor screen is the same for both the Variable and Data View screens, it is important to notice the *subtle* differences in desktop features between these two screens found within the data editor (compare Fig. C.5 and Fig. C.6).

- Click on the **Variable View** tab in the data editor screen to produce Fig. C.5.

Notice the column names are like those in Fig. C.5. You create (define and label) new variables using the **Variable View** (see Chapter 2).

	Name	Type	Width	Decimals	Label	Values	Missing	Columns	Align	Measure
1	gend	Numeric	1	0	gender	{0, male}...	None	8	Right	Nominal
2	faed	Numeric	2	0	father's educati	{2, < h.s. grad}	None	8	Right	Ordinal
3	maed	Numeric	2	0	mother's educ	{2, < h.s.}...	None	8	Right	Ordinal
4	alg1	Numeric	1	0	algebra 1 in h.	{0, not taken}..	None	8	Right	Nominal
5	alg2	Numeric	1	0	algebra 2 in h.	{0, not taken}..	None	8	Right	Nominal
6	geo	Numeric	1	0	geometry in h.	{0, not taken}..	None	8	Right	Nominal

Fig. C.5. SPSS data editor: Variable view.

- Click on the **Data View** tab in the data editor to produce Fig. C.6.

Notice the columns change to **var** or to the names of your variables if you have already entered them (see Fig. C.6). You enter (input) data using the **Data View**.

	gend	faed	maed	alg1	alg2	geo	trig	calc	mathgr	grades	mathach	mosaic	visual
1	1	10	10	0	0	0	0	0	0	4	9.00	31.0	8.75
2	1	2	2	0	0	0	0	0	0	5	10.33	56.0	4.75
3	1	2	2	0	0	0	0	0	1	6	7.67	25.0	4.75
4	0	3	3	1	0	0	0	0	0	3	5.00	22.0	1.00
5	1		3	0	0	0	0	0	0	3	-1.67	17.5	2.25
6	1	3	2	0	0	0	0	0	1	5	1.00	23.5	1.00
7	0	9	6	1	1	1	0	0	0	6	12.00	28.5	2.50

Fig. C.6. SPSS data editor: Data view.

Set Your Computer to Print the SPSS Syntax (Log)

In order to have your computer print the SPSS commands on your output, as shown throughout the book, you will need to set your computer using the following:
- Click on **Edit => Options.**
- Click on the **Viewer** tab under **Data** near the top left of the **Options** window to get Fig. C.7.

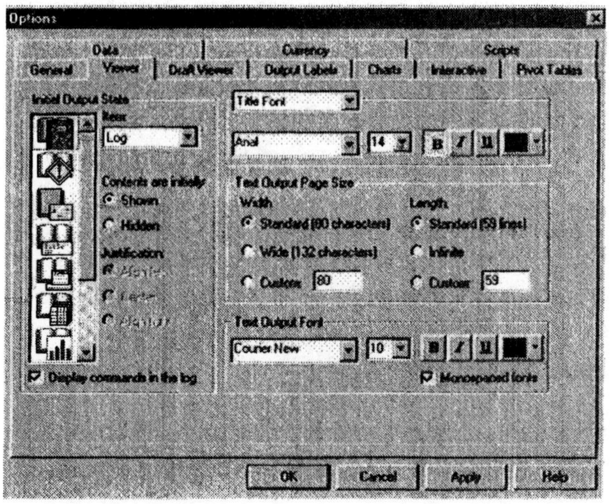

Fig. C.7. Edit: Options.

- Check **display commands in log** near the lower left of the window.
- Leave the other defaults as is.
- Click on **OK.** Doing this will always print the syntax on your output unless someone unclicks this check on this computer.

APPENDIX D

Making Tables and Figures

Don Quick

Tables and figures are used in most fields of study to provide a visual presentation of important information to the reader. They are used to organize the statistical results of a study, to list important tabulated information, and to allow the reader a visual method of comparing related items. Tables offer a way to detail information that would be difficult to describe in the text.

A figure may be just about anything that is not a table, such as a chart, graph, photograph, or line drawing. These figures may include pie charts, line charts, bar charts, organizational charts, flow charts, diagrams, blueprints, or maps. Unless the figure can dramatically illustrate a comparison that a table cannot, use a table. A good rule is to use a table for numbers and text and to use figures for visual presentations.

The meaning and major focus of the table or figure should be evident to the readers without them having to make a thorough study of it. A glance should be all it takes for the idea of what the table or figure represents to be conveyed to the reader. By reading only the text itself, the reader may have difficulty understanding the data; by constructing tables and figures that are well presented, the readers will be able to understand the study results more easily.

The purpose of this appendix is to provide guidelines that will enhance the presentation of research findings and other information by using tables and figures. It will highlight the important aspects of constructing tables and figures using the *Publication Manual of the American Psychological Association, Fifth Edition* (2001) as the guide for formatting.

General Considerations Concerning Tables

Be selective as to how many tables are included in the total document. Determine how much data the reader needs to comprehend the material, and then decide if the information would be better presented in the text or as a table. A table containing only a few numbers is unnecessary; whereas a table containing too much information may not be understandable. Tables should be easy to read and interpret. If at all possible, combine tables that repeat data.

Keep a consistency to all of your tables throughout your document. All tables and figures in your document should use a similar format, with the results organized in a comparable fashion. Use the same designation measure or scale in all tables, figures, and the text.

In a final manuscript such as a thesis or dissertation, adjust the column headings or spacing between columns so the width of the table fits appropriately between the margins. Fit all of one table on one page. Reduce the data, change the type size, or decrease line spacing to make it fit. A short table may be on a page with text, as long as it follows the first mention of it. Each long table is on a separate page immediately after it is mentioned in the text. If the fit and appearance would be improved, turn the table sideways (landscape orientation, with the top of table toward the spine) on the page.

Each table and figure must be discussed in the text. An informative table will supplement but not duplicate the text. In the text, discuss only the most important parts of the table. Make sure the table can be understood by itself without the accompanying text; however, it is never independent of the text. There must be a reference in the text to the table.

Construction of the Table

Table D.1 is an example of an APA table for displaying simple descriptive data collected in a study. It also appears in correct relation to the text of the document. (Fig. D.1 shows the same table with the table parts identified.) The major parts of a table are: the number, the title, the headings, the body, and the notes.

Table D.1. *An Example of a Table in APA Format for Displaying Simple Descriptive Data*

Table 1

Means and Standard Deviations on the Measure of Self-Direction in Learning as a Function of Age in Adult Students

Age group	n	Self-directed learning inventory score	
		M	SD
20-34	15	65	3.5
35-40	22	88	6.3
50-64	14	79	5.6
65-79	7	56	7.1
80+	--[a]	--	--

Note. The maximum score is 100.
[a] No participants were found for the over 80 group.

Table Numbering

Arabic numerals are used to number tables in the order in which they appear in the text. Do NOT write in the text "the table on page 17" or "the table above or below." The correct method would be to refer to the table number like this: (see Table 1) or "Table 1 shows..." Left-justify the table number (see Table D.1). In an article, each table should be numbered sequentially in the order of appearance. Do not use suffix letters with the table numbers in articles. However, in a book table numbers may be numbered within chapters; e.g. Table 7.1. If the table appears in an appendix, identify it with the letter of the appendix capitalized, followed by the table number; for instance Table C.3 is the third table in Appendix C.

Table Titles

Include the variables, the groups on whom the data were collected, the subgroups, and the nature of the statistic reported. The table title and headings should concisely describe what is contained in the table. Abbreviations that appear in the body of the table can sometimes be explained in the title, however, it may be more appropriate to use a general note (see also comments below on **Table Headings**). The title must be italicized. Standard APA format for journal submission requires double spacing throughout. However, tables in student papers may be partially single spaced for better presentation.

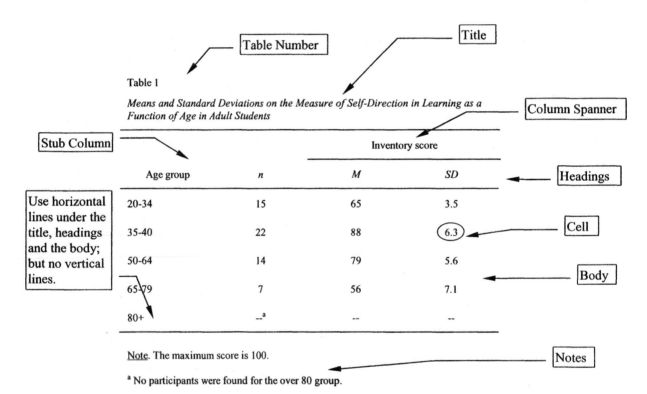

Fig. D.1. The major parts of an APA table.

Table Headings

Headings are used to explain the organization of the table. You may use abbreviations in the headings; however, include a note as to their meaning if you use mnemonics, variable names, and scale acronyms. Standard abbreviations and symbols for non technical terms can be used without explanation (e.g., *no.* for *number* or *%* for *percent*). Have precise title, column headings, and row labels that are accurate and brief. Each column must have a heading, including the **stub column**, or leftmost column. Its heading is referred to as the **stubhead**. The stub column usually lists the significant independent variables or the levels of the variable, as in Table D.1.

The **column heads** cover one column, and the **column spanners** cover two or more columns -- each with its own column head (see Table D.1 and Fig. D.1). Headings stacked in this manner are called **decked heads**. This is a good way to eliminate repetition in column headings but try to avoid using more than two levels of decked heads. **Column heads, column spanners**, and **stubheads** should all be singular, unless referring to a group (e.g., children). Table spanners, which cover the entire table, may be plural. Use sentence capitalization in all headings.

Notice that there are no vertical lines in an APA style table. The horizontal lines can be added by using a "draw" feature or a "borders" feature for tables in the computer word processor, or they could be drawn in by hand if typed. If translating from an SPSS Table or box, the vertical lines must be removed.

The Body of the Table

The body contains the actual data being displayed. Round numbers improve the readability and clarity more than precise numbers with several decimal places. A good guideline is to report two digits more than the raw data. A reader can compare numbers down a column more easily than across a row. Column and row averages can provide a visual focus that allows the reader to inspect the data easily without cluttering the table. If a cell cannot be filled because the information is not applicable, then leave it blank. If it cannot be filled because the information could not be obtained, or was not reported, then insert a dash and explain the dash with a note to the table.

Notes to a Table

Notes are often used with tables. There are three different forms of notes used with tables: a) to eliminate repetition in the body of the table, b) to elaborate on the information contained in a particular cell, or c) to indicate statistical significance:

- A *general note* provides information relating to the table as a whole, including explanations of abbreviations used:

    Note. This could be used to indicate if the table came from another source.

- A *specific note* makes a reference to a specific row or column or cell of the table and is given superscript lowercase letters, beginning with the letter "a":

    [a]$n = 50$. Specific notes are identified in the body with superscript.

- A *probability note* is to be included when one or more inferential statistic has been computed and there isn't a column showing the probability, p. Asterisk(s) indicate the statistical significance of findings presented within the table. Try to be consistent across all tables in a paper. The important thing is to use the fewest asterisks for the largest p value. It is common to use one asterisk for .05 and two for .01. For example:

    *$p < .05$.   **$p < .01$.

Notes should be listed with general notes first, then specific notes, and concluded with probability notes, without indentation. They may be single spaced for better presentation. Explain all uses of dashes and parentheses. Abbreviations for technical terms, group names, and those of a similar nature must be explained in a note to the table.

Constructing a Table in Microsoft Word XP or 2000

For this step-by-step example the ANOVA was chosen from previous examples in the book. See Fig. D.2. The data are transferred from the standard SPSS output to an APA table.

ANOVA

grades in h.s.

	Sum of Squares	df	Mean Square	F	Sig.
Between Groups	18.143	2	9.071	4.091	.021
Within Groups	155.227	70	2.218		
Total	173.370	72			

Fig. D.2. An example of the type of default table generated from a SPSS ANOVA output.

The finished table should look like Table D.2. This explanation is accomplished using MS Word XP but using MS Word 2000 will be similar. Any earlier version will have some problems with line spacing. You will also need to adjust the number of columns and rows for the type and amount of data that you need to present.

Table D.2. *An Example of an ANOVA Table in APA Format*

Table 2 ◄————

The **Table Number** is double spaced but the **Table Title** is single spaced. The **Title** is in italics but the **Table Number** is not.

One-Way Analysis of Variance of Grades in High School by Father's Education

Source	df	SS	MS	F	p
Between groups	2	18.14	9.07	4.09	.02
Within groups	70	155.23	2.22		
Total	72	173.37			

The **Headings** and **Body** of the table are actually built using Word's table function. Type your **Table Number** and **Title**. Then on the next line after the title, insert a 6x4 table:

- **Table => Insert => Table...** (See Fig. D.3).
- For our example of the ANOVA set it to 6 columns and 4 rows. Leave everything else as is. See Fig. D.4.
- Click **OK.**

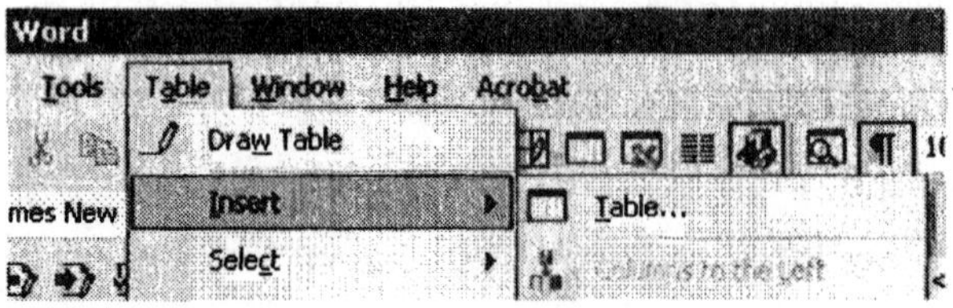

Fig. D.3. Using MS Word to make a table.

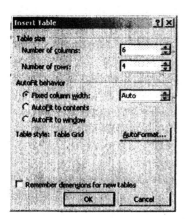

Fig. D.4. Inserting a 6x4 table.

> This is for the single ANOVA table. You will need to adjust the number of columns and rows for the type and amount of data that you need to present.

Compare your table to Table D.3.

Table D.3.

APA uses no vertical and just a few horizontal lines so it is best to remove them all and then put back the ones that are needed:
- Select the table by clicking anywhere inside the table, then: **Table => Select => Table.**
- **Format => Borders and Shading...** to get Fig. D.5.
- Select the **Borders** tab, if it's not already selected.
- Under **Settings** click the box to the left of **None** to remove them.
- Click **OK.**

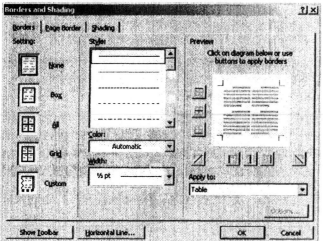

Fig. D.5. Clearing the borders.

To add the correct lines in for an APA table:
- Clicking anywhere in the top row and **Table => Select => Row.**
- **Format => Borders and Shading...** to get Fig. D.6.
- Make sure the solid line **Style** is selected and the **Width** is **1/2 pt.**

- In the **Preview** picture click the **Upper** and **Lower** bar buttons. This inserts the top two lines in the table.
- Click **OK**.
- Select the last row in your table.
- Click the **Lower** bar button only. This inserts the bottom line in the table.
- Click **OK**.

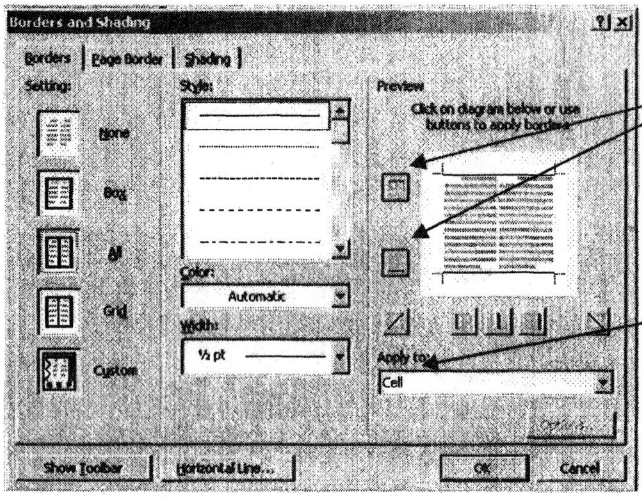

Upper and Lower bar buttons

Fig. D.6. Setting the horizontal lines.

Note: the **Apply to** is set to **Cell** but since you have selected the entire row it will look like a solid line across the table.

Compare your table to Table D.4.

Note: If you can't see the gridlines, turn them on to better see where the rows and cells are. They won't show when printed. Click **Table => Show Gridlines**

Table D.4.

The text in the body of an APA table is equal distance between the top and bottom of the cell:
- Select the table by clicking anywhere inside the table, then: **Table => Select => Table.**
- Click **Format => Paragraph...**
- Set **Line spacing** to **Single** (see note on Fig. D.7).
- Set **Spacing** to **Before** and **After** to **6pt** (see Fig. D.7).
- Click **OK**.

Enter the headings and data into each cell; the SPSS printout will have all of the information to accomplish this. Don't worry about wrapping and aligning at this time. That is easier to do after the data are entered.

Compare your table to Table D.5.

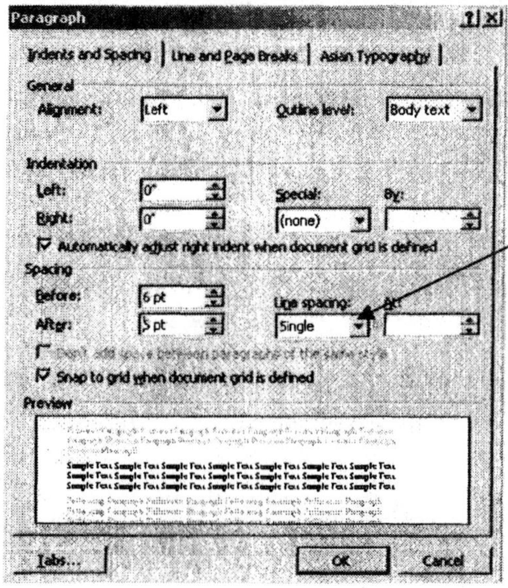

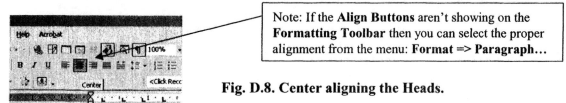

Note: With normal SPSS tables with numerical data and short heads, **Single** and the **6pt** before and after sets the text equal distant in the cell. Wrapped text will come out single spaced which is better presentation for student papers and dissertations. However, if you have text that wraps and the journal requires that all text be double spaced then you will need to **Double** space only those cells that wrap.

Fig. D.7. Setting line spacing within the cell.

Table D.5.

Source	*df*	*SS*	*MS*	*F*	*p*
Between groups	2	18.14	9.07	4.09	.02
Within groups	70	155.23	2.22		
Total	72	173.37			

In an APA table the **Heads** should be center aligned in the cell and the **Stubs** are left aligned. The numbers in the **Cell** are decimal aligned and centered under the Heads. Notice also that "Between groups" wrapped. Let's first align the **Heads** and **Stubs**, then fix that wrap and finally align the data off of the **Heads**. To center align the **Heads**:

- Select the **Header Row** of your table by clicking anywhere in the top row and **Table => Select => Row**.
- Click the **Center** align button in the Formatting Toolbar, see Fig. D.8.
- The stub column should already be left aligned; if not, then select the cells and click the **Align Left** button.

Note: If the **Align Buttons** aren't showing on the **Formatting Toolbar** then you can select the proper alignment from the menu: **Format => Paragraph...**

Fig. D.8. Center aligning the Heads.

When MS Word creates a table it will generally make all of the columns the same width. To fix the wrap on the "Between groups" cell, that column will need to be widened slightly and then to keep the table within the margins the data columns will need to be decreased slightly. This may be a trail and error process to get the right spacing for your text.

- Click anywhere on the **Stubs** column.
- **Table => Table Properties...** to get Fig. D.9.
- Click the **Column** Tab.
- Set the **Preferred width** to 1.4".
- Click the **Next Column** button and set it to 1.0".
- Repeat for all of the columns, setting them to 1.0".
- Click **OK**.

Note: This can also be accomplished by dragging the vertical column separator lines until the "Between groups" is not wrapped and then dragging the other column separator lines so that they are within the margins. However this produces uneven column spaces. We recommend the method outlined.

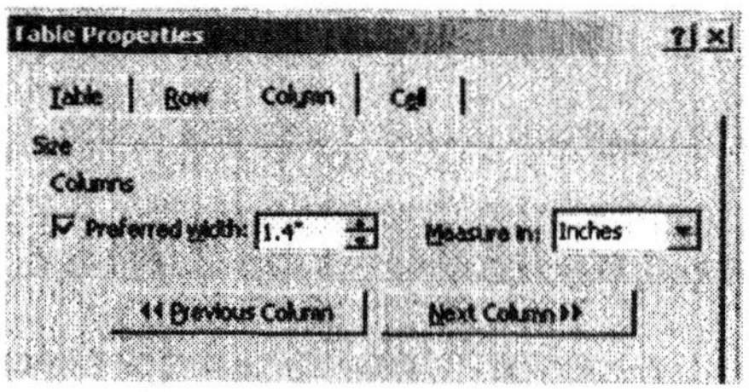

Fig. D.9. Adjusting the column widths.

Compare your table to Table D.6.

Table D.6.

Source	df	SS	MS	F	p
Between groups	2	18.14	9.07	4.09	.02
Within groups	70	155.23	2.22		
Total	72	173.37			

To set the **Cell** columns so that they are all centered under its **Head**, you will need to set the **Tabs** for each column of data cells to a **Decimal Tab**. We recommend this method of setting all columns the same and then adjusting them separately so they look right, because it requires less individual column adjustment:

- Select just the data cells by clicking in the upper left one, hold the shift key down, and then click in the lower right cell.
- **Format => Tabs...** to get Fig. D.10.
- Clear all of the Tabs in the selected cells first by clicking the **Clear All** button.
- Click **Alignment Decimal**.
- Type .35" in the **Tab stop position** box.
- Click the **Set** button.
- Click **OK.**

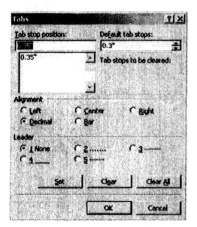

Fig. D.10. Setting the decimal tabs.

Compare your table to Table D.7.

Table D.7.

Source	*df*	*SS*	*MS*	*F*	*p*
Between groups	2	18.14	9.07	4.09	.02
Within groups	70	155.23	2.22		
Total	72	173.37			

The *df* column looks like it could be adjusted slightly to the right and the *p* column slightly to the left. We show you this so that you will know how to get a perfect decimal alignment of the data under the column head text. This may be trail and error depending on your data.

- Select the cells of the *df* column by clicking first on the top data cell, "2," hold the **Shift key** down, and the click on the bottom data cell, "72."
- **Format => Tabs...**
- Clear all of the Tabs in the selected cells first by clicking the **Clear All** button.
- Click **Alignment Decimal**.
- Type .45" in the **Tab stop position** box, to set decimal tap .45" from the left edge of the cell.
- Click the **Set** button.
- Click **OK.**
- Repeat for the *p* column but set it to .25" to set decimal tap .25" from the left edge of the cell.

Compare your finished table to Table D.8.

Table D.8.

Table 2

One-Way Analysis of Variance of Grades in High School by Father's Education

Source	df	SS	MS	F	p
Between groups	2	18.14	9.07	4.09	.02
Within groups	70	155.23	2.22		
Total	72	173.37			

Adjusting the SPSS Output to Approximate the APA Format

The preceding example shows how the standard SPSS output can be used to create a table in APA format. However, this does require some knowledge of your word processing program's table creation capabilities in order to accomplish this task. It also requires retyping the data into the table. You can adjust SPSS so that the output will approximate the APA format. We would not recommend submitting this to an APA journal, but it may be acceptable for student papers and some graduate program committees.

In SPSS follow these commands <u>BEFORE</u> running your SPSS analysis of your data:
- Click **Edit => Options**.
- Under the **Pivot Tables** tab select **Academic 2.tlo** (see Fig. D.11).
- Press **OK**.

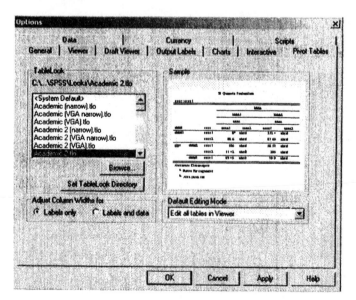

Fig. D.11. Setting SPSS for an approximate APA format output.

- Run the SPSS statistical analysis.

Your outputs will look similar to Table D.9, which approximates an APA table. In order to transfer it to MS Word:

- On the SPSS output, **right click** on the table that you want to transfer.
- Select **Copy objects** from the short menu presented, see Fig. D.12.

Fig. D.12. Copying tables from SPSS.

- Place the curser in the MS Word file where you want to put the table.
- Select **Paste** in MS Word.

You can then move it and format it like any other image in MS Word, but it can not be edited.

Table D.9. *An Example of the SPSS "Academic" Output*

Table 2

One-Way Analysis of Variance of Grades in High School by Father's Education

ANOVA

grades in h.s.

	Sum of Squares	df	Mean Square	F	Sig.
Between Groups	18.143	2	9.071	4.091	.021
Within Groups	155.227	70	2.218		
Total	173.370	72			

Using Figures

Generally, the same concepts apply to figures as have been previously stated concerning tables: they should be easy to read and interpret, be consistent throughout the document when presenting the same type of figure, kept on one page if possible, and it should supplement the accompanying text or table. Considering the numerous types of figures, I will not attempt to detail their construction in this document. However, one thing is consistent with all figures. The figure number and caption description are located below the figure and the description is detailed, similar to that of the title of a table. See Fig. D.12.

Some cautions in using figures:

1) Make it simple. Complex diagrams that require lengthy explanation should be avoided unless it is an integral part of the research.
2) Use a minimum number of figures for just your important points. If too many figures are used, your important points may be lost.
3) Integrate text and figure. Make sure your figure compliments and enhances the accompanying text.

Correlation of math achievement with

mosaic pattern test

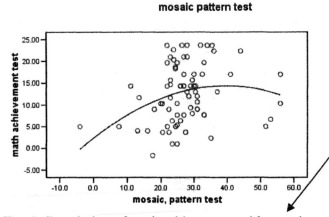

Fig. D.12. An example of using a figure in APA with caption.

Note: The figure number is italicized but the caption itself is not. Also, the caption text is sentence case (only the first word is capitalized).

Fig. 1. Correlation of math achievement with mosaic pattern test.

Appendix E

Answers to Odd Numbered Interpretation Questions

Chapter 1

1.1   Compare the terms active independent variable and attribute independent variable. What are the similarities and differences?

An *attribute independent variable* is a characteristic or a "part" of you. Some common attribute variables such as ethnicity, gender, and IQ are not easily changed. Other attributes such as age, income, job title, personality traits, and attitudes can change over time. An *active independent variable* is manipulated or varied by the experimenter or some collaborating group (school, clinic, etc.). The researcher or collaborating group actively gives different groups different treatments during the study. The most common active variable is when a control and experimental group receive different treatments. The participants might be randomly assigned to groups or be in intact groups such as school classes.

1.3.   What is the difference between the independent variable and the dependent variable?

The concept of independent and dependent variable confuses many students. The independent variable is the *presumed* cause; it should precede the dependent variable. The scores or values for the dependent variable "depend on" the independent variable. For example, you might have a new weight reduction plan, say reduced carbohydrates. One group follows a low carbohydrate diet while the other group eats their normal diet (the independent variable). Then to determine if the low carb system works the researcher might make weight measurements before the study and at the end. Thus, the researcher is hoping that the treatment (the independent variable), causes a change in weight (the dependent variable).

1.5   Write a research question and a corresponding hypothesis regarding variables of interest to you but not in the HSBdata set. Is it an associational, difference, or descriptive question?

Of course the answers to this question will vary greatly. An associational question will most likely involve two normally distributed variables. For example, "Is there an association between IQ scores and SAT scores for high school seniors?" Difference questions usually compare the results of two to four groups. For example, "Are there differences between three different weight loss programs in regard to the average weight loss?" Although it should be the easiest, often students misunderstand descriptive questions. Descriptive questions do NOT compare groups or associate variables. You might ask, "What is the average weight loss of all participants in the study?" Or, "what is the average age of all participants in the study?" Descriptive questions are not answered with inferential statistics such as a *t* test.

Chapter 2

2.1.   What steps or actions should be taken after you collect data and before you run any analyses?

a) Decide how to code each variable (i.e., what numbers/values to use with each type of response).
b) Check the completed questionnaires to see if participant responses are clear and consistent with your coding rules; clean up problems.
c) Define and label variables with SPSS.
d) Enter the data; the data can be coded directly from the original questionnaires or from a coding sheet.
e) Compare the data that you entered with that on the questionnaires.
f) Finally, check again, running some simple statistics to look for errors in the data. For example, if you have a field where the scores range from 1 to 5, the maximum value in any field should not be greater than 5.

2.3.   Why would you print a codebook?

Codebooks serve as a dictionary for your data. It provides you a way to check what was entered for each variable as value codes and labels, the variable name and label, special missing value codes, and the level of measurement.

2.5.   Why and why not would you use a data entry form?

Why: sometimes the data being entered is from a long or messy questionnaire or instrument. In these cases a data entry form helps you not make data entry errors. Sometimes the instrument or survey itself is laid out in such a manner that it is difficult to enter the data directly into SPSS. *Why not*: If the instrument is clearly laid out it is often simpler and more accurate to enter the data directly into SPSS from the instrument because an intermediate step is not used.

Chapter 3

3.1.   If you have categorical, ordered data (such as low income, middle income, high income) what type of measurement would you have? Why?

Ordinal. The key here is that the data are ordered. Low income is clearly lower than middle income, but the data are not interval or normal because the distances between the low, middle, and high income categories are probably not equal, and our definition of approximately normal specifies that there be five or more ordered categories. This is a little tricky because the term categorical is often associated with nominal; however, if the categories are ordered, the variable can not be nominal.

3.3.   What percent of the area under the standard normal curve is between the mean and one standard deviation above the mean?

Approximately 34%. The exact percent is 34.13.

3.5.   Why should you not use a frequency polygon if you have nominal data? What would be better to use to display nominal data?

Frequency polygons and histograms are designed for use with normally distributed or scale data. The correct ways to display nominal data are the frequency distribution or the bar chart.

Chapter 4

4.1.   Using Output 4.1: a) What is the mean visualization score? b) What is the range for grades in h.s.? c) What is the minimum score for mosaic pattern test? How can that be?

a) 5.24
b) The range equals 6, the high score minus the low score, 8 - 2 = 6.
c) -4.0. At first this may seem like an error. However, if you check the codebook, you will see that visualization scores go from -4 to 16. The -4 score also verifies that at least one person scored the lowest possible score, which is probably negative due to a penalty for guessing wrong.

4.3.   Using Output 4.2b: a) How many participants have missing data? b) What percentage of students have a valid (non-missing) scores for both motivation and competence? c) Can you tell from Output 4.1 and 4.2b how many are missing both motivation and competence scores? How?

a) 4
b) 94.7%
c) In Output 4.1b, you can see that there were 73 competence scale scores and 73 motivation scale scores. In Output 4.2b you can see that only 71 had both of the scores. Therefore, no one is missing both motivation and competence scores.

4.5.   Using Output 4.5: a) 9.6% of what group are Asian Americans? b) What percentage of students have visualization retest scores of 6? c) What percent had scores of 6 or less?

a) This is the percentage of subjects in the study who made a valid answer to this question and listed themselves as Asian Americans. It does not include those who left the question blank or checked more than one ethnic group.
b) There is no missing data in this category, so the valid percent and the percent are both the same, and the answer is 5.3%.
c) 70.7%. This is read from the cumulative percent column.

Chapter 5

5.1.   Using your initial HSB data file, compare the original data to your new variables: a) How many math courses did participants number 1 take? b) What should *faedrRevis* be for participants 2, 5, and 8? c) What should the pleasure scale score be for participant 1? d) Why is comparing a few initial scores to transformed scores important?

a) None
b) 1, missing, and 2, respectively.
c) 3.25.
d) It is easy to make an error in the calculation process, thus, giving you wrong data after transformation. A few data point checks is reassuring and gives you confidence in your data. The computer will not make computation errors, but you might give it the wrong recoding or computing instructions.

5.3.   Why did you reverse questions 6 and 10?

These two questions are negatively worded. Thus, for items 02 and 14, a 4 is high pleasure and 1 is low pleasure, but for these two (item 06 and 10) it is the opposite. Therefore we cannot add these four items together unless we reverse the coding on items 06 and 10 so that a 4 = 1, 3=2, 2=3 and 1=4. Then all four items will have high pleasure equal to 4.

5.5.   When would you use the Mean function to compute an average? And when would the Mean function not be appropriate?

If participants have completed most items on a construct or scale composed of several questions, the SPSS "Mean" function allows you to compute the average score on that variable for *all the participants* by using the average of their responses for the items that they did answer.

When computing a multiple item scale it is important *not to use* the Mean function if respondents only answered one or a few items. For example, if the construct of math anxiety was being measured and math anxiety was composed of responses to 7 items, but some respondents only completed 2 or 3 of the seven items, the Mean function would give a biased answer.

Chapter 6

6.1.   Compare and contrast a between groups design and a within groups design.

This is a fairly simple concept but is often confused by beginners. In a *between subjects design,* different people get different treatments or have different levels of the independent variable. In other words, there are treatments between the levels of the independent variable. For example, you might want to see if one 8th grade math curriculum is more effective than another. Each set of students would receive a different curriculum.

In a *within subjects design* the same people get multiple treatments. This design is sometimes referred to as a repeated measures design. The most common example of this design is a pre-test posttest design. All students take the pretest and the same students take the posttest. Another example is when a group of people are being monitored over time. Twenty people might enter an exercise program and their blood pressure and cholesterol levels might be measured each week for 10 weeks. The dependent variable in a within subjects design is sometimes referred to as change over time. In other words, "was there a significant change in the cholesterol levels and blood pressure levels over the 10 week period?" is a within subjects design question. It is also a within subjects design if pairs of subjects are matched and then compared.

6.3.   Provide an example of a situation in which a researcher could appropriately choose two different statistics. Explain your answer.

There are many possible answers to this question. As demonstrated by the discussion of the general linear model, there are usually at least two choices of an inferential statistic for analyzing any set of variables (e.g., *t* or eta; see Fig. 6.2). Another example of choices has to do with basic assumptions related to the statistics. There are a series of judgments that researchers make in the selection of statistics. For example, a judgment is made about whether a variable is approximately normally distributed or not. You might have a data set where the skewness of the data is 1.0. Would you use a nonparametric or parametric statistic? In this case you could justify the use of either type of statistic. Another common answer to this question relates to choosing ANOVA or correlation. If the independent variable has 2-4 *ordered* levels, you could run a correlation, although we recommend that you run an ANOVA. Remember the five or more ordered levels in Fig 6.1 is a guideline not a rule.

6.5.   Interpret the following related to effect size:

a) $d = .25$ Small or smaller than typical
b) $r = .35$ Medium or typical
c) $R = .53$ Large or larger than typical
d) $r = .13$ Small or smaller than typical
e) $d = 1.15$ Much larger than typical
f) eta $= .38$ Large or larger than typical

6.7.   What statistic would you use if you had two independent variables, income group (< $10,000, $10,000-$30,000, > $30,000) and ethnic group (Hispanic, Caucasian, African-American), and one normally distributed dependent variable (self-efficacy at work).

Factorial ANOVA (This would be a 3 X 3 factorial ANOVA).

6.9.   What statistic would you use if you had three normally distributed independent variables, one dichotomous independent variable and one normally distributed dependent variable?

Multiple regression

Chapter 7

7.1.   In Output 7.1: a) What do the terms "count" and" expected count" mean ? b) What does the difference between them tell you?

a) The count is the actual number of subjects in that cell. For example, in this data set 10 males did not take geometry and 29 females did not take geometry. The expected count is what you would expect to find in the cell given the marginal totals if there were no relationship between the variables.

b) If the expected count and the actual count are fairly close together there is probably not a significant difference for the chi-square. If, however, there is a large difference, as in this case, you would expect to find a significant chi-square.

7.3. Because father's and mother's education revised are at least ordinal data, which of the statistics used in 7.2 is the most appropriate to measure the strength of the relationship: phi, Cramer's V, or Kendall's tau-b? Interpret the results. Why are tau-b and V different?

The key here is "at least ordinal." Because both variables are at least ordinal, Kendall's tau-b is the appropriate measure. The tau-b of .572 is a large effect size (see Table 6.5). The formula for Kendall's tau-b assumes ordinal data whereas the formula for Cramer's V assumes nominal data and ignores the order of the levels.

7.5. Write a sentence or two describing the results of Output 7.4 that you might include in a research report.

In this case, ethnicity and reported ethnicity had a high level of reliability using Cohen's Kappa. (Kappa = .86). There were only few cases where there was not agreement between ethnicity and reported ethnicity.

Chapter 8

8.1. Why would we graph Scatterplots and regression lines?

The most important reason is to check for violations in the assumptions of correlation and regression. Both the Pearson correlation and regression assume a linear relationship. Viewing the scatterplot lines allows the researcher to check to see if there are marketed violations of linearity (e.g., the data may be curvilinear). In regression, there may be better fitting lines such as a quadratic (one bend) or cubic (two bends) that would explain the data more accurately. Graphing the data also allows you to easily see outliers.

8.3. In Output 8.3, how many of the Pearson correlation coefficients are significant? Write an interpretation of a) one of the significant and b) one of the nonsignificant correlations in Output 8.3. Include whether or not the correlation is significant, your decision about the null hypothesis, and a sentence or two describing the correlations in nontechnical terms. Include comments related to the sign (direction) and to the effect size.

There are two significant correlations: 1) visualization with math achievement test and 2) grades in high school with math achievement. There are several possible answers to the rest of this question.
a) There was a significant positive association between scores on a math achievement test and grades in high school ($r_{(73)} = .504, p < .001$). In general those who scored high on the math achievement test also had higher grades in high school. Likewise, those that did not score well on the math achievement test did not do as well on their high school grades. The effect ($r = .50$) was larger than typical. The null hypothesis stating that there was no relationship can be rejected.

b)   There was not a significant relationship between the visualization test scores and the mosaic pattern test scores ($r_{(73)} = .03$, $p = .798$). There is little evidence from this data set to support a relationship between these two variables. The null hypothesis is not rejected.

8.5.   Using Output 8.5 find the regression weight (B) and the standardized regression (beta) weight. a) How do these compare to the correlation between the same variables in Output 8.2? b) What does the regression weight tell you? c) Give an example of a research problem in which Pearson correlation would be more appropriate than bivariate regression, and one in which bivariate regression would be more appropriate than Pearson Correlation.

a)   The term regression weight refers to the unstandardized (B) coefficient for grades, which is 2.142. The *bivariate* regression *(R)* and the standardized (beta) coefficient are the same; in this case .504. This is also the same as the Pearson correlation in Ouput 8.2. So with two variables the correlation (r = .504) and the bivariate regression *(R = .504)* are the same.

b)   The unstandardized coefficient (B) allows you to build a formula to predict math achievement based upon grades. B is the slope of the best fit regression line.

c)   The key here is that bivariate regression gives you the ability to predict from one variable to another, where correlation shows the strength of the relationship, but does not involve prediction. Correlation is more appropriate than bivariate regression is when there is no clear independent or antecedent variable (perhaps both variables were assessed at the same time) and there was no intention to predict.

Chapter 9

9.1.   a) Under what conditions would you use a one-sample *t* test?
   b) Provide another possible example of its use from the HSB data.

a)   It is not uncommon to want to compare the mean of a variable in your data set to the mean of a variable in another data set for which you do not have the individual's scores. One example of this is comparing a sample with the national norm. You could also compare the mean of your sample to that from a different study. For example, you might want to replicate a study involving GPA, and ask how the GPA in your study this year compares to the GPA in the replicated study of 10 years ago, but you only have the mean GPA (not the raw data) from that study.

b)   We could, possibly compare the means for other variables in the HSB data set with national norms for the visualization test, the mosaic pattern test, or the math achievement test. Comparing our data with national norms could help us justify that the HSB data set is similar to all students or tell us that there is a significant difference between our HSB data and national norms.

9.3.   a) Compare the results of Output 9.2 and 9.3.
   b) When would you use the Mann-Whitney U test?

a) Note that although the two tests are based on different assumptions, the *p*s were similar for the *t* and M-W that used the same variables, and the results that were significant did not change. Males and females were significantly different on math achievement (*p*=.009 and .010, respectively) and on visualization scores (*p*=.020 and .040), but there was not a significant difference between males and females on grades in high school (*p*=.369 and .413).

b) The Mann-Whitney U is used to compare two groups, as is a *t* test, but you should use M-W when you have ordinal (not normally distributed) dependent variable data. The M-W can also be used when the assumption of equal group variances is violated.

9.5.   Interpret the reliability of visualization test and retest scores using Output 9.5.

There is pretty good support for the reliability of visualization and retest scores with this sample. The visualization scores were higher than the retest scores, but there was a very high correlation between the two sets of scores (*r* = .88), a typical measure of reliability. The paired t test, however, shows that there is a significant difference between the average visualization scores and the average retest scores (*t* = 3.22; *p* = .002). In general, the same people scored significantly higher on the visualization test than on the visualization retest. Unless there is some reason (a negative event, less time, etc.) that the average retest score should be lower, this *t* test result would make one question the similarity between the two tests. However, if there had been a positive intervention between pretest and posttest, one would expect posttest scores to be higher.

Chapter 10

10.1.   In Output 10.1: a) Describe the *F*, *df*, and *p* values for each dependent variable as you would in an article. b) Describe the results in nontechnical terms for visualization and grades. Use the group means in your discussion.

a) There is a significant difference between father's education groups on grades in high school F (2,70) = 4.09, p = .021 and on math achievement scores F (2,70) = 7.88, p = .001. There is not a significant difference on visualization scores. In order to fully interpret these results, you need to use post hoc tests (see Output 10.2 and the interpretation section). Note that between groups degrees of freedom is 2 because there are 3 groups 3-1 = 2. The degrees of freedom within is the total minus the number of groups or 73-3 = 70.

b) There is not a significant difference in average student visualization scores among the groups of students who have fathers with a high school or less education, with some college education, or with a B.S. or more. There is one or more significant difference among the father's educational level groups in regard to their child's grades in high school. Students who had parents with a B.S. or better received average grades of 6.53 which using the codebook is approximately a 3.25 GPA, half way between mostly Bs and half As and half Bs. Students who had parents with some college had mean grades of 5.56, about a 2.75 GPA. Students whose parents had high school degree or less (mean = 5.34) had an average about 2.65.

In Output 10.1 we did not run post hoc tests. To see if these group differences are statistically significant, we would need to use a post hoc test as we did in Output 10.2.

10.3. In Output 10.3, interpret the meaning of the sig. values for math achievement and competence. What would you conclude, based upon this information, about differences between groups on each of these variables?

Using the Kruskal-Wallis test, there is a significant difference somewhere among the three parental educational levels on math achievement (chi-square = 13.384, df = 2, N = 73, p = .001). There are no differences on the competence scores among the parental education groups.

If you review the Mean Rank table it is fairly clear to see that the mean ranks for competence scales are similar (36.04, 35.78, and 36.11). It is also appears that the mean ranks on math achievement are quite different (28.43, 43.78, and 48.42). Students who had parents with BS or more seemed to score higher on math achievement than did those who had parents with a high school degree or less. However, it is less clear if there are significant differences between the group in the middle (some college) and the one above or below it. To test these comparisons statistically would require post hoc analysis, probably with Mann-Whitney tests.

10.5. In Output 10.4; a) Is the interaction significant? b) Examine the profile plot of the cell means that illustrates the interaction. Describe it in words. c) Is the main effect of gender significant? Interpret the eta squared. d) How about the "effect" of math grades? e) Why did we put the word effect in quotes? f) Under what conditions would focusing on the main effects be misleading?

a) No. F = .34, p = .563. That is convenient because it means that we can interpret the main effects without concern that they might be misleading.

b) Males did better than females regardless of whether they had high or low high school math grades. Note that the lines are nearly parallel, indicating that the difference is about the same for the less than A-B grades group and the mostly A-B math grades group.

c) Gender is significant (p < .001). Eta squared is .163. This indicates that about 16% of the variance in math achievement can be predicted by gender. Taking the square root of eta squared you get an eta = .415, which is a larger than typical effect.

d) The math grades "effect" is also statistically significant (p < .001). By looking at the total means or the plot, we can see that students with high (most A-B) math grades scores had higher average math achievement scores.

e) We put "effect" in quotes because this is not a randomized experiment so we can not know if male gender or high math grades is the cause of higher math achievement.

f) If there is an interaction you must interpret the interaction first. Under that condition the interaction can make the results of the main effects misleading.

For Further Reading

American Psychological Association (APA). (2001). *Publication manual of the American Psychological Association* (5th ed.). Washington, DC: Author.

Chen, P. Y., & Popovich P. M. (2002). *Correlation: Parametric and nonparametric measures.* Sage University Papers Series on Quantitative Applications in the Social Sciences, 7–139. Thousand Oaks, CA: Sage.

Cohen, J. (1988). *Statistical power and analysis for the behavioral sciences* (2nd ed.). Hillsdale, NJ: Lawrence Erlbaum Associates.

Gliner, J. A., & Morgan, G. A. (2000). *Research methods in applied settings: An integrated approach to design and analysis.* Mahwah, NJ: Lawrence Erlbaum Associates.

Huck, S. J. (2000). *Reading statistics and research* (3rd ed.). New York: Longman.

Leech, N. A., Barrett, K. C., & Morgan, G. A. (2004). *SPSS for intermediate statistics: Use and interpretation.* Mahwah, NJ: Lawrence Erlbaum Associates.

Morgan, S. E., Reichart T., & Harrison T. R. (2002). *From numbers to words: Reporting statistical results for the social sciences.* Boston: Allyn & Bacon.

Newton R. R., & Rudestam K. E., (1999). *Your statistical consultant: Answers to your data analysis questions.* Thousand Oaks, CA: Sage.

Nicol, A. A. M., & Pexman, P. M. (1999). *Presenting your findings: A practical guide for creating tables.* Washington, DC: American Psychological Association.

Nicol, A. A. M, & Pexman, P. M. (2003). *Displaying your findings: A practical guide for creating figures, posters, and presentations.* Washington, DC: American Psychological Association.

Rudestam, K. E., & Newton, R. R. (2000). *Surviving your dissertation: A comprehensive guide to content and process* (2nd ed.). Newbury Park, CA: Sage.

Salant, P., & Dillman, D. D. (1994). *How to conduct your own survey.* New York: Wiley.

SPSS. (2003). *SPSS 12.0: Brief guide.* Chicago: Author.

Vogt, W. P. (1999). *Dictionary of statistics and methodology* (2nd ed.). Newbury Park, CA: Sage.

Wainer, H. (1992). Understanding graphs and tables. *Educational Researcher, 21*(1), 14–23.

Wilkinson, L., & The APA Task Force on Statistical Inference. (1999). Statistical methods in psychology journals: Guidelines and explanations. *American Psychologist. 54*, 594–604.

Index[1]

---

[1] Commands or output terms used by SPSS but not common in statistics or research methods books are in bold.

Index

Index